THE
SRI VAISHNAVA BRAHMANS

THE SRI VAISHNAVA BRAHMANS

BY

DEWAN BAHADUR K. RANGACHARI

GYAN PUBLISHING HOUSE
New Delhi - 110002

THE SRI VAISHNAVA BRAHMANS

ISBN :9788121200431

Published in 2014 in India by
Gyan Publishing House
23, Ansari Road, Daryaganj,
New Delhi - 110002
Phones : 23261060, 23282060 Fax : 23285914
e-mail : books@gyanbooks.com
website : gyanbooks.com

Laser Typesetting at : Vinayak Printers, Delhi
Printed at : Salasar Imaging System, Delhi

PREFACE.

This study of the Sri Vaishnava Brahmans aims at recording the customs of the people with which it deals as they are regarded within the community itself, the community to which the author belongs and within which he has therefore spent his long life. Outside authorities may disagree with some of his conclusions. But the paper is intended not as a critical study so much as a record of traditions, customs and ceremonies as understood by those who adhere to them and as interpreted by one of their number who is also an anthropologist—*Editor.*

CONTENTS.

		PAGE
	Preface ...	iii
1.	Introductory ...	1
2.	Vishṇu Worship ...	2
3.	Vaishnavism of South India ...	5
4.	Āzhvārs ...	9
5.	Āchāryas ...	17
6.	Rāmānuja ...	19
7.	Conception of God as laid down by Rāmānuja ...	24
8	Soul and Immortality ...	30
9.	Matter or Prakṛti ...	33
10.	Initiation into Vaishnavism ...	34
11.	The Vaḍagalai Sri Vaishnavas ...	37
12.	The Tengalai Sri Vaishnavas ...	42
13.	The Daily Observances of Orthodox Sri Vaishnava Brahmans ...	48
	Getting up from sleep ...	49
	Evacuation of the urine and faeces ...	50
	Washing ...	51
	Sipping of the water ...	52
	Cleaning of the teeth ...	53
	Bathing or Snānam ...	53
	Putting on the ūrdhva puṇḍram ...	56
	Offerings of water and rice to devaṛshis and forefathers (Devaṛshi pitṛ tarpaṇam) ...	59
	Morning prayers to God (Morning sandhyāvandanam) ...	60
	Repetition of the ashṭākshararn ...	68
	Ādhāraśakti tarpaṇam...	70
	Brahmayajñam ...	74
	Aupāsanam ...	79
	Abhigamana ārādhanam ...	83
	Upādānam ...	84
	Mādhyāhnika snānam ...	85
	Mādhyāhnikam ...	85
	Ārādhanam or worship ...	87
	Vaiśvadēvam ...	92
	Panchamahāyajñam ...	92
	Bhōjanam (taking one's food) ...	93
	Svādhyāyam ...	97
	Sandhyāvandanam ...	97
	Yōgam ...	98

	PAGE
14. Archaka Sri Vaishnava Brahmans	99
The chakrābja maṇḍala dīkshai ceremony	101
15. The Pratishṭhā Ceremony of Utsava Vigrahas in Temples	114
The ankurārpaṇam ceremony	115
16. The Daily Worship in Temples according to the Pāncharātra System	134
Entrance into the temple	135
The Archaka purifying himself to be fit for the worship of God	135
The worship of God...	141
17. Brahmōtsavam or Car Festival	149
18. Index	156

LIST OF ABBREVIATIONS.

Bhag. Gītā	Bhagavad Gītā.
Brihad. Up.	Brihadāraṇyaka Upanishad.
Chand. Up.	Chāndōgya Upanishad.
Keno. Up.	Kenopanishad.
K. Up.	Kaṭhopanishad.
S.B.E.	Sacred Books of the East.
Tait. Up.	Taittirīya Upanishad.
Vish. Pur.	Vishṇu Purāṇa.

The Sri Vaishnava Brahmans.

1. Introductory.

The Sri Vaishnava Brahmans form now an exclusive group adopting certain customs based on beliefs in which they have implicit faith. But in most of their general ritualistic observances they do not differ from the other groups of Brahmans. As a matter of fact all Brahmans, to whatever section they belong, follow one of the Vedas and in the ceremonies they have to perform they adopt the rituals as laid down in the sūtras pertaining to their Vedas. For example a Sri Vaishnava Brahman and a Vaḍama Brahman both belonging to Ṛg Veda or Yajur Veda, perform their religious rites according to the Gṛhya sutras of the Ṛg or Yajur Veda. Although there is uniformity in the essential features of their religious rites, the various sections introduce certain details which necessarily differ from one another, as they are based on their religious beliefs.

Sri Vaishnava Brahmans as a distinct sect and as a separate class, more or less in the present form, must have come into existence only after the time of the great reformer Rāmānuja Āchārya. But according to the traditional account there seems to have been a separate existence of this group since the time of Nāthamunigal. Further there is a belief current amongst several of the Sri Vaishnava community that the Sri Vaishnava Brahmans existed as a separate class from very early times, almost suggesting that they constitute a very distinct class quite different from the other sections of the Brahmans. A careful scrutiny of the Vaishnava traditional account at once disproves this claim. It is quite possible that amongst Brahmans several would have belief in Vaishnavism, but such would not have completely seceded from the Smārta Brahmans as a distinct class. A few families may have seceded from their own section on account of their belief in Vaishnavism. Some of the chief Āchāryas (religious teachers) of the Sri Vaishnavas appear to have been Vaḍama Brahmans by birth according to their own traditions. One Gōvinda Āchārya, who accompanied Yādavaprakāśa and Rāmānuja to Benares, became a Śaivite Brahman and later on he was again converted into a Sri Vaishnava Brahman. Yādavaprakāśa, a Smārta Advaitin, under whom Rāmānuja began to study, became later in his career a Sri Vaishnava and a true disciple of Rāmānuja. Some say that even the great Rāmānuja, the upholder of Sri Vaishnavism, was born of Smārta parents. It is clear from observation and traditional accounts that there was not much distinction observed between the Smārta Brahmans and Sri Vaishnavas, until the time of Rāmānuja. Sri Vaishnava Brahmans always sought as their teachers for Vedic study either Sri Vaishnava Brahmans or Smārta Brahmans indiscriminately. In the absence of priests (purōhits) amongst Sri Vaishnavas, Smārta Brahmans are usually called in to assist them in the performance of various rites and ceremonies.

The distinct teachings of Rāmānuja must have certainly helped the Sri Vaishnavas to form a distinct class by themselves, and probably the ranks of this exclusive group swelled from frequent additions from amongst the Smārta Brahmans. This accretion of members which began in Rāmānuja's time continues still, and even now it is possible to trace close relationship between Smārtas and Vaishnavas in certain families. There are some families, though few, amongst Sri Vaishnavas whose members observe pollution when there is death of a member in certain Smārta families which belong to the same gōtra as their own. No doubt such cases are becoming rare and probably no cases will easily be found of this kind after a few years. Sṛi Vaishnavas of some villages, such for example, as Valavanur, Savalai, Pērangiyur in South Arcot District and Pādhur, Tekkulur, Panappākam and Chettimaniyam in the Chingleput District, are considered not equal in status to some orthodox Sri Vaishnava families. Those who claim some superiority such as Tātāchārs, Chakravartis and Nāvalpākkattārs do not have any marital relationship with the Sri Vaishnavas of these villages, even though the latter are undoubtedly Sri Vaishnavas. A good example of Smārtas becoming Vaishnavas is afforded by the Thummagunta Drāviḍas some of whom have become Vaishnavas, but still take girls in marriage from Smārta families. They do not, however, give in marriage girls born in their families to members of the Smārta families. The Smārta Brahmans living in Esanur wear dress and castemarks like the Sri Vaishnavas, but their women dress like Smārta ladies and observe only the customs usual amongst the Smārta Brahmans.

In this connection we may also mention the Mukkāniars and Śōzhiers amongst whom there are both Smārta and Vaishnava families related to one another.

It should not be thought that Vishnu is worshipped as a god only by Sri Vaishnavas. Even Smārta Brahmans adore Vishnu as their God. The only difference between the Vaishnavas and Smartas in this matter is that the former recognize Vishnu as the only supreme deity and would not acknowledge any other as such, whereas the latter recognize the Trimūrtis—Brahma, Vishnu and Śiva—as God's manifestations, some giving prominence to Śiva and others to Vishnu.

2. Vishnu Worship.

According to some modern critics Vishnu worship in India can undoubtedly be traced as far back as the fourth century after Christ. Dr. Bhandarkar states that Vāsudēva and Sankarshaṇa were worshipped as gods in the Mahratta country about the first century before Christ (100 B.C.)*

The worship of God under the name of Vishnu can be traced to the epics and even to the Vedas. No doubt the term Vishnu occurs in the Vedas, but according to some modern scholars the Vedic gods are believed to be numerous and different, and Vishnu was not recognized as the supreme deity by men during Vedic times. But the orthodox Sri Vaishnavas who are well versed in Vedas hold that Vishnu was recognized by the Vedas as the supreme deity. They think that the views held by modern critics are due to a misconception. According to them the various parts of the Vedas were not written

* Page 48 Vaishnavism, Saivism and minor religious systems.

at different times with long intervals, but were brought into existence simultaneously. They also aver that the different parts of the Vedas were compiled with definite purposes. It would be wrong to expect to find general and philosophical ideas of God in the portions written especially for guidance in carrying on various rituals, ceremonies, etc. It would be equally wrong to expect to find in the philosophical portions ideas about the conducting of rites and ceremonies.

Modern critics and scholars generally hold that the Vedic periods were several and that the idea of God varied with these periods. In other words, they recognize three phases of thought in the Ṛg Veda, namely, nature-worship, monotheism and monism. To the earliest seers of the Vedic hymns natural objects such as the moon, sky, stars, sea, dawn or nightfall appear to be gods. This regarding of natural objects as God and worshipping them as such is believed to constitute the pantheistic stage.

When man began to think more about himself and his own agency he was induced to project himself and think of the spiritual agencies in his own form. So anthropho-morphism followed pantheism. Dyaus, Varuṇa, Mitra, are all considered to be Vedic gods. Sūrya, Pūshan, Agni, Sōma, Parjanya, etc., are also Vedic gods.

In this connection we may quote what Barnett, one of the modern scholars, says about these :—

"Most of them (gods) are taken from the religion of the people, and dressed in new garb according to the imagination of the priest; and a few are priestly inventions altogether. There is Dyaushpitā, the Sky-father, with Prithvī-Mātā, the Earth-mother; there are Vāyu, the wind spirit, Parjanya, the rain-god, Sūrya, the sun-god and other spirits of the sky such as Savitā; there is the Dawn goddess, Ushas. All these are or were originally deified powers of nature; the people, though their imagination created them, have never felt any deep interest in them, and the priests who have taken them into their charge, though they treat them very courteously and sing to them elegant hymns full of figures of speech, have not been able to cover them with the flesh and blood of living personality. Then we have Agni, the fire-god, and Sōma, the spirit of the intoxicating juice of the sōma plant, which is used to inspire the pious to drunken raptures in certain ceremonies; both of these have acquired a peculiar importance through their association with priestly worship, especially Agni, because he, as bearing to the gods the sacrifices cast into his flames, has become the ideal Priest and Divine Paraclete of Heaven. Nevertheless all this hieratic importance has not made them gods in the deeper sense, reigning in the hearts of men. Then we find powers of doubtful origin, Mitra, Varuṇa, and Vishnu and Rudra, and figures of heroic legend, like the warrior Indra and the twin charioteers called Aśvinā and Nāsatyā. All these with many others, have their worship in the Rig Veda : the priests sing their praises lustily, and often speak now of one deity, now of another, as being the highest divinity without the least consistency." (*Hindu Gods and Heroes—Wisdom of the East*—pages 12–14.)

"Sūrya and Savitā are worshipped as nature-power and not as personal Gods."

"The Ṛg-Veda is essentially a priestly book; but it is not entirely a priestly book. Much of the thought to which it gives utterance is popular in origin and sentiment, and is by no means of the lowest order. On this ground-work the priests have built up a system of hieratic thought and ritual of their own, in which there is much that deserves a certain respect. There is a good deal of fine poetry in it. There is also in it some idea of a law of righteousness: in spite of much wild and unmoral myth and fancy, its gods for the most part are not capricious demons but spirits who act in accordance with established laws, majestic and wise beings in whom are embodied the highest ideals to which men have risen yet. Moreover, the priests in the later books have given us some mystic hymns containing vigorous and pregnant speculations on the deepest questions of existence, speculations which are indeed fanciful and unscientific, but which nevertheless have in them germs of powerful idealism that is destined to arise in centuries to come. On the other hand, the priests have cast their system in the mould of ritualism. Ritual, ceremony, sacrifice, professional benefit—these are their predominant interests. The priestly ceremonies are conceived to possess a magical power of their own; and the fixed laws of ritual by which these ceremonies are regulated tend to eclipse, and finally even to swallow up, the laws of moral righteousness under which the gods live. A few generations more, and the priesthood will frankly announce its ritual to be the supreme law of the universe. Meanwhile they are becoming more and more indifferent to the personalities of the gods, when they have preserved any; they are quite ready to ascribe attributes of one deity to another, even attributes of nominal supremacy, with unscrupulous inconsistency and dubious sincerity; for the personalities of the different gods are beginning to fade away in their eyes, and in their mind is arising the conception of a single universal Godhead." (L. D. Barnett—Hindu Gods and Heroes—pp. 42-44.)

"Priests" Barnett says "sing to Vāyu, Sūrya and Agni considering each of them as Gods." This is only an assumption on the part of Mr. Barnett according to the orthodox Sri Vaishnava Brahmans. They think that Mr. Barnett does not seem to understand the real mentality of the Hindu Vedic men. To interpret the text of the Vedas, as understood by the Vaidiki Brahmans who know the Vedas, it is absolutely necessary to know certain explanations which are usually given orally. Since these explanations are not generally reduced to writing, misreading and misinterpretation become possible. The remarks of Mr. Barnett are quoted at length just to show how modern European scholars think of the Hindu conceptions of God from Vedic times. Whatever may be the view of the modern European critics and scholars, it is not certainly supported by the Sri Vaishnavas. All the remarks made by Mr. Barnett, they say, would disappear if he understands the mentality and viewpoint of the Vaidiki Brahmans well-versed in the Vedas. They maintain that the idea of one God is certainly derivable from the Vedas, and that the various gods mentioned and worshipped are only subordinate and do not refer to the supreme deity. Mr. Barnett says that Dyaushpitā, Prithvīmāta, Vāyu, Parjanya, Sūrva and Ushas were originally held to be deified powers of nature. But according to the Hindu conceptions, these are not to be considered as gods, but only as spirits. If they refer to God in them, they think only of the spirit of God existing in them, as they form part of the universe.

The conception that in the sōma sacrifice the intoxicating spirits of the sōma plant is made use of is not correct. The sōma juice used is not an intoxicating juice at all. The European scholars have made the mistake of considering this as such. The rules given to make the sōma juice are such that it could never be an intoxicating stuff—*See* the article "Sōma juice is not liquor" by N. B. Pavgee, Poona—pages 70-79 in the Third Oriental Conference Report, Madras, 1924.

3. Vaishnavism of South India.

A devout Sri Vaishnava thinks that he should strive his best to obtain mōksha or salvation and that this is possible only through an Āchārya or a religious teacher. Without the intervention of an Āchārya, however learned one may be, he cannot hope to attain mōksha. In support of this view many a Vaishnava often quotes the examples of the wicked Kshatrabandhu and the good and pious Puṇḍarīkāksha who both obtained salvation only through an Āchārya. In the case of both these men Nārada appeared to be their Āchārya. According to Rahasyāmnāyam every person desirous of obtaining mōksha is expected to seek an Āchārya and to show always respect towards him and to his Āchāryas and so on up to God. God is considered to be the greatest Āchārya for the whole world, as he is the master of everything in this universe. All Sri Vaishnavas firmly believe that God being all merciful He would not allow the souls to get away from Him and that He would do everything that is just to save them from going astray from Him. This view is inculcated by every Sri Vaishnavite Āchārya from Rāmānuja downwards. Rāmānuja in his introduction to the Gītā Bhāshya says "God in his infinite mercy assumed various forms without putting away his own essential god-like nature, and time after time incarnated himself . . . descending not only with the purpose of relieving the burden of the earth, but also to be accessible to men, even such as we are, so revealing himself to the world as to be visible to the sight of all, and doing such other marvellous deeds as to ravish the hearts and eyes of all beings, high and low." Vēdānta Dēśika, another preceptor of the Sri Vaishnavas expresses himself in a similar strain in the introductory chapter of his Rahasyatrayasāram, a work written in "Maṇi-pravāḷam" (a mixture of Tamil and Sanskrit) and highly prized by the Vaḍagalai Sri Vaishnavas. In it he says that the Lord gave the Vedas in former days to Brahma and when these sacred Vedas were stolen from Brahma God secured them back to Brahma. He brought into existence śāstras and caused them to be taught to men through Brahma. Through Sanat-Kumaras, sons of Brahma, he sought to promulgate good ideas. God tried to keep up the correct way (sampradāyam) through the Maharshis Nārada, Parāśara, Śuka and Śaunaka. These ṛshis did their best. Then Vyāsa was created and he was induced to write the great epic—the Mahābhārata—for the enlightenment of the people of the world. Next God himself became incarnate in this world as Hamsa,

Matsya, Hayagrīva, Nara Nārāyaṇa, Gītāchārya and as the avatārs Rāma and Kṛshṇa, and in these forms taught tatvas and several good things. He caused the proper views expressed by himself to be promulgated by such wise men as Bhīshma; he gave out to the world many truths by Pāncharātra śāstras. Finally he himself incarnated as ten avatārs in the form of Parāṅkuśa, Parakāla, etc. Just as clouds drink water from the sea and pour down this water as rain, so essential for the up-keep of all living beings, these Āzhvārs gave out in their own mother tongue (Tamil) the essence of the Vedic teachings. In the land of Agastya the Lord became incarnate in the form of several saints as prophesied in the stanza found in the Bhāgavata Purāṇa and quoted below:—

"Kalau khalu bhavishyanti nārāyaṇa parāyanāḥ kvachit kvachinmahābhāgā dramiḍēshu cha bhuriśaḥ | tāmbraparṇī nadī yatra kṛtamālā payasvinī | kāvēricha mahābhāgā pratīchīcha· Mahānadī ||" This when rendered freely into English runs thus:— "It is in Kaliyuga that some devoted exclusively to Nārāyaṇa are to arise here and there in some places; but they are to be born in larger numbers in the region of the Drāviḍa country, by the side of the rivers Tāmbraparṇī, Vaigai, Pālār, and in the region of the famous Kāvēri and in the Mahānadī (Periyār) which flows to the west."

On noting the birth places of the ten Āzhvārs it looks as if the prophecy alluded to in the stanza already quoted is fulfilled. The great saint Saṭhakōpa or Nammāzhvār was born in the land of Tāmbraparṇī and in the same region Madurakavi also was born; Peria Āzhvār and his daughter in the region of the Vaigai; Poigai, Pēy and Bhūtat Āzhvars belong to the Pālār region as well as the great Tirumahisai.

As the stanza quoted above is not found in certain manuscript copies and printed editions of Bhāgavata Purāṇa some critics maintain this stanza to be an interpolation and believe the insertion to have taken place long after the appearance of these Āzhvars. According to some critics the whole chapter dealing with Āzhvārs, Āchāryas and Avatārs is said to be an interpolation. However this may be, it is clear that this interpolation should have taken place long before the time of Vēdānta Dēśika because he bases his views expressed in Rahasyatrayasāram on this ślōka of Bhāgavata Purāṇa.

On the other hand, the learned amongst this community of Brahmans hold this not to be an interpolation. They hold that Bhāgavatam was in existence long before the time of the Āzhvārs and that the passage relating to the birth of Āzhvārs is not an interpolation. They hold that many of the Tamil stanzas of the Prabandha echo the sentiments expressed in the Bhāgavata Purāṇa, and they say that in some cases they are almost similar to ślōkas in the Bhāgavata Purāṇa.

Vishnu, or Nārāyaṇa as he is generally called, is considered to be the supreme Deity by all the Sri Vaishnavas. Nārāyaṇa is considered to be ever in close association with Lakshmī. She shares all powers and responsibilities with Nārāyaṇa and is on a par with him. This idea is held by every learned Vaḍagalai Sri Vaishnava and in support of this they quote or refer to the Chatuślōkī of Śrī Āḷavandār (see page 18 for the Chatuślōki). In these four stanzas Āḷavandār maintains that Lakshmī shares with Nārāyaṇa the bed, the vāhana, and that the dēvas with their wives are her servants. Her splendour is as boundless as that of her lord and he too cannot measure it. The three worlds are flourishing on account of her grace only. In all his Vibhūtis, she is associated with him and is never found separately. This is the view held by all Vaḍagalai Sri Vaishnavites. But the Tengalai Sri Vaishnavas do not consider her to belong to the same category as Nārāyaṇa and hold that Śrī or Lakshmī is on a lower plane than Nārāyaṇa and on a par with other lives—including the souls of human beings.

The chief doctrines held by the Vaḍagalai section of the Sri Vaishnavas at the earliest times are the following and they hold good even now. 1. The Lord (Nārāyaṇa) with Śrī Lakshmī is the supreme being; 2. Souls and God are different; 3. By resigning oneself to God salvation is obtained; 4. Conscious volition and thought of Him at the time of death (especially for the faithful) is unnecessary; 5. An Āchārya should be sought by every one; 6. Moksha can certainly be attained by having an Āchārya (preceptor or teacher).

The following Tamil stanza of Tirumahisai Āzhvār expresses well the Vaishnavite conception of God and his Grace:—

> " இன்றாக நாளையே யாக இனிச்சிறிதும்
> நின்றாக நின்னருளென் பாலதே—நன்றாக
> நானுன்னை யன்றி யிலேன்கண்டாய் நாரணனே!
> நீயென்னை யன்றி யிலை."

" Whether to-day, to-morrow, later on or a long time after, your grace is certainly mine. O Nārāyaṇa, I very well know that I am not without you and you without me."

All Sri Vaishnava Brahmans hold the Āzhvārs and Āchāryas in very great veneration, so much so, that the images of Āzhvārs and chief Āchāryas are set up in many a temple and are worshipped. This reverence and worship is due to the belief that the Āzhvārs and the Āchāryas represent *amśams* of God. Their great learning and piety is attributed to the presence of the *amśams* of God.

Rāmānuja, the great reformer, is the first of the recent Āchāryas to be represented by an image in a temple. Annually utsavams are celebrated to him in the month of Chittirai. His nakshatra day is "Tiruvādirai," and this nakshatram is taken into consideration while fixing the utsavam in the Chitra month. Next to him the two great Āchāryas Śri Vēdānta Dēśika and Śrī Maṇavāḷa Mahā Munigal, who are the special Āchāryas of the Vaḍagalai and Tengalai sects are similarly treated. The festival of Vēdānta Dēsika is celebrated in the month of Puraṭṭāsi on śrāvaṇam day and that of Maṇavāḷa Mahā Munigal in the month of Arpisi on mūlam day.

This tendency to represent Āchāryas by images is now seen to be working in the minds of some. Recently the swami of the Ahōbila Maṭṭ, who is now the head of the maṭṭ, established in the maṭṭ an idol for one of his predecessors who happened to be his own Āchārya. Similarly images of their Āchāryas are set up by a few Sri Vaishnavas in Conjeeveram and Kumbakonam. Generally, however, Sri Vaishnavas who do not belong to the Ahōbila Maṭṭ have a different mentality and so they are not disposed to set up images for any of their recent Āchāryas subsequent to Vēdānta Dēśika or Maṇavāla Mahā Munigal.

Every Sri Vaishnava Brahman of the Vaḍagalai and Tengalai sects remembers the succession of Āchāryas and Āzhvārs prior to his own up to the Supreme Being who is considered to be the great Āchārya for the whole universe, by repeating daily or whenever he has to do anything of the nature of a religious ceremony the names of his Āchāryas and Āzhvārs up to God. The following is usually remembered and repeated by a Vaḍagalai Sri Vaishnava on occasions when he has to remember his Āchāryas up to God:—

"Asmat Gurubhyōnamaḥ; asmatparamagurubhyōnamaḥ; asmat sarva gurubhyōnamaḥ; Śrīmatē Vēdānta Guravēnamaḥ; Śrīmatē Rāmūnujāyanamaḥ; Śrī Parāṅkuśāyanamaḥ (Śrīmatē Mahā Pūrṇāyanamaḥ); Śrīmad Yāmunamunayenamaḥ; Śrī Rāma Miśrāyanamaḥ; Śrī Puṇḍarīkākshāyanamaḥ; Śrīman Nāthamunayēnamaḥ; Śrīmad Śaṭhakōpāyanamaḥ; Śrīmad Vishvaksēnāyanamaḥ; Śriyainamaḥ; Śrīdharāyanamaḥ."—

"Asmaddēśikam asmadīya paramāchāryān aśēshān gurūn Śrīman Lakshmaṇa yōgi Pungava Mahā Pūrṇam Munim Yāmunam Rāmaṁ padma vilōchanam munivaram nātham śaṭha dvēshinam sēnēśām Śriyamindirā sahacharam Nārāyaṇam samśrayē ||—"

Some also repeat the following Tamil stanza composed by Vēdānta Dēsika in addition to the above two Sanskrit ślōkas. Those who do not know Sanskrit understand the Tamil much better and know what they are repeating.

"என்னுயிர் தந்தளித்தவரைச் சரணம்புக்கி
யானடைவே யவர்குருக்கள் நிரைவணங்கி
பின்னருளால் பெரும்பூதூர் வந்தவள்ளல்
பெரியநம்பி ஆளவந்தார் மணக்கால்நம்பி
நன்னெறியை யவர்க்குரைத்த உய்யகொண்டார்
நாதமுனி சடகோபன் சேனைநாதன்
இன்னமுதத்திரு மகளென்றி வர்களைமுன்னிட்
டெம்பெருமான் திருவடிக ளடைகின்றேனே."

This when translated runs as follows:—

"I am surrendering myself to him who initiated me into the knowledge of myself and am saluting the line of his Āchāryas; then, I am also saluting respectfully these Āchāryas, *viz.* the most merciful Emberumānar who was born in Sriperumbudur, Mahā Pūrṇa (also called Periya Nambi), Āḷavandār, Maṇakkāl Nambi (also called Śrī Rāmamiśra), Puṇḍarīkākshar who initiated into the secrets of Prapatti Maṇakkāl Nambi, Nāthamuni, Saṭhakōpan and Sēnaināthan (Vishvaksēnar) and Lakshmī who is as sweet and dear to God as amritam; and with their help I am reaching the feet of Śriyappati (husband of Śrī, *i.e.*, God)."

In all the stanzas quoted above the order of the preceptors is the same. At first one thinks of his own immediate Āchārya, then his Āchārya's preceptors, next the prominent Āchāryas, Vēdānta Dēśika and Rāmānuja. After this the preceptors Maṇakkāl Nambi, Uyyakkoṇḍār and Nāthamunigal are mentioned. Then Śaṭhakōpan or Nammāzhvar is thought of and he is the only one of the Āzhvārs mentioned though there are ten of them.

This is because he is the only Āzhvār who is entitled to a place in the list of gurus. So far beings of this world are thought of. Then follow Sēnēśa, Śrī Lakshmi and Śrīman Nārāyaṇa, all inhabitants of the superhuman celestial region Śrī Vaikunṭham.

4. Āzhvars.

The Āzhvārs who are recognized and whose writings have been codified into what is now called "The Nālāyiraprabandham" are twelve in number. They are detailed below according to their traditional dates of birth which is stated in each case :—

I. Ancient—

Poigai Āzhvār (Sārayōgin). Born B.C. 4203.
Bhūtat Āzhvār (Bhūta yōgin). Born B.C. 4203.
Pēyāzhvār (Mahat or Bhrānta yōgin). Born B.C. 4203.
Tirumahisai Āzhvār. Born B.C. 4203.

II. Middle—

Nammāzhvār (Śaṭhakopan). Born B.C. 3102.
Maduraikavi Āzhvār. Born B.C. 3102.
Kulaśēkhara Āzhvār. Born B.C. 3075.
Periya Āzhvār (Vishṇuchitta). Born B.C. 3056.
Āṇḍāḷ (Gōdā). Born. B.C. 3005.

III. Recent—

Toṇḍaraḍippoḍi Āzhvār (Bhaktānghrirēṇu). Born B.C. 2814.
Tiruppāni Āzhvār (Yōgi Vāhana). Born. B.C. 2760.
Tirumangai Āzhvār (Parakāla). Born B.C. 2706.

In the above enumeration of Āzhvārs it is seen that some are recent and some middle while others are ancient. The nearest dates of birth of all these Āzhvārs as held by the orthodox Sri Vaishnava community are also given. On going through the dates of birth we find that all of them were born before Christ and the last of them about 2,700 years before Christ; in other words the last of them was born 4,627 years ago and the earliest or the first 6,130 years ago. Several amongst modern critics are not disposed to give to the Āzhvārs any antiquity and so they place them only in the 4th, 5th or 6th century A.D. The dates given according to the traditional account are considered by them to be fanciful and untrustworthy. There are a few critics who say that the Āzhvārs must have been contemporaneous with Rāmānuja or that they flourished after him. Both these views are considered by Sri Vaishnavas to be preposterous and to have no basis of any kind to support them.

The heirarchy and the dates in which the various Āzhvārs flourished and which the Sri Vaishnavas believe as true is based on their Guruparamparas which is a traditional account of their Āchāryas and Āzhvārs. The account given in the Guruparamparas of the Āzhvārs and Āchāryas down to Rāmānuja, the great Reformer, is similar in both the Vaḍagalai and Tengalai Guruparamparas.

As regards the individual lives of these Āzhvārs and Āchāryas modern scholars question the ages assigned to some of them. Some of the Āchāryas are held to have lived 25 years, while others to the ripe age of 135. These ages are considered by the present day English knowing scholars to be rather high, and they allow only 80 or 90 years of age as the maximum. Sri Vaishnavas consider that these scholars ignore two important facts. In the first place, the Āzhvārs and prominent Āchāryas were men of great intellectual capacity and ability and so they were above the average level of men in general. Secondly, even ordinary men are now known to live over 130 years of age, if we believe the accounts given in the daily paper "Hindu" and a review, the "Indian Review." For example there is in one of the issues of the daily "Hindu" in the month of August 1927 a photograph of a person named zara Aga whose present age is 146 years. The same photograph was also reproduced by the Indian Review in the September number of the year 1927, in page 600. The "Swadesamitran" a Tamil daily published at Madras, in its issue of 11th October 1927, announced that a Muhammadan Saint named Syed Habib Alat Roon, who hailed from Medina and who was living at Hyderabad (in Nizam's Dominions) breathed his last in his 130th year.

The Sri Vaishnava Brahmans do not worry themselves as to the correctness or otherwise of the dates of birth or the periods in which their Āzhvārs flourished. They are content with the view stated in their Guruparamparas and believe in the traditional account given in it. To most orthodox Vaishnavites it is immaterial whether an Āzhvār was born ten thousand years ago, or in recent times ; they are particular only about the correctness of their views and the proper understanding of such truths as are set forth by the Āzhvārs and Āchāryas. According to these men, the antiquity or modernness of the Āzhvārs and Āchāryas do not in any way detract from the value of the spiritual truths promulgated by them and the faith excited remains unaffected by such accidents.

Most of these Āzhvārs composed and promulgated their views in Tamil, although a few amongst them have also written in Sanskrit. However, it is the Tamil writings of these Āzhvārs that are prominent and these have been codified into the 4,000 or the Nalāyiraprabandham. All the writings contained in this Prabandham are in the form of verses full of piety and devotion. These verses are called "Pāśurams" in Tamil. The religious truths enshrined in them are not very different from those inculcated in the Sanskrit Vedas and important Purāṇas. Consequently the Prabandham is considered to be as sacred as the Vedas and in confirmation of this view it is often spoken of as the Tamil Vedás. The equality of the Prabandham with the Sanskrit Vedas is recognized and so both of them are referred to to-day by the use of the term "Ubhaya Vēdāntam".

From the Prabandham many stanzas may be quoted to prove that the views held regarding God and this world are exactly the same as are expressed in the Sanskrit Vedas. As examples a few stanzas are selected and are quoted below. From a perusal of these it will be seen that Āzhvārs expressed ideas about God and Tatvas almost identical with what is found in Vedic writings and Sanskrit Purāṇas. First we may quote from "Tiruccanda Vrittam" of Tirumahisai Āzhvār:—

பூநிலாய வைந்துமாய்ப் புனற்கணின்ற நான்குமாய்
தீநிலாய மூன்றுமாய்ச் சிறந்தகா லிரண்டுமாய்
மீநிலாய தொன்றுமாகி வேறுவேறு தன்மையாய்
நீநிலாயவண்ணம் நின்னை யார் நினைக்கவல்லரே.

(திருச்சந்தவிருத்தம்—1)

"Oh! My Lord! you are the supporter of the five qualities pertaining to earth (sound, touch, form, taste and smell), the four qualities of water (sound, touch, form and taste), the three qualities of fire (sound, touch and form), the two qualities belonging to air (sound and touch) and the single quality of sound possessed by ether or sky; you are also the supporter of devas and other things that are separate from you. Who can or who is able to guess how you are supporting and your true self."

ஐந்துமைந்து மைந்தமாகி அல்லவற்று ளாயுமாய்
ஐந்துமூன்று மொன்றுமாகி நின்றவாதி தேவனே!
ஐந்துமைந்து மைந்துமாகி அந்தரத்தணைந்து நின்று
ஐந்துமைந்து மாயநின்னை யாவர்காண வல்லரே.

(திருச்சந்தவிருத்தம்—3)

"Oh! Lord, who is the First! You are the supporter of the five elements (earth, water, fire, air and ether), of the five senses of knowledge (touch, sight, hearing, taste and smell), of the five senses of action (mouth, hands, feet, buttocks (thighs!) and organs of excretion and generation), the *five tanmātras* of śabda, sparśa, rūpa, rasa and gandha, and thus you are supporting not only these twenty-four tatvas, but you are permeating all the living beings (so far the reference is to the Līlā vibhūti of God or existence on this earth or universe). You are also staying in Paramapada wherein you are the supporter of five śaktis, five jñānēndriyas, and five karmēndriyas, the five enjoyable sensual effects (all unconnected with this earth and hence different in nature) and the influencer of bhōgasthānam, bhōgōpakaraṇam, munis and muktas." (This latter part refers to his Nitya vibhūti or his existence in Vaikunṭha.)

நின்றியங்கு மொன்றலா வுருக்கடோறு மாவியாய்
ஒன்றியுள் கலந்துநின்ற நின்னதன்மை யின்னதென்று
என்றும்யார்க்கு மெண்ணிறந்த ஆதியாய்! நின்னுந்திவாய்
அன்று நான்முகன் பயந்தவாதி தேவனல்லையே!

(திருச்சந்தவிருத்தம்—5)

"Oh Lord who is the First Cause! You are permeating as ātman all the lifeless and living things that are varied in shape and form; and how you do this will remain inexplicable for ever and to all wise men. Are you not the creator of the four-faced Brahma from your navel formerly?"

தன்னுளே திரைத்தெழுந் தரங்கவெண்ட டங்கடல்
தன்னுளே திரைத்தெழுந் தடங்குகின்ற தன்மைபோல்
நின்னுளே பிறந்திறந்து நிற்பவும் திரிபவும்
நின்னுளே யடங்குகின்ற நீர்மைநின்க ணின்றதே !

(திருச்சந்தவிருத்தம்—10)

"Just as the ocean having waves that arise and spread in it and which has white spaces, possesses also the power of causing the subsidence of the waves in itself, so you alone have the power by which all movable and immovable things originate and die and finally get absorbed in you."

உலகுதன்னை நீபடைத்தி யுள்ளொடுக்கி வைத்திமீண்டு
உலகுதன்னுளே பிறத்தி ஓரிடத்தை யல்லையால்
உலகுநின்னொ டொன்றிநிற்க வேறுநிற்றி யாதலால்
உலகில்நின்னை யுள்ளசூழல் யாவருள்ள வல்லரே ?

(திருச்சந்தவிருத்தம்—12)

"You have created the universe ; you have kept the universe within yourself ; again you have appeared in this world as avatars ; it is impossible to think of you as belonging to a place ; the whole universe is your body and yet you have a separate existence in Vaikuṇṭha. Hence who could know your wonderful states ?"

ஏகமூர்த்தி மூன்றுமூர்த்தி நாலுமூர்த்தி நன்மைசேர்
போகமூர்த்தி புண்யத்தின் மூர்த்தியெண்ணில் மூர்த்தியாய்
நாகமூர்த்தி சயனமாய் நலங்கடற் கிடந்துமேல்
ஆகமூர்த்தியாய வண்ணமென் கொல் ? ஆதி தேவனே !

(திருச்சந்தவிருத்தம்—17)

"Oh Lord ! the cause of everything in this universe, who is existing in Vaikuṇṭha as Paravāsudēva and who appears as the three vyūhas Sankarshaṇa, Pradyumna and Aniruddha, as the four mūrtis Pradhāna, Purusha, Avyakta and Kāla, as the Bhōga mūrti in which all the good is embodied, as the Puṇya mūrti and innumerable mūrtis and finally lying on the Ādi Śesha, on the ocean of milk and as Archāvatāra. Who can understand all this !"

காணிலும் உருப்பொலார் செவிக்கினாத கீர்த்தியார்
பேணிலும் வரந்தர மிடுக்கிலாத தேவரை
ஆணமென் றடைந்துவாழும் ஆதர்காள் ! எம்மாதிபால்
பேணிநும் பிறப்பெனும் பிணக்கறுக்க கிற்றிரே.

(திருச்சந்தவிருத்தம்—69)

"Oh blind men that worship the various dēvatas whose very forms are hideous, whose stories are most unpleasant to hear, who even if sought for help are incapable of giving you the help you very much desire and those who thereby become worse, can you not get rid of the samsāra in which you are entangled by worshipping the true one God who is mine ?"

தானே உலகெல்லாம்
தானே படைத்திடந்து
தானே உண்டுமிழ்ந்து
தானே யாள் வானே.

"Permeating everything in this universe, creating all the universe, swallowing the universe and giving out the same, He is the Lord of everything."

All the writings of Āzhvārs are full of bhakti of the higher kind only. The extreme doctrine of prapatti or self-surrender underlies their outpourings. They firmly believed in the efficacy of this and believed in the intimate relationship between man and God. This becomes apparent when the following Tamil stanza is read:—

"இன்றாக நாளையே யாகஇனிச் சிறிதும்
நின்றாகநின் னருளென்பாலதே--நன்றாக
நானுன்னை யன்றியிலேன் கண்டாய் நாரணனே!
நீ யென்னை யன்றி யிலை."

(நான்முகன் திருவந்தாதி—7)

"Whether to-day, to-morrow, later on or a long time after, your grace is certainly mine. O Nārāyaṇa, I very well know that I am not without you and you without me."

Nammāzhvār, another Āzhvār, says in his Tiruvāimozhi:—

எனதாவியுள்கலந்த பெருநல்லுதவிக் கைம்மாறு
எனதாவிதந் தொழிந்தேன் இனிமீள்வ தென்பதுண்டே?
எனதாவி யாவியும்நீ பொழிலேழு முண்டவெந்தாய்!
எனதாவியார்? யான்ஆர்? தந்தநீ கொண்டாக்கினையே.

(திருவாய்மொழி—II-3, 4)

"In return for thy great and good gift the mingling of my spirit with Thee—I have entirely yielded up my spirit to Thee" (free translation).

பிறந்தவாறும் வளர்ந்தவாறும் பெரியபாரதம் கைசெய்து ஐவர்க்குத்
திறங்கள் காட்டியிட்டுச் செய்துபோன மாயங்களும்
நிறந்தனூடு புக்குஎனதாவியை நின்றுநின்று உருக்கியுண்கின்ற இச்
சிறந்தவான்சுடரே! உன்னை யென்றுகொல்? சேர்வதுமே.

(திருவாய்மொழி—V-10, 1)

This when freely rendered:—

"Thou splendid light of Heaven, Thou art in my heart melting and consuming my spirit. When shall I become one with Thee."

All the Āzhvārs when they speak of God view Him as their teacher, father, mother, child or beloved. In most cases the last is the view largely held. Many a critic is of opinion that the use of the symbolism of love is objectionable and wrong. Such a critic has no conception of the higher love and he generally thinks the sensual attraction to be the chief characteristic of love. Higher love as understood and felt by some men and women is certainly far above the level of the love that could be described only as bestial. It cannot be considered as a mere search after new sensations. The reputed women Sītā, Sāvitrī and Damayantī of the Purāṇas are ever remembered and their memories treasured up because their love was of a higher kind. In the higher love the souls of man and woman are attracted and whether they are near each other or separated widely from each other through difficulties, mutual love or attraction is felt by them. Even death cannot break this link of mutual love.

The Vaishnavite Āzhvārs, when they look upon God as their beloved, are actuated only by the higher aspect of love. All their passions and longings are redirected to God and they feel helpless in the absence of His presence and highly satisfied when he is present. In short when God is absent they have a sense of desolation and in his fellowship they feel joy because of the preciousness of His love. The attachment to God in the case of some Āzhvārs is so great that they are indifferent to all else in this world.

Like the Āzhvārs a Vaishnavite devotee merely tries to withdraw his desires from the creation, only to centre them on the Creator, *i.e.*, he lifts his desires from earth to heaven. According to Maṇavāḷa Mahāmuni "The pleasure which arises for the ignorant from sense-objects, the same is called bhakti when directed to God; in the case of Nammāzhvār this bhakti has become love for the beautiful Lord, hence for Āzhvārs there arises the love type of devotion."

Although many of those who use the symbolism of bride and bridegroom are quite free from all traces of the sensual contacts (and so morally impeccable), there are some who misunderstand this symbolism. Sri Vaishnavas can only consider this as being abnormal. As an example it is only necessary to draw attention to what Mr. Chintamani Vaidya says in his book "Epic India." There he writes: "We entirely disbelieve the truth of these stories; no more mischievous though well intentioned misrepresentations have ever sullied the fair name of a great man" (p. 422) and he adds further on "it is surely something exasperatingly inconsistent when those who recite Śrī Kṛshṇa's Bhagavad Gītā should themselves believe that Śrī Kṛshṇa indulged in amours with the gōpīs of Brindāvana which in others would at once be set down as deeply irreligious" (p. 446). "To this I need add nothing" says Barnett in the preface to his book "The Heart of India". A Sri Vaishnava would say that both Barnett and Mr. Vaidya are evidently thinking only of love as usually understood by ordinary, not spiritual, mortals. Further, this incident, which evidently alludes to the "Rāsakrīḍa" according to the Śrī Bhāgavata Purāṇa, occurred when Śrī Kṛshṇa was a boy of only 7, 8 or 10 years of age. It is certainly preposterous to say that Kṛshṇa indulged in amours with the gōpīs of Brindāvan at this age. No South Indian Vaishnavite of any learning thinks of this love towards Kṛshṇa as of the same nature as the ordinary passion of love as understood by the common people.

Since the Prabandhas or the writings of the Āzhvārs were in Tamil, which is the language of the people, they were widely read. So the doctrines inculcated in these writings were clearly understood by the men. These teachings appealed to them better and they became the general property of the people.

From the writings of Āzhvārs it is clear that they did not countenance and uphold caste principles in the matter of God and salvation. Any person, endowed with good character and possessing good learning, was considered to be a great man fit to be respected. Even a Brahman by birth may accept as his guru for mere learning any man of any caste provided the guru possesses the necessary culture and character. So to this extent the caste system was disregarded, though not for other purposes. In support of this we may quote two pāsurams or stanzas of the Āzhvārs:—

> " பழுதிலா வொழுகலாற்றுப் பலசதுப் பேதிமார்கள் !
> இழிகுலத்தவர்களேனும் எம்மடியார்களாகில்
> தொழுமினீர் கொடுமின் கொண்மின் என்று நின்னோடுமொக்க
> வழிபட வருளினாய்போல் மதிள் திருவரங்கத்தானே !
>
> (திருமாலை—42)
> (தொண்டரடிப்பொடியாழ்வார்)

The above when translated is as follows:—

"God in the fort of Srirangam said as follows:—'Oh men! descended from Brahma, who are free from all mistakes and who are well versed in Vedas! People who are my real devotees must be treated with respect by you even if they are of low birth; teach them things that you know and learn from them things that they know; saying thus you seem to have ordained to treat your devotees as your equals and show them respect accordingly."

Nammāzhvār also expresses a similar sentiment in his Tiruvāimozhi III-7, 9:—

> " குலந்தாங்கு ஜாதிகள் நாலிலும் கீழிழிந்து எத்தனை
> நலந்தானிலாத சண்டாள சண்டாளர்களாகிலும்
> வலந்தங்கு சக்கரத்தண்ணல் மணிவண்ணற் காளென்றுள்
> கலந்தார் அடியார்தம் அடியார் எம்மடிகளே.
>
> (திருவாய்மொழி—III-7, 9)

"If we descend below the four castes and come to chaṇḍāḷas who, however lacking in virtue are true worshippers of God who has in his right hand the hakra, their servant's servants are my masters and their feet are mine to worship."

Amongst Vaishnava devotees it is possible to quote many examples of men of lower castes being held in great respect. Even amongst the Āzhvārs, there were men of castes other than Brahman and of even low caste.

Even Rāmānuja held similar views. But to add that he admitted into the Brahman caste a large number of people of other castes seems to Sri Vaishnavas to be preposterous and to show absence of an intimate knowledge of Vaishnavism and Vaishnavite Brahmans. To Rāmānuja men who believed in Vishnu as the Supreme Being and followed the principles of Vaishnavism were all Vaishnavites and they were all equal in religious views and so are entitled to great respect. But Rāmānuja never interfered with the social order and in fact he seems to have upheld and favoured the Varṇāśrama Dharma. All men to whatever caste they may belong are entitled to the grace of God but this does not mean that he ignored caste principles.

Sri Vaishnavism is always connected with Rāmānuja, at any rate in South India, because Vaishnavism was crystallized and was clearly understood only after him. The Viśiṣṭādvaita views constitute the central ideas of the Vaishnavites, and though held by many of Rāmānuja's predecessors, it is only after the writing of Śrī Bhāshya of Rāmānuja that people had definite and clear views about God, Soul and

Matter. To-day every Sri Vaishnava in South India who claims to know something of his religion believes God to be immanent both in this material world and in the spiritual universe. God is to them not merely a mental abstraction remaining aloof from the world looking down upon men as an autocrat. God is conceived by them as existing in soul and matter, and in fact everything is dependent upon Him. In other words Sri Vaishnavas think that God joins them in their experiences of life, shares in their views and works for the upbuilding of the world.

In the succession list of Āchāryas and Āzhvārs which every devout Sri Vaishnava remembers, and which is already quoted, the Āzhvārs are referred to by only one name, that of Nammāzhvār. Of the beings of this world Āzhvārs are considered to be the most prominent and greatest and amongst them Nammāzhvār holds a very high place both on account of his personal character and his writings. His writings are more philosophical and contain much of the religious beliefs and treats of everything from a high plane. His writings are believed to be the epitome of the teachings of the Vedas Ṛg, Yajus and Sāma. The Tiruvāimozhi, which is the best known and the most popular of his works, is believed to be the repository of grand truths echoed in the Sāma Veda. It is the clearest and most succinct exposition of the eternal truths of the Vedas. It consists of 1,102 stanzas divided into 10 chapters.

Since the writings of the Āzhvārs and Āchāryas have a profound influence on the Vaishnavite movement, it is necessary to take a brief view of the lives, and doings of at least the most important personages amongst them. Of the Āzhvārs Nammāzhvār may be singled out as a representative of his class.

Nammāzhvār was born at Sri Nagari on the 43rd day of the present Kaliyuga. He is considered to be the *amśam* of Vishvaksēna (Senaināthan), the leader of the divine hosts. He was called Māran by his parents, because, as a child, he ate no material such as milk, etc., which are usually given as food to children and yet he maintained his health and grew well. He was laid in a cradle tied to a tamarind tree, which is held to be a sacred tree even now. Some of the orthodox Sri Vaishnavas keep along with other materials of worship a bit of the bark of this tamarind tree.

He had not any kind of touch with this world even afterwards. It is generally held that he was endowed with all perfections even from his childhood. Since he was not connected with this world and its affairs, he never knew the ways of the world. Because of his perfection in all ways people think that he should be considered to be superior to all the other Āzhvārs. He is therefore described as the soul and the other Āzhvārs as his body, Bhūtat Āzhvār, Poigai Āzhvār and Pēyāzhvār represent his head, eyes and face respectively; his neck and hands are Tirumahisai, Kulaśēkhara and Tiruppāṇa Āzhvārs respectively; his breasts and navel are Toṇḍaraḍippoḍi and Tirumangai Āzhvārs respectively; and the Āzhvār Madurakavi forms his feet.

Nammāzhvār is believed to have seen directly the Lord and thus realized in himself and in the infinite Nature the powers of the Supreme being. He was always anxious to save humanity without distinction of caste, creed or sex. It was this that made him pour forth his religious ideas and views in the language of the people, Tamil, in his Tiruvāimozhi already referred to. He was very short lived, as he died in his 35th year.

Madurakavi, born at Tirukkoilur who was considered to be the *amśam* of Kumuda, an angel near God in Vaikuṇṭha, was the shield and shadow of Nammāzhvār. Madurakavi survived his master and lived for 50 years after him. He travelled about widely in South India singing Prabandhams and proclaiming his master's story.

5. Āchāryas.

Now coming to the line of Āchāryās the first of them was Nāthamuni. He was born according to tradition, 3,641 years after the great Saint Nammāzhvār. That is to say he was born in the year 3684 of Kaliyuga. As he was endowed with yogic powers he was often called the Yōgi or Nāthamuni Yōgi. While staying at Vīranārāyāṇapuram he heard the recital by Sri Vaishnavas of the pāsuram "ஆராவமுதே" (Ārāvamudē) in the presence of God Rājagōpāla in the temple. Learning from them that it might be possible to find some one who knew all the *pāsurams* (stanzas) of the Āzhvārs and especially those of the great Nammāzhvār at Srinagari (Tirunagari), he met in that place one Parānkuśadāsa, one of the disciples of Madurakavi. On being questioned Parānkuśadasa said that he knew only the ten stanzas usually called "கண்ணிநுண் சிறுத்தாம்பு" and continued that anyone who reverentially and with faith repeats the stanzas 12,000 times may find favour in the eyes of the Nammāzhvâr and thus be blessed with his glorious presence.

Nāthamunigal carried out the repetition of Madurakavi's stanzas successfully under Parānkuśadāsa's guidance and in response to this prayer Saṭhakōpan (Nammāzhvār) appeared to Nāthamuni in a vision and asked him what he wanted. To this Nāthamuni replied that he wished to be taught the Prabandhams of the Āzhvārs and be instructed in the spiritual knowledge. Then Saṭhakōpa (Nammāzhvār) endowed Nāthamuni with divine vision and taught him the three Rahasyās, the Prabandham, the essence of various schools of philosophy and systems of religion and the mysteries of the eight-fold path of yoga. Nāthamuni resided there for a time devoting himself to the service of the Lord Ādinātha and Saṭhakōpa.

Nāthamuni as soon as he learnt the Prabandhams caused them to be set to music with the assistance of his nephews, Bhadrāksha and Rāma Miśra.

Nāthamuni was succeeded by Uyyakoṇḍār (Puṇḍarīkāksha), born in the year 3927 of Kaliyuga. He was directed by his master to communicate the secrets of religion to his grandson, Yāmuna Muni (or Āḷavandār). As Uyyakoṇḍār was unable to carry out the wishes of his master before his death, he desired the best of his disciples, Maṇakkāl Nambi (Rāma Miśra), to fulfil his master's wish by initiating Yāmunāchārya into the secrets.

Maṇakkāl Nambi was born in the year 3932 of Kaliyuga. When this Āchārya (also called Rāma Misra) was about 85 years of age, Yāmunāchārya was born (in the year 4017 of Kaliyuga), and as soon as he heard of the birth of this grandson to Nāthamunigal he hurried to the birth place and on the 12th day from the birth of the child caused him to be named "Yāmunāchārya" in accordance with the directions of his own master Uyyakoṇḍār (Puṇḍarīkāksha). Yāmunāchārya when of age began the study of Vedas and Śāstras and very soon became an efficient and well-read scholar. Later on in his life he had a contest with Akkiāḷvān and won a victory over him. As the result of this success he was given by the Rāja a large portion of his kingdom. From that time Yāmunāchārya lived like a prince and he was also named "Āḷavandār" after this victory over Akkiāḷvān. Maṇakkāl Nambi (Rāma Miśra) could not meet Āḷavandār, and so instead of going empty handed he used to supply daily the green leaves of the plant "Tutuvalai" (*Solanum trilobatum*), a solanaceous plant, of which Āḷavandār was very fond, for six months. Then Maṇakkāl Nambi discontinued the supply of these green leaves for four days successively. Āḷavandār (Yāmunāchārya) noticing the absence of the preparation of this green leaf questioned the cook. On hearing from the cook that Maṇakkāl Nambi who was bringing these leaves daily did not do so for the last four days, he ordered the cook to direct Maṇakkāl Nambi to him when he would come. On the fifth day Maṇakkāl Nambi came and was taken before Āḷavandār. On seeing Āḷavandār Maṇakkāl Nambi told him that he was entrusted by his grand-father's request with some treasure to be bequeathed. This aroused the attention of Āḷavandār and so he followed Maṇakkāl Nambi, who gradually instilled into Āḷavandār's mind spiritual truths. As the result of this Upadeśa Āḷavandār renounced the world and became a sanyāsin.

As a spiritual teacher Āḷavandār became a great sanyāsin and even Rāmānuja owes a great deal to his indirect influence. That, his doctrines and mode of thinking were entirely based upon Viśiṣṭādvaita philosophy is very clear from one of his writings '*Stōtra Ratnam*." He also insisted upon the view now held by every Vaḍagalai Sri Vaishnava that Lakshmī or Śrī was endowed with Vibhutvam just like Nārāyaṇa and that she was with him always, everywhere and in all Vibhūtis.

Āḷavandār's Chatuślōkī describes Lakshmī and he considers both God and Lakshmī as equal—

"(1) The best of purushas, *i.e.*, God, is your dear husband; Ādiśēsha is your bed and he is your seat; Garuḍa, the lord of birds, the embodiment (svarūpa) of vedas is your vāhanam (carrier); the prakriti (primordial matter) which bewitches everybody is your curtain. Brahma, Rudra, and dēvatas with their wives are your male and *man* servants; you are yourself called Śrī; Oh Lakshmi! who is full of good and auspicious qualities how shall we describe you!

"(2) Your mahimā (greatness in everything) which is boundless and ever-loving like that of your husband cannot be measured even by the God of your heart, who is also the most powerful or knowing. Oh Lakshmī! who is the one mistress of all the worlds and who is the wife of the Bhagavān, the Lord of all the lōkas, I, who know your mercy that is shown by you to those who throw themselves at your feet, have now begun to worship without fear, knowing that I am your servant and a prapanna

"(3) The three worlds that were decaying by the want of your mercy shown by the ambrosia of your sight are now flourishing as they are having now your protection;

without your grace who is dear to the heart of Bhagavān having eyes like lotus flowers men cannot obtain the highest bliss of attaining aiśwarya (dharma, artha and kāma), enjoying pure jīvātma and reaching God through archirādi mārga.

"(4) The Supreme Being who is without any change, who is limitless and is far above all things and who is called Brahman, the Supreme Being who likes his most wonderful form with angas called Paravāsudēva and the Supreme Being whose incarnations are manifested for his own pleasure is inseparably associated with you, Oh, Lakshmi who is capable of assuming the different forms appropriate to God's forms."

6. Rāmānuja.

The great reformer Rāmānuja who succeeded Āḷavandār was born at Bhūtapuri (now called Sriperumbudur) in the year Pingala, in the month of Chitrai, on a Thursday, śukla paksha panchamī under Ārdrā star (4118 of Kaliyuga=1017 A. D.), as the son of Āsuri Kēśava Sōmayājī and Kantimatī (sister of Śrīśaila Pūrṇa). According to some Āsuri Kēśava Somayājī was a Vaḍama Brahman of Yajus Śākhā, Āpastamba Sūtra and of Hārita gotra.

Rāmānuja, when he was of the proper age, began his general and Vedic studies under Yādavaprakāśa, an Advaitic sanyāsin. Even while studying under this Advaitic sanyāsin he seems to have differed from his master in the interpretation of certain passages in the Vedas. According to the traditional account three instances are given and they are as described below:—

The first occasion to differ occurred when the Upanishad statement "Satyam jñānam anantam Brahma (Tait. Up. II-i, 1) was explained by Yādavaprakāśa. This statement when translated into English is "Brahman (God) is Truth, Knowledge and Infinity." In explaining this passage Yādavaprakāsa held that the three attributes Truth, Knowledge and Infinity could not be predicted of Brahman, just as a cow could not be considered to be at the same time broken-horned, hornless and full horned. In other words Brahman cannot simultaneously be the possessor of various attributes. To Rāmānuja this explanation was not satisfactory and on being pressed to give his own explanation he gave out his own explanation as follows:—The attributes Truth, Knowledge and Infinity are mutually exclusive of one another and so are not incompatible in one and the same Being. The attribute Truth precludes all idea of momentary change; it is meant to fully establish that the existence of God is eternal. The second attribute of Knowledge is intended to establish that God is an all-knowing spirit and free from Achit, *i.e.*, removes all possibility of the presence of Achit (lifeless matter in His nature). The attribute Infinity is meant to establish that Brahman is without limits or conditions, i.e., it puts an end to all conceptions of limitation of his essence.

"Truth, therefore, is the term which characterises Brahman as eternal, distinguishing it from what is non-eternal; Knowledge is the term which characterises Brahman as spirit or life distinguishing it from what is non-spirit or non-life; and Infinity which characterises Brahman as infinite distinguishing it from what is non-infinite (*i.e.*, conditioned by space-limits or mode limits). These attributes and infinite others can co-exist in Brahman without mutual contradiction, as redness, softness, perfume, etc., can harmoniously co-exist in the flower. The analogy of the cow is not appropriate in this case; the analogy of the flower as quoted, or the sun having light and heat co-existing is appropriate. And therefore to try to postulate an attributeless Brahman or a Brahman in whom different attributes cannot co-exist, is neither logical, nor consistent with the affirmatory character of the Vedic passage in question." ("Life of Sri Rāmānuja"—Govinda Acharya—pages 30-31.)

The second one in which Rāmānuja differed from the explanation given by Yādavaprakāśa is given below:—

"Tasya yathā kapyāsam puṇḍarīkam ēvam akshīni." (Chand. Up.—Ch. I, sec. vii, 6-7.)

The explanation given by Yādavaprakāsa being blasphemous in character, Rāmānuja was very much affected and tears ran down his eyes. The hot tears of indignation caused by the wanton sacrilege coursed down his cheeks and fell on Yādava's thighs and scalded them severely. On this he asked Rāmānuja to say why he was crying and he explained the whole situation and said that the true explanation of the passage should be thus:—The eyeṣ of the golden Person or God in the Sun are like the lotus blooming under the influence of the welcome rays of the Sun.

"Sir" cried Rāmānuja "can you not see that *ka* means water, and *pibati* means to drink. Water drinker is thus *kapi*, the sun or the lotus-stalk. *Asa* is to open (vikasanē) or to rest (upa vasanē). *Puṇḍarika* is the lotus. And therefore God in the sun is He whose eyes are like the *lotus growing in deep water which blooms under the balmy beams of the sun, or lotus which rests on its stalk below.*" It is to repudiate God to deny him Person; and when the Vedas postulate such a Personality it is doubly to repudiate Him by reading blasphemous similies into the Vedas, where reverential gravity and grandeur are intended. Such constructions betoken nothing short of heresy." ("Life of Rāmānuja"—Govinda Acharya—page 32.) This reply was too much for Yādavaprakāśa and so he asked Rāmānuja to leave him as he cannot calmly take in his instruction. And Rāmānuja departed without saying anything.

The third occasion for difference of opinion arose in explaining the following passages:—

"Sarvam khalvidam Brahma." (Chand. Up. III, 10-1.)

"Nēha na nāsti kinchana." (Brihad. Up. VI, 4—19.)

Yādava was one day explaining the above Vedānta texts as if they meant that soul (man) and God were identical. The first passage means:—***All this is indeed Brahman,*** and the second means *there is not the least diversity here.* According to Yādava, the first passage meant that *all this cosmos is God*; the second passage meant that ***all the diversities that are*** *seen in the cosmos are illusory.* Rāmānuja took objection to these interpretations and said that the cosmos can never be identical with Brahman (God) nor can it be proved unreal. For the first passage *all this indeed is Brahman* meant that the cosmos is permeated with his spirit, *i.e.*, full of God; in other words the cosmos has no existence independent of God; it exists by his Will. He is its Creator, Preserver and Destroyer. He is its Ruler and rules by his immanence. And the second passage meant that the diversity of the cosmos is real inasmuch as it is sustained by the unity of God; and therefore who so sees the diverse cosmos as severed from God sees not aright. There is but one God neither two nor many. In Him is All. That is the meaning of the text. Cosmos is not denied inasmuch as its existence is eternal-substantially, though it exteriorly undergoes adjectival change. It is an axiom that *nothing can come out of nothing.* The cosmos is real. It is in God, who is thus One only, not many. This passage is thus an assertion, not a negation of the cosmos." ("Life of Rāmānuja"—Govinda Acharya, page 43.)

Soon after finishing his studies Rāmānuja vacillated a little and had certain doubts. So he requested Tirukachi Nambi to lay before Varadarāja, God at Conjeeveram, his doubts and get them cleared. The Sri Vaishnavas believe that Tirukacchi Nambi was a privileged being having the power of holding conversation with God Varadarāja. One day Tirukacchi Nambi mentioned Rāmānuja's doubt to Varadarāja who is said to have anticipated the questions and answered them as follows:—

(1) I am the Supreme Reality or Truth.

(2) I and souls are different, *i.e.*, there is essential difference between God and soul.

(3) By faith in me and final surrender (Prapatti) men reach me (*i.e.*, attain salvation).

(4) Thought of me at the time of death (antima smriti) is not essential for the faithful.

(5) Such a one gets released from Samsāra and attains mōksha.

(6) The questioner (Rāmānuja) should choose as his Āchārya Mahā Pūrṇa. Rāmānuja's doubts disappeared and he respectfully accepted the answers communicated by Tirukachi Nambi.

Āḷavandār met two Sri Vaishnavas at Srirangam hailing from Kānchī and heard from them about Rāmānuja's studying Vedānta under Yādavaprakāśa and also about the differences that arose between the master and the pupil in the explanation of Vedanta texts. On hearing all about Rāmānuja he hurried to Kānchī where he was received with due honours by his disciple Tirukachi Nambi. While paying his respects and worshipping Varadarāja in his temple he saw Yādavaprakāśa coming with his followers. Being anxious to know Rāmānuja, Āḷavandār asked if he was amongst the followers. Then Rāmānuja was shown to Āḷavandār and he was mightily pleased with Rāmānuja and sent after him his silent prayers. He prayed to God on the Hastagiri hill that Rāmānuja should become the bearer of the torch of the Sri Vaishnava faith.

Rāmānuja one day heard Mahā Pūrṇa reciting Āḷavandār's śloka and was very anxious to meet Āḷavandār. So both Mahā Pūrṇa and Rāmānuja proceeded together to Srirangam, but to their grief they came too late to see Āḷavandār alive. However, they both saw the remains of Āḷavandār and at once they swooned. On recovering from the swoon Rāmānuja exclaimed that he was unlucky and that he should give up the struggle and resign himself to fate. Mahā Pūrṇa encouraged him by soothing words, persuaded him to take a last look on the earthly remains of Yāmunāchārya (Āḷavandār). Rāmānuja on looking at the mortal remains saw three of the fingers of the right palm of Āḷavandār folded. On questioning those that were with the sage they informed Rāmānuja that "He was always full of expressions of unbounded gratitude towards Vyāsa and Parāśara; his devotion to Sri Saṭhakōpa was a thing by itself; and he used to regret that age and infirmities did not allow him to write a Viśishṭādvaita Bhāshya on the Brahma Sūtras of Vyāsa.' Rāmānuja is said to have cried aloud "If I am allowed to remain on the earth long enough, if it be true that my Lord here is pleased with his humble servant, and if the Divine One deigns to grant my prayers, I have, before all of you, given my word that I will, to the best of my ability, carry out his last wishes. If my service is accepted, I pray that the closed fingers open." Rāmānuja is said to have seen the fingers opening.

Extract from Prapannāmritam:—Rāmānuja very soon read the sign and exclaimed "I hereby promise to enter the Vaishnava faith; to devote myself, my time and energies to the task of saving humanity. I shall lead them to the true Faith, shall perfect them in the knowledge of the inner meanings of the Sacred Collect, and shall make them live out the doctrine of Prapatti." One of the fingers of Yāmuna opened. Rāmānuja continued "I shall embody the teachings of the Vedas, the Sastrās and of the great gurus in a commentary on the Vyāsa Sūtras, and place the means of salvation within the easy reach of all." Another of Yāmuna's fingers opened of itself. Rāmānuja went on "I shall select a holy Vaishnava and name him after the sage Parāsara, who in the Vishnu Purāna, had unanswerably established the prominence of the Supreme Self, his relation to the jīva and the path to liberation." The last finger of Yāmunāchārya unclosed.

Rāmānuja returned to Conjeeveram and was doing service to Varadarājaswāmi. Mahā Pūrṇa left Srirangam to induce Rāmānuja to come to Srirangam. At the same time Rāmānuja left Kānchī with a view to go to Srirangam. Both Māha Pūrṇa and Rāmānuja met accidentally at Madurāntakam and Rāmānuja pressed to be initiated into Vaishnavaite secrets. Agreeably to his wishes Mahā Pūrṇa initiated him and both went back to Conjeeveram.

Later in life Rāmānuja renounced family life and became a sanyāsi of the Viśishṭādvaita form. The main differences between an Advaitic sanyāsi and a Sri Vaishnava sanyāsi are in the staff and personal dress. The former usually carries with him a bamboo staff and the latter carries three bamboo sticks tied together as his staff. The Viśishṭādvaita sanyāsi retains his hair (kuḍumi), sacred thread and usually performs his daily rites such as sandhyāvandanam, worship of God, whilst the Advaitic sanyāsi has no tuft of hair and removes his sacred thread. He does not perform the usual sandhyā, etc., which he performed before becoming a sanyāsi.

Sometime after becoming a sanyāsi Rāmānuja sought Gōshṭi Pūrṇa for further initiation. He after testing Rāmānuja a number of times and finding him to be really well-devoted and sincere in his desire to obtain knowledge of God initiated him into the mysteries of the sacred words of the "Ashṭākshari" mantra. But Rāmānuja proceeded to the temple at Tirukkottiyur and from its gopuram proclaimed to the Sri Vaishnavas after gathering them all the secrets communicated to him by Gōshṭi Pūrṇa. On hearing about this incident Gōshṭi P[illegible]ṇa became angry and asked Rāmānujā why he thus disobeyed the sacred injunction. Rā[illegible]ānuja replied that he divulged the secrets to all the Sri Vaishnavas so that they may all hand down to posterity these secrets. By this all of them have become your disciples and are therefore ever freed from the bonds of material existence. I felt compassion for the Sri Vaishnavas and others of mankind and so this emboldened me to behave as I did and, if I incur any sin, it is likely to affect me only as an individual and the merit of the wholesale salvation goes to you. On hearing this explanation which showed the large-heartedness of Rāmānuja, Gōshṭi Pūrṇa was mightily pleased and from that moment he had the greatest regard for Rāmānuja.

Rāmānuja's greatness consists in his establishing firmly the Viśishṭādvaita philosophy, so well developed in his Śrī Bhāshya. It should not, however, be thought that he was the originator of this system of philosophy. It was in vogue even before his time. It was taught before Rāmānuja's time by Bōdhāyana, Tanka, (also called Vākyakāra) Bhagavat Śrī Vatsānka Miśra, Nāthamuni and Āḷavandār. Many of these Āchāryās promulgated this system of philosophy, but were not able to stem the theory of Advaitism so ably advocated by Śankara Āchāryā. Śankara Āchārya based his Bhāshya on Vedas and Upanishads.

In the face of the doctrine of Śankara Āchārya the theory of love and bhakti could not be easily established. The one great attempt of the Āzhvārs and Āchāryās that preceded Rāmānuja was to preach the doctrine of bhakti or prapatti to disprove the theory of Māyā or illusion.

It was left for Rāmānuja to lay the foundation of Viśishṭādvaita on a very firm basis by means of his writing the Śrī Bhāshya. He established the monotheistic principles on the basis of Brahma Sūtras and Upanishads and thus succeeded in opposing successfully the Advaitic philosophy.

From the explanations given by Rāmānuja in opposition to those given by Yādavaprakāśa, his teacher, it is evident that he had Viśishṭādvaitic views from his early age. Further he was influenced very much by the writings of Āzhvārs and Āchāryās, and in fact we may say that he realized in his own experience the ancient wisdom. So instead of trying to find out what his original views are it would be better to consider him as having propounded clearly and succinctly the wisdom of the wise of all times.

As the result of his inspiration from various sources his thoughts were moulded and he set forth a deeply religious view of God, soul and matter. His chief aim seems to have been to preach the doctrine of salvation through bhakti and to make it out to be the central teaching of the Upanishad, the Brahma Sūtra and the Gītā. It would not be an exaggeration if Rāmānuja's attempt in the Śrī Bhāshya is described as an effort surpassing in merit and completeness any previous effort in the same direction.

He was undoubtedly the spokesman of his age. He proclaimed to the world the doctrine of Prapatti or self-surrender to God to be the means of salvation. He also took care not to reject the rituals and the regulations laid down according to the Vedas. In short as remarked by an European scholar "the teaching of Rāmānuja presents to us the highest intellectual altitude in all its varied history by Indian Theism."

7. Conception of God as laid down by Ramanuja.

To have a clear view of what Rāmānuja tried to establish regarding the idea of Brahman or Absolute Being, which was then acquiesced in and followed by his disciples and followers, it is necessary to dwell on Śankara's view of Brahman as developed in Advaitism and elaborated in his Bhāshya on the Vedānta Sūtras. Śankara holds that Brahman is the only real thing and all else including ourselves and our experiences are non-existent and hence unreal. The belief in our individual existence arising from our bodily experience and its entanglement in the samsāra is said to be an error. The higher knowledge showed the whole world and its inhabitants enveloped in ignorance and in the grip of illusion. So, from Śankara's standpoint God is impersonal and consequently indifferent to the love or suffering of the humanity. A Brahman thus devoid of all guṇas (Nirguṇa Brahman) cannot be expected to satisfy the cravings of an intense religious insight. Further it is impossible to infer the existence of such a one by any means, perception, inference or scriptures.

Rāmānuja accepts the existence of the Absolute Being and does not hold that everything in this universe outside the Being is unreal or illusory. On the other hand to him everything is real. He preaches that there is a very intimate relation between the soul, matter and God. According to him God permeates and forms the basis of everything in this universe. God is not merely a transcendental Absolute Being above and beyond the finite Universe, but as already stated God is both immanent and transcendent. Although the conscious (chit) and unconscious (achit) objects of the Universe co-exist with God, they yet derive their existence from Him and are sustained through Him. The pluralistic Universe is real in precisely the same sense as God is real. Thus matter and soul are dependent on God as their ground and they are what they are because of the Brahman. God is the Soul and controlling power of the Universe.

"According to our view, on the other hand, Brahman, which has for its body all sentient and non-sentient beings, whether in their subtle or their gross state is always—in its effected as well as in its casual condition—free from all shadow of imperfection and a limitless ocean as it were of exalted qualities. All imperfections, and suffering and all changes belong not to Brahman, but only to the sentient and non-sentient beings which are its modes." (S.B.E.—48th Vol., Thibaut, page 544.)

"The highest Brahman which is denoted by the term "Being" is the substantial and also the operative cause of the world, that it is all knowing, endowed with all powers; that its purposes come true; that it is the inward principal, the support and ruler of everything; and that distinguished by these and other qualities it constitutes the Self of the entire world." (S.B.E.—48th Vol., Thibaut, page 78.)

In Śrī Bhāshya Rāmānuja says as follows about God:—"He who knows me as unborn and without a beginning, the Supreme Lord of the worlds" (Bhag. Gītā X, 3); "All beings abide in me, I abide not in them. Nay, the beings abide not in me—behold my wordly power. My Self bringing forth the beings supports them but does not abide in them" (Bhag. Gītā IX, 4, 5); "I am the origin and the dissolution of the entire world; higher than I there is nothing else; on me all this is strung as pearls on a thread" (Bhag. Gītā, VII-6, 7); "Pervading this entire universe by a portion (of mine) I abide" (Bhag. Gītā, X-42); "But another the highest person, is called the highest Self, who pervading the three worlds supports them, the Eternal Lord. Because I transcend the perishable and am higher than the Imperishable even, I am among the people and in the Veda celebrated as the Supreme Person" (Bhag. Gītā XV-17 and 18).

"He transcends the fundamental matter of all beings, its modifications, properties and imperfections; he transcends all investing (obscuring) influences, He who is the Self of all. Whatever (room) there is in the interstices of the world is filled by Him; all auspicious qualities constitute His nature. The whole creation of beings is taken out of a small part of His power. Assuming at will whatever form He desires He bestows benefits on the whole world effected by Him. Glory, strength, dominion, wisdom, energy, power, and other attributes are collected in Him, Supreme of the Supreme, in whom no troubles abide, Ruler over high and low, Lord in collective and distributive form, non-manifest and manifest, universal lord, all seeing, all knowing, all powerful, Highest Lord. The knowledge by which that perfect, pure, highest, stainless homogeneous (Brahman) is known or perceived or comprehended—that is knowledge: all else is ignorance." (Vish. Pur. VI-5, 82–87.)

"To that pure one of mighty power, the highest Brahman to which no term is applicable, the cause of all causes, the name "Bhagavat" is suitable. The letter *bha* implies both the cherisher and the supporter, the letter *ga* the leader, mover and creator. The two syllables *bhaga* indicate the six attributes—dominion, strength, glory, splendour, wisdom, dispassion. That in Him the universal Self, the Self of the beings all beings dwell and that He dwells in all, this is the meaning of the letter *va*. Wisdom, might, strength, dominion, glory, without any evil qualities, are all denoted by the word *bhagavat*. This great word *bhagavat* is the name of Vāsudeva who is the highest Brahman and of no one else. This word which denotes persons worthy of reverence in general is used in its primary sense with reference to Vāsudeva only; in a derived sense with regard to other persons." (Vish. Pur. VI-4, 72 pp.)

"Where all these powers abide, that is the form of Him who is the universal form: that is the great form of Hari. That form produces in its sport forms endowed with all powers, whether of gods, men or animals. For the purpose of benefiting the worlds, not springing from work (Karma) is the action of the unfathomable one; all pervading, irresistible." (Vish. Pur. VII-7, 69–71.)

"Him who is of this kind, stainless, eternal, all pervading, imperishable, free from all evil, named Vishnu, the highest abode" (Vish. Pur. I-22, 53); "He who is the highest of the High, the Person, the highest Self, founded on Himself; who is devoid of all the distinguishing characteristics of colour, caste and the like; who is exempt from birth change, increase, decay, and death; of whom it can only be said that He ever is. He is everywhere and in Him everything abides; hence He is called Vāsudeva by those who know. He is Brahman, eternal, supreme, imperishable, undecaying; of one essential nature and ever pure, as free from all defects. This whole world is Brahman, comprising within its nature the Evolved and the Unevolved; and also existing in the form of the Person and in that of time" (Vish. Pur. I-2, 10–14). "The Prakriti about which I told and which is Evolved as well as Unevolved, and the Person—both these are merged in the highest Self. The highest Self is the support of all, the highest Lord; as Vishnu he is praised in the Vedas and the Vedānta texts" (Vish. Pur. VI-4, 38, 39). "Two forms are there of that Brahman, one material, the other immaterial. These two forms, perishable and imperishable, are within all things: the imperishable one is the highest Brahman, the perishable one this whole world. As the light of a fire burning in one place spreads all round, so the energy of the highest Brahman constitutes this entire world" (Vish. Pur. I-23, 53—55). "The energy of Vishnu is the highest, that which is called the embodied soul is inferior; and there is the third energy called Karma or Nescience, actuated by which the omnipresent energy of the embodied soul perpetually undergoes the afflictions of the worldly existence. Obscured by Nescience the energy of the embodied soul is characterised in the different beings by different degrees of perfection." (Vish. Pur. V-7, 61-63.)

These and other texts teach that highest Brahman is essentially free from all imperfection whatsoever, comprises within itself all auspicious qualities, and finds its pastime in originating, preserving, reabsorbing, pervading, and ruling the universe; that the entire complex of intelligent and non-intelligent beings (souls and matter) in all their different estates is real and constitutes the form, *i.e.* the body of the highest Brahman, as appears from those passages which co-ordinate it with the Brahman by means of terms such as śarīra (body), rūpa (form), tanu (body), amśa (part), śakti (power), vibhūti (manifestation of power), and so on; that the souls which are a manifestation of Brahman's power exist in their own essential nature, and also, through their connexion with matter, in the form of embodied souls (Kshetrajña); and that the embodied souls, being engrossed by Nescience in the form of good and evil works, do not recognize their essential nature, which is knowledge, but view themselves as having the character of material things.—The outcome of all this is that we have to recognize Brahman as carrying plurality within itself, and the world, which is the manifestation of his power, as something real. (S.B.E.—Thibaut, Vol. 48, pp. 86—89.)

According to the view of Śankara, the texts in some Upanishads negative the existence of plurality. But Rāmānuja replies thus:—"But what all these texts deny is only plurality in so far as contradicting that unity of the world which depends on its being in its entirety an effect of Brahman, and having Brahman for its inward ruling principle and its true Self. They do not, on the other hand, deny that plurality on

Brahman's part which depends on its intention to become manifold—a plurality proved by the text "May I be many, may I grow forth." (K. Up. VI, 2-3.)

Along with Rāmānuja all orthodox Sri Vaishnavas hold that Brahman, the sole cause of the world, is known only through the Vedas or Śāstras. He cannot be the object of our senses, nor can we have a perception of this object. Ordinary generalizations from our own experience could neither prove nor disprove his existence. Intelligence, however, points to the reality of Brahman and it must be admitted that this reality lies in a region beyond that which can be actually seen or understood by finite intelligence. Rāmānuja in his Śrī Bhāshya says "With regard to supersensuous matters, Scripture (Vedas) alone is authoritative, and that reasoning is to be applied, only to the support of the Scripture (Vedas). (S.B.E., Vol. 48, p. 426.) As the possession, on the Brahman's part, of various powers (enabling it to emit the world) rests exclusively on the authority of the word of the Veda and thus differs altogether from other matters (which fall within the sphere of the other means of knowledge also), the admission of such powers is not contrary to reason. Brahman cannot either be proved or disproved by means of generalizations from experience." (S.B.E.—Thibaut's 48th vol., p. 474.)

Rāmānuja insists throughout his writings that God must always be thought of in two aspects, one, the Supreme Lord beyond our comprehension, but thought of by men as existing in Vaikuṇṭha and the other the personal aspect of the Supreme. It is these two aspects that are often referred to as the two Vibhūtis of God by Āḷavandār and the Āzhvārs in the Prabandhams.

It is generally held that God manifests himself in various forms, but out of his mercy he has assumed and exists in five special forms. These five forms are as described below :—

(1) *Para Rūpa.*—God is believed to exist in the higher world, beyond the experience of human beings. This form of existence is often, in writings of Rāmānuja, Āchāryās and Āzhvārs, referred to as *Nitya Vibhūti.* The place where God exists in this Vibhūti is called *Vaikuṇṭhalōka.* There he is conceived to manifest Himself as described in Vaikuṇṭha Gadya of Rāmānuja. He is believed to be invested with his weapons and ornaments, *viz.*, Śankha, Chakra, Gadā, Sārṅga, Padma, Khaḍga, Kaustubha, Śrīvatsa and Vanamālā (the conch, the discus, the mace, the bow, the lotus, the sword, the gem on his breast, a mole on his breast and a garland of flowers). In this form he is known as *Para Vāsudeva* or *Paratatva.*

The remaining four manifestations belong to this universe and hence are included under the term *Līlā Vibhūti.*

(2) *Vyūhas* or forms assumed by God :—These manifestations of God are three in number and are called Sankarshana, Pradyumna and Aniruddha. These are supposed to occupy the three Vishnulōkās Amōda, Bhuvana and Pramōda forming parts of this material universe. Devas living in these worlds are said to worship them and they will continue to do so until praḷayam.

The six divine attributes jñāna, bala, aiśvarya, śakti, tējas and vīrya are found only in Para Vāsudeva or Vāsudeva, the full manifestation of God. The three Vyūhas divide these qualities amongst them and so each manifestation possesses only two of these divine attributes as shown below:—Sankarshaṇa—jñāna and bala; Pradyumna—aiśvarya and vīrya; Aniruddha—śakti and tējas. These manifestations are meant to take care of the world in its evolution and involution, to prevent evils befalling the jīvātmas whilst they are enslaved and are in bondage of samsāra and to help the Bhaktas or the devoted.

Sankarshaṇa presides over the jīvas and he is responsible for the involution of the universe; he teaches truth to the world. Creation of all pure objects and the teaching of the dharma (good law) are Pradyumna's duties; he is also the organizer of the four varṇas and he presides over "manas." Aniruddha looks after the promulgation of knowledge in the world and protecting it; he is the responsible deity for miśra śrishṭi (mixed creation).

(3) *Vibhava Vigrahas.*—His incarnations in this world are known by the name Avatārs. Some Avatārs like Rāma and Kṛishṇa are considered Sākshād Avatārs or full and direct incarnations, while others are included under Amśāvatārs as in the case of Āzhvārs and some world teachers.

(4) *Antaryāmin.*—God exists in atomic form in the heart of men and generally invisible. But he may become manifest when one meditates on Him with proper concentration of mind and controlling his Buddhi. Even the manifestation is believed to be like "a flash of lightning in the heart of a blue cloud." The real meaning and appearance can be learnt only through initiation.

(5) *Archā Vigraha.*—God is believed to exist in an invisible form in idols made of stone, wood, metal or even masonry. He is of the nature of intellect. God in this form can be made to enter the idols by the force of concentration and the recital of Vedas accompanied by proper rituals. So long as the idols are not polluted and as long as they are worshipped continuously the in-dwelling energy of God resides in them. The moment worship is stopped and idols are neglected or polluted this energy departs from the idols and after this they are not worthy of worship. The idols are usually made in human forms in general, but are invested with some special features such as the possession of more than two arms.

The idols are described in the Āgamas as follows:—"An object of stone, wood or metal, usually fashioned in the form of a human being, in which certain spiritual forces are focussed by the concentrated will-power of high initiates, for the purpose of aiding a worshipper in acquiring that stability of mind necessary to him for the contemplation of the ALL, as laid down in the Upanishads". About Archā Pillai Lokacharya says in his Arthapanchaka as follows:—"The Archā form consists in the images of Bhagavān (God) which accommodate themselves to the various tastes of His creatures, having no fixed form, but that which the worshipper may choose and desire to call Him by; all knowing, but seeming as if not knowing; all powerful, but seeming as if powerless; all sufficient, but seeming as if needy; thus seeming to exchange places, the worshipped with the worshipper and choosing to be ocularly manifest to him in temples and homes, in short at all places and at all times desired."—(Extract from Govindachar's translation). The Āzhvārs also voice forth the above sentiments. For example Poigai Āzhvār in the "Iyarpa" expresses the same idea in the Tamil stanza quoted below:—

> "தமருகந்தது எவ்வுருவம் அவ்வுருவம் தானே
> தமருகந்தது எப்பேர் மற்றப்பேர்—தமருகந்தது
> எவ்வண்ணம் சிந்தித்து இமையா திருப்பரே
> அவ்வண்ணம் ஆழி யானும்."

This in English runs as follows:—

"God with his chakra in his right hand assumes that form which is desired by his devotees; his name also will be that name which his devotees wish him to bear; he will be of that quality which his devout devotees consider him to possess whenever they think of him."

In all these forms enumerated above the Vadagalais think that Śrī or Lakshmī, the Divine mother is associated with the Lord. In support of this they often quote the four ślōkas of Chatuślōkī of Āḷavandār. The Tengalais do not deny this, but say that Lakshmī has no "Vibhutvam" like God and that she is only inferior to God and belongs to the Jīva-kōṭis. But Vadagalais invest Lakshmī with "Vibhutvam" and she is on a par with God and not inferior in any sense.

To understand clearly the mentality of the Sri Vaishnavas as regards their conception of the Abstract Deity it is necessary to know what Rāmānuja has to say in this connexion. Rāmānuja holds that the human mind as it is constituted cannot conceive the Lord as an abstract essence. Such a conception is impossible to our intellectual nature and our moral nature revolts from it. He says "By concrete pictures alone is our otherwise indefinite consciousness rendered definite; in other words what is formless is by such pictures rendered into form." If God is considered to be an Absolute Being, not having any relation to things in this world, it is very difficult to think of him as being the cause; and further, for knowledge relation of things is absolutely necessary. Mere abstraction without any relationship to things cannot constitute knowledge. Constituted as we are, how can we have conception of God, devoid of all qualities and destitute of everything which makes up man's idea of Divine Being. The true and full nature of God cannot be described by our speech nor can it be visualised by symbolism. But God at the same time may be present amongst us holding personal relationship to ourselves. Personal experiences are not denied in scientific enquiries and in ordinary sense perceptions and as such they may be accepted without demur even in religious enquiries. Our conceptions of God are meant only to insist and show his relationship to us, and it is never meant to represent God's full nature. Men can conceive of God in their own form and they can only talk of him in terms of which they are capable. It is essential to think that man is only one of the so many things in this Universe and he is entirely dependent on God for everything. God is not an instrument meant for the advancement of human ends. Saying that beautiful flowers and animals are created for the enjoyment of men is not true.

The Hindu thinkers bring out the sense of otherness of the Divine by the use of the negatives. "There the eye goes not, speech goes not, nor mind, we know not, we understand not, how one would teach it" (Keno-Up. 3). But the human mind finds it extremely difficult to resign itself to absolute silence or negative descriptions. Man is a talking animal.

He insists on interpreting the religious mystery in terms of his own experience. The completely other, the absolutely unlimited, seems to be akin to the utterly indefinite. The human mind craves for something definite and limited and so uses its resources for bringing down the supreme to the region of the determined. We cannot think of God without using our imagination. The religious seer needs the help of the imagination to express his vision. The highest category we can use is that of self-conscious personality. We are persons "purushas" and God is perfect personality (uttamapurusha).

"To admit various descriptions of God is not to lapse into polytheism." (Radhakrishnan—Hindu View of Life, pages 26–29.)

8. Soul and Immortality.

The soul is as much a reality as God himself. It is quite distinct from Brahman and it exists from all eternity and it cannot lose its distinction for all time. If it were to cease to be distinct at any time, its very existence would be ended and it cannot become absorbed and become one with Brahman. It is preposterous to find one substance passing over into the nature of another substance and consequently the individual soul and the highest self cannot enter into real union. If the soul is not capable of separate existence then seeking of release from bondage has no meaning and striving for mōksha is useless.

The soul is an independent agent in one sense. The essential feature of jīva (soul) is the consciousness of self. It retains its character of knowing even in its embodied state. Even though it is made to pass through the process of birth and death several times, it maintains its identity all through. But the power of knowledge, which is its essential feature, becomes contracted when under bondage and expanded in the state of release.

The soul is undoubtedly different from the body, the senses, the vital breath and even buddhi. In the human plane it is merely attached to the gross body which has the five senses and vital breath as its instruments.

Though the soul is endowed with an individuality of a kind, it should be considered at the same time as a part of Brahman. Inasmuch as the soul is an inhabitant of the universe it exists in God. We should remember that God being an inner ruler he also dwells in the soul. As a matter of fact he is in all conscious beings and as such they are thus "qualified" forms of Brahman. The qualifying element (Viśēshaṇa) is found in the limiting conditions attached to the successive births in the samsāra. The soul, therefore, cannot exist apart from God. So souls are regarded as the effects of Brahman. But the change effected in the soul relates only to the contraction and expansion of knowledge and so it is not a change of state in the essential nature as is the case with ether, etc.

When we say that the soul is intrinsically a part of Brahman, we must remember that it is no portion cut out from the whole into separate independence for Brahman admits of no division. The individual soul or jīva is no doubt comprised within the supreme self and at the same time it differs from the most high and so is distinct in one sense.

Souls are found embodied and their energy is certainly inferior to that of Brahman or Vishnu. "The souls cannot escape the consequences of their past lives, and they are again thrust into the world at the new creation with appropriate endowments. The souls are of necessity attached to bodies until release."

The embodiment of the soul is, as already stated, due to being engrossed by karma in the form of good and evil works.

Jīva is atomic in form. "The atomic jīva has his seat in the hritpadma. In spite of the atomic size of the jīva through its attribute of knowledge which expands and contracts, it is able to feel pleasure and pain all over the body, even as the flame of the lamp, though tiny in itself, illumines many things by means of its light which is capable of contraction and expansion. It can apprehend objects far away in space and remote in time. The cognition of the souls, as in the case of God, is eternal in character, self-sustained, extends over all things and is valid; albeit its range is narrowed on account of defects such as the past karma and the like. The plurality of souls is evident from the distribution of pleasures and pains. Until liberation, they are bound to prakriti, which serves as a vehicle (Vāhana) to the jīva, even as a horse does to the rider. The bondage to the body, "This muddy vesture of decay" obstructs the vision of the eternal and prevents the soul from recognizing its kinship with God." (Radhakrishnan—Indian Philosophy, Vol. II, page 691.)

"Thus the self also, although dwelling in one part of the body only, is conscious of sensations taking place in any part of the body." (S.B.E.—48th vol.—Thibaut, page 548.)

"Just as a lamp, although abiding in one place only, enters through the light proceeding from it into connexion with many places; so the soul also, although limited to one place, may through its light-like consciousness enter into several bodies. It may do this as well as in this life the soul, although abiding in one spot of the body only, viz., the heart, pervade the whole body by means of its consciousness and thus makes it its own. There is, however, the following difference between the two cases. The non-released soul has its intellectual power contracted by the influence of karma, and hence is not capable of that expansive pervasion without which it cannot identify itself with other bodies. The released soul, on the other hand, whose intellectual power is non-contracted is capable of extending as far it likes, and thus to make many bodies its own." (S.B.E., Thibaut, Vol. 48, p. 765.)

When freed from the body the souls go to heaven regain their innocence and face God. In this heaven, God abides in his wonderful divine form possessing the charm of eternal youth. In the released state souls are in the satva form. "This ideal world is inherent in God. It is a state already individualized. This condition cannot be identified with the state of souls and matter in pralaya. Apart from the world body, Īsvara has an ideal materiality, a sort of plastic stuff, through which he displays his boundless power of appearing diverse and multiple, though he is inwardly one and the same. Yet his essence is to be distinguished from this Nitya Vibhūti also." (Radhakrishnan—Indian Philosophy, Vol. 2, p. 686.)

"All evil is the issue of past wrong. It is the product of the soul's life in the samsāra, the fruit of its own act. For this God is in no way responsible. Above the endless succession of existences he dwells in light where no shadow of wrong can dim his glory. Such life is even possible from embodied spirits in the world above; how much more then for the Most High Self." (S.B.E., Vol. 48, p. 648.)

"So scripture testifies with the utmost emphasis that Brahman 'free from evil, from old age, from grief'." (S.B.E., Vol. 48, p. 608.)

Mōksha or salvation is understood by Rāmānuja and his followers in South India to be the release of the soul from its bondage or samsāra (limiting barriers). Rāmānuja does not accept the theory of complete absorption of soul into the absolute. Though the released soul may attain the nature of God, there will always be an Almighty Power above him to worship and to adore. In the released state all souls are alike. "Of him who has freed himself from his ordinary name and form, and all the distinctions found thereon, and has assumed the uniform character of intelligence, it may be said that he is of the character of Brahman." (S.B.E., Vol. 48, p. 100.)

Although the released souls keep up their individuality, or the character of Brahman, they do not attain identity with God. Like God they are atomic in size, but they cannot permeate everything and thus be all-pervading. It is true that souls can enter into several bodies and experience different worlds created by the Lord, but they are not capable of creating these worlds. The work of creation is the exclusive characteristic of God. In the Bhagavat Gītā it is said that the released soul attains only the same attributes as the Highest Self. "Abiding by this knowledge, they, attaining, to an equality of attributes with me, do neither come forth at the time of creation nor are troubled at the time of general destruction." (Bhag. Gītā, XIV, 2.)

"Intelligence, therefore, bliss, and the other essential qualities of the soul which were obscured and compacted by karma, expand and thus manifest themselves when the bondage due to karma and the soul approaches the highest light." (S.B.E., Vol. 48, p. 758.)

"Where the texts speak of the soul's becoming equal to, or having equal attributes with, Brahman the meaning is that the nature of the individual soul which is a mere mode of Brahman is equal to that of Brahman, *i.e.*, that on putting off its body it becomes equal to Brahman in purity. The soul when it has reached the highest light and freed itself from all bondage, is conscious of itself as separate from the highest self." (S.B.E., Vol. 48, pp. 758 and 759.)

"Śruti and Smriti alike declare that the connexion of the individual souls with bodies of different kinds—divine, human, animal and so on—depends upon the karma of those souls; compare 'He who performs good works becomes good, he who performs bad works becomes bad. He becomes pure by pure deeds, bad by bad deeds.' In the same way the reverend Parāśara declares that what causes the difference in nature and status between Gods, men, and so on, is the power of the former deeds of the souls about to enter into a new creation. 'He (the Lord) is the operative cause only in the creation of new beings; the material cause is constituted by the potentialities of the beings to be created. The being to be embodied requires nothing but an operative cause; it is its own potentiality which leads its being into that condition of being (which it is to occupy in the new creation)'. Potentiality here means karma." (S.B.E., Vol. 48, p. 478.)

9. Matter or Prakrti.

According to Rāmānuja prakriti also is uncreated, although there may be changes in its form. "Some texts declare a distinction of nature between non-intelligent matter, intelligent beings, and Brahman, in so far as matter is the object of enjoyment, the souls the enjoying subjects and Brahman the ruling principle. 'From that the Lord of Māyā creates all this; in that the other one is bound up through the Māyā; know prakriti to be Māyā, and the great Lord the ruler of Māyā." (S.B.E., Vol. 48, page 141).

Matter or Prakriti is called Māyā. Primeval matter is in a subtle condition, which forms the totality of non-intelligent things. The prakriti is called Māyā because it is capable of producing various wonderful effects.

"Other texts, again, aim at teaching that the highest Self to whom non-intelligent beings stand in the relation of body, and hence of modes, subsists in the form of the world, in its causal, as well as in its effected aspect and hence speak of the world in this its double aspect as that which is (the Real)." (S.B.E., 84th Vol., page 140.)

"Matter in its subtle state subserves ends, in so far only as it is dependent on the Supreme Person who is the cause of all. We by no means wish to deny unevolved matter and all its effect in themselves, but in so far only as they are maintained not to have their Self in the Supreme Person. For the fact is that they constitute His body and He thus constitutes their Self; and it is only through this their relation to Him that the Pradhāna, and so on are capable of accomplishing their several ends. Otherwise the different essential natures of them all could never exist—nor persist, nor act." (S.B.E., Vol. 48, page 358.)

Matter like Soul is uncreated and exists from all eternity. It exists in two different conditions, namely, a subtle state when it does not possess the qualities by which it is ordinarily known, when there is no distinction of individual name and form and when matter is unevolved (avyakta) and the gross state when it becomes associated with Souls. The subtle state exists in the state of Pralaya when Brahman is in the causal condition (kāraṇāvasthā). It is during the period of creation that matter is evolved and becomes gross. In obedience to the will of God souls enter into connexion with material bodies corresponding to the degree of merit or demerit obtained by them in previous forms of existence. God is now, along with souls and matter as his body in his effected condition (kāryāvasthā). The existence of matter from eternity cannot be proved either by perception or inferences. The belief in its existence is dependent only on the authority of the Vedas. Compared with the Soul, prakriti is more dependent on the Lord and so has no freedom and choice of its own, like the Soul. Prakriti is only an object of experience bhōgya, liable to changes and indifferent to the ends of man.

Smritis also maintain that Souls and Prakriti are eternal. In the Bhagavat Gītā the following statements occur:—

"Do thou know both Nature and the Soul to be without beginning, and know all effects and qualities to have sprung from Nature. Nature is declared to be the cause of the activity of cause and effects, whilst the soul is the cause of there being enjoyment of pleasure and pain. For the Soul abiding in Nature experiences the qualities derived from Nature, the reason being its connexion with the qualities, in its births in good and evil wombs." (Bhag. Gītā. XIII, 19--21). "Goodness, Passion and Darkness—these are the qualities which, issuing from Nature, bind in the body the embodied Soul, the undecaying one" (Bhag. Gītā. XIV—5). "All beings at the end of a kalpa return into my Nature, and again, at the beginning of a kalpa, do I send them forth. Presiding over my own Nature again and again do I send forth this vast body of beings which has no freedom of its own being subject to Nature. With me as ruler Nature brings forth all moving and non-moving things and for this reason the world does ever go round." (Bhag. Gītā, IX—7, 8, 10.)

Further on Rāmānuja in his Śrī Bhāshya says "that from that, *i.e.* from matter in its subtle causal state when it is not yet divided, the Lord of all creates the entire universe." From this statement about Creation we understand that Prakriti exists in a two-fold state according as it is either cause or effect. During a praḷaya it unites itself with Brahman and abides in its subtle state, without any distinction of names and forms; it then is called the "Unevolved," and by other similar names. At the time of creation, on the other hand, there reveal themselves in Prakriti, goodness and other gunas, it divides itself according to names and forms, and then is called the "Evolved" and so on, and, transforming itself into fire, water, and earth, it appears as red, white and black. In its causal condition it is *aga, i.e.*, unborn, in its effected condition it is caused by light, i.e., Brahman. (S.B.E. Thibaut., Vol. 48, page 368.)

10. Initiation into Vaishnavism.

As already stated the Sri Vaishnava Brahmans do not differ from the Smārta Brahmans so far as samskāras enjoined by the Sūtras are concerned. But every Sri Vaishnava Brahman has to be initiated into the secrets of the Vaishnavite religion by a

Vaishnavite religious teacher. This first initiation into Vaishnavism is called the Panchasamskāra ceremony. This initiation is usually performed by a grihastha who is learned and well versed in Śāstras. It is also done by the sanyāsis and maṭhādhipatis.

The person seeking initiation goes to the religious teacher and after the preliminary prostration and offering of the usual fruits, flowers, betel leaves and nuts requests to be initiated. The initiate should be a Brahmachārī, a grihastha and a person who has not passed through the ceremony of Upanayana is not fit for initiation. Though it has become a formal ceremony, it was in former times a living ceremony and the initiate was capable of understanding the importance of the initiation. The frame of mind most essential for the initiation was there.

The person seeking initiation is usually told to come on a particular day fixed by the Achārya, provided he is satisfied with the candidate. In case he is not satisfied, the candidate is asked to wait for a time. The actual ceremony of Panchasamskāra consists of the five distinct items tāpa, punḍra, nāma, the mantras and yajana (branding, wearing caste marks, naming, repeating of mantras and worship of God given). As a matter of fact the name of the ceremony Panchasamskāra is given to it on account of its consisting of these five items.

The branding or tāpa is usually done on the shoulders with chakra mark on the right shoulder and the śankha mark on the left, the chief emblems of Vishnu. (See plate IV-A.) These marks are made of silver or copper and are attached to the ends of sticks of the same metal. For purposes of branding these sticks are heated in a fire in which the sudarśana hōmam has been performed. If the Āchārya is a grihastha (married man), he heats the sticks, after himself doing the hōma and brands the initiate. If, on the other hand, the Āchārya happens to be a sanyāsi, he requests a grihastha to do the sudarśana hōmam and then receives the heated rods bearing the emblem from him and does the branding. The sanyāsins of Vadagalai persuasion cannot touch any metal under any circumstances. So the heated rods are not directly touched. They are covered with betel or plantain or mango leaves and then the covered end is taken hold of by the hand and the branding is then done. Some Āchāryas such as those of the Ahōbila Mutt and a few Tengalai Āchāryas do not consider the sudarśana hōmam as necessary and so they dispense with it.

The punḍra or caste mark is put on in twelve places (hence the name dvādaśapunḍram) beginning with the forehead. While making these marks in their appropriate places they have to pronounce the mantra pertaining to it or at least the name of one of the twelve. The full details of wearing the dvādaśapunḍram are described in detail under the daily ceremonies of a Sri Vaishnava Brahman.

The name to be adopted by the person should be that of one of the recognized names of Vishnu. If the name already borne by the initiate corresponds to any one of Vishnu's names, it is recognized and no new name is given, but if otherwise a new name is given. As regards naming of men it is mostly the name of some God that is given and amongst Sri Vaishnavas it is only the name of the God Vishnu. In this connexion it is interesting to note that one of the Āzhvārs insists upon giving to an individual the name of Vishnu and not the names of objects. (cf. Pāsurams of Periya Āzhvār Tirumozhi IV).

> " மானிடசாதியில் தோன்றிற்று ஓர்மாணிட ஜாதியை
> மானிடசாதியின் பேரிட்டால் மறுமைக் கில்லை
> வானுடைமாதவா! கோவிந்தா! வென்றழைத்தக்கால்
> நானுடை நாரணன் தம்மன்னை நரகம்புகாள்."
>
> மலமுடை யூத்தையில் தோன்றிற்று ஓர்மல வூத்தையை
> மலமுடை யூத்தையின் பேரிட்டால் மறுமைக்கில்லை
> குலமுடைக் கோவிந்தா! கோவிந்தா! வென்றழைத்தக்கால்
> நலமுடை நாரணன் தம்மன்னை நரகம்புகாள்.
>
> (பெரியாழ்வார்திருமொழி—IV—6, 4, 5)

The above translated into English is as follows:—

(1) If a being who is one of the human kind is called by a name common to the human beings, heaven is not attainable; in case he is called Mādhava! Gōvinda! (which are names of God) the mother of this person who is named after Nārāyaṇa will not enter (naraka) hell.

(2) If a person whose body consists of a mass of dirt and who is born from another person whose body is also similarly composed is named after a being who is also like the human being in structure, heaven is not attainable; if, on the other hand, he is named Gōvinda! Gōvinda! the mother of this person called only by one of Nārāyaṇa's names, he will not go to hell.

The fourth and most important item is the repetition of the *mūla mantra* and *dvaya mantra* into the right ear of the initiate in such a low tone that it could be heard only by the person who undergoes initiation. These mantras are held to be most sacred and very important by all Sri Vaishnavas.

The fifth item is the presenting of an idol for worshipping. This item is only a formal thing in the ceremony now done.

After this ceremony of branding the initiate very often requests to be initiated in the reading of Rāmāyaṇa, Śrī Bhāshya, etc. These works are not generally to be read without an initiation. The Āchārya utters in the hearing of the candidate the beginning (words which form the commencement) of these works. This is done because no Sri Vaishnava can begin the reading of any of these without being initiated. From an elaborate real initiation this has now dwindled into an empty formal ceremony. Originally initiation meant, making the candidate catch the real spirit of the work.

To call oneself a Sri Vaishnava Brahman this initiation is necessary. Even non-Brahmans undergo the ceremony of Panchasamskāra if they are to become Vaishnavas. Of course in all the twice born castes wearing the sacred thread, initiation takes place only after the performance of the thread-wearing ceremony to the individual concerned.

As already mentioned, during the time of Rāmānuja all Sri Vaishnava Brahmans observed more or less the same common principles as regards rituals and doctrines. As they had to contend against other religions they all united together and observed the same customs and held similar beliefs. This was inevitable as they all had the same Āzhvārs and Āchāryas who all wrote in the same strain. Until several years after the death of Rāmānuja (A.D. 1137) there were no dissentient voices. But after Rāmānuja's death differences soon arose in interpretations and this led to doctrinal differences and observances. At first the differences were only in philosophical explanations but as time rolled on the differences became larger and larger in number and at last when Pillai Lōkācharya and Vēdānta Dēśika appeared the Sri Vaishnavas became sharply divided into the two sections Tengalais and Vadagalais, the former recognizing Pillai Lōkācharya and the latter Vēdānta Dēśika as their respective teachers. From this time onwards these two sections remain separate and the differences are becoming keener and keener day after day and are becoming more bigoted and losing the spirit of toleration to a very great extent. For the sake of clearness the two sections of Vaishnavites will be dealt with separately.

11. The Vadagalai Sri Vaishnavas.

The Vaḍagalais or the Northerners as the name is sometimes interpreted, recognize Rāmānuja as their chief Āchārya and after him Tirukkurukaippillān—shortly referred to as Pillān. Subsequent to Pillān there were several recognized as Āchāryas until we come to Vēdānta Dēśika. Their names and successors are shown below in a tabular form:—

Rāmānuja.
|
Tirukkurukai
Pillan.
|
Engaḷ Āzhvān.
(Vishnu Chittan).
|
Naḍādur Ammāl.
(Varadā Chāriar).
|
Appullār.
|
Vēdānta Dēśika.

After Rāmānuja the Āchārya of eminence and of keen intellect capable of preaching to the world was only Vēdānta Dēśika. Like Rāmānuja he was a reformer of a very high order and a universal teacher in virtue of his versatile intellect.

As long as Rāmānuja was alive, Sri Vaishnavas attached equal importance to the religious views expressed both in Sanskrit and Tamil writings. To Rāmānuja and his followers during his lifetime the Vedas written in Sanskrit along with the other Śāstras also written in the Sanskrit language and the Tamil Prabandhams with the commentaries in Tamil called "The Six Thousand" were equal in sanctity. Both were held in high estimation. Soon after Rāmānuja's death certain Āchāryas took more kindly to the Tamil Prabandhams than to the Sanskrit Vedas and Śāstras. This was natural because Tamil being their own mother-tongue, Tamil writings appealed to their minds with greater force than a foreign language like Sanskrit. Great intellectual effort was needed to master the Sanskrit language so as to be able to understand thoroughly the views expressed in Sanskrit religious works. The followers of such Āchāryas began to pay exclusive attention to the Prabandhams and Tamil commentaries on the same, and totally neglected the Sanskrit writings. The followers of such Āchāryas became crystallized as the Tengalai sect of the present day. While some Āchāryas showed a greater inclination to the study of Tamil Prabandhams alone, others continued like Rāmānuja to consider both the Tamil Prabandhams and the Sanskrit Vedas and Śāstras as equally good and the followers of such Āchāryas are now known as the Vaḍagalai sect.

The Viśishṭādvaita philosophy so ably developed by Rāmānuja in his commentaries on the Brahma Sūtras usually called "The Śrī Bhāshya" was promulgated by all the teachers that followed Rāmānuja until Vēdānta Dēśika. It was left to Vēdānta Dēśika once again to preach and promulgate this philosophy to its fullest extent and resuscitate it from its decadence. The Vaḍagalai Sri Vaishnavas of the present time adopt practically the tenets as promulgated by Vēdānta Dēśika. To understand the influence of this great soul it is necessary to speak about this universal teacher and his doings.

Vēdānta Dēśika was born at Tūppil (at present a part of Conjeeveram town) in the year 1269 A.D. Ananta Sūri his father was a devout Sri Vaishnava who had performed a yāga. Hence he was called Ananta Sūri Sōmayājī. He was the descendant of one of the seventy-four simhāsanādhipatis established by Rāmānuja. Vēdānta Dēśika's mother Thothārambhā was the sister of Ātrēya Rāmānuja, better known as Appullār, the successor of Naḍādur Ammal (Varada Chariar) as the Ubhayasimhāsanādhipati. Vēdānta Dēśika lived for 100 years. He died in the year 1369 A.D. (14th November 1369).

As already stated, amongst the Āchāryas that came after Rāmānuja, Vēdānta Dēśika is considered to be the greatest and in many respects equal to Rāmānuja. Just like Rāmānuja, Vēdānta Dēsika had to establish once again the Viśishṭādvaita philosophy and thus prove the supremacy of Vaishnavism over other religious beliefs especially Advaitism. This was his chief aim. To do this successfully he had to promulgate the Viśishṭādvaita philosophy and teach the tenets in such a way as to appeal to the people in general. The difficulties he had to overcome were greater than those Rāmānuja encountered. The latter reformer had only to deal with the Advaitism of Śankara, but the former had to contend not only against Advaitism but also against Jainism. After Rāmānuja's death Jainism gained ground and gradually began to spread amongst the masses. At the time when Vēdānta Dēśika began his religious teachings these religions had attained great prominence. Further in many respects the period in which Vēdānta Dēśika flourished was a most momentous and troublesome one in South India. Just then the Mahomedans had penetrated South India. Their fanaticism, crusading spirit against other religions and their discipline enabled them to become irresistible. The people of the country, being in a weakened condition, could not withstand the struggle with other religions. So they were looking on with despair at all the desecrations of their temples and religion. Just at this juncture the two great men Vēdānta Dēśika and Vidyāraṇya appeared on the scene and successfully maintained their religions Vaishnavism and Śaivism respectively. In opposing the spread of other religions both these men were interested and so both of them united in stemming the progress of other religions. Their organizing genius, faith and patience enabled them to restore the faith of the panic-stricken people in their own religion and to bring about its triumph over other religions in this part of India.

No doubt all the Srivaishnavas, both the Vadagalais and the Tengalais followed the Viśishṭādvaita philosophy. As the Tengalais adopted mainly Prabandhams to the exclusion of Sanskrit they were unable to maintain this philosophy in the face of the development of other Hindu religions and Muhammadanism. So Vēdānta Dēśika (also named Venkaṭanātha) had to contend against the Tengalai views and Śaivism.

Vēdānta Dēśika continued the work of Rāmānuja and his position was a peculiar one. He joined hands with Vidyāraṇya, a worthy rival who continued the work of Śankara Āchārya, in opposing the spread of other religions. As both Dēśika and Vidyāraṇya were men of extraordinary intellect and encyclopædic knowledge and as they both disliked the spread of other religions equally, they preached and worked to establish the faith of the Hindus. Vēdānta Dēśika upheld his own view of the Viśishtādvaita philosophy against the Tengalais and against Advaitism.

Judging from Vēdānta Dēśika's writings, which are about 120 in number, his activity was many-sided. Possessing a versatile intellect, it was possible for him to make his teachings thorough. So far as his daily life was concerned he was extremely kind, sincerely pious, and his habits were saintly though simple. His name is revered by posterity because he was not only the embodiment of everything that was good and great, but also for his deep erudition and sterling virtues as man. By rescuing from degradation he rendered valuable services to Vaishnavism at the most critical period. It would not be an exaggeration if people told that no saint ever lived in more critical times and no one overcame the difficulties with such success and glory.

Vēdānta Dēśika possessed an extraordinary power of rousing the religious spirit in human minds. His writings have appealed and moulded the minds of many and in several directions. He wrote both in Tamil and Sanskrit and like Rāmānuja he held both the languages equal and treated the Prabandhams and Vedas and Śastras with the same respect and regard. The subject-matter of his writings is as varied as his intellect. He wrote to the satisfaction of poet, saint, philosopher and the ordinary level of human beings. In fact his writings appealed to and appeased all kinds and grades of men. Added to this the intellectual feat of his life presented to the world a model of saintly simplicity and divine purity. In the matter of devotion to God, he was the foremost and unique. He has rendered the greatest possible service to the humanity by the purity of his devotion to God. So it is no wonder that his own people loved him very much, that he was a terror to his enemies and that he was admired by both.

His literary greatness is well-known to scholars and it was acknowledged even by Advaitins. Appayya Dīkshitar, an orthodox Brahmin and an Advaitin of a high order, has written a commentary called Dēśika's Yadāvābhyudayam on one of Vēdānta Dēśika's works.

Vēdānta Dēśika was a grihastha throughout his life and never adopted the sanyāsi's life. Thus he proved to the world that it is not necessary to be a sanyāsi for being an Āchārya and to do religious and propagandist work. He successfully showed to the world that a householder's life is also as dignified as that of a sanyāsi and that it is well suited for the attainment of mōksha. All his teachings were done in the very homes of men who were desirous of knowledge. No one had to seek the Āchārya in a secluded place. Consequently religious instruction spread widely and rapidly. The mode of teaching adopted by him led to the marvellous increase of scholars to hear him and the Viśishṭādvaitic philosophic ideas thereby became more general and popular.

This great person is considered to be a great saint and he is not only worshipped in the form of an idol, but is also ever remembered by Sri Vaishnavas of the Vaḍagalai persuasion. Whenever they do their domestic worship of God they never fail to invoke this great saint's blessings and pray that he may be with them and shed his wholesome influence on their character and life "for a century more" referring of course to his period of existence in this world. As the prayer is repeated almost everyday by the Vaḍagalai Sri Vaishnavas, it may be said that Vaḍagalai Sri Vaishnavas are praying indirectly for his eternal presence. It is also a custom amongst the Vaḍagalai Brahmans to offer holy offerings in the form of betel, fruits and money to Vēdānta Dēśika during every ceremony.

Being a strict follower of Rāmānuja he promulgated Rāmānuja's ideas of God, soul and matter in a more elaborate form as religious treatises and lectures. All his lectures are now collected together and are called Rahasyams as they contain views about tatvas and God. Most of these lectures were delivered to a mixed audience and in a mixed language called "Maṇipravāḷam." It is probable that his audience were well versed in this mixed language—Tamil interspersed with Sanskrit—during his days.

With Rāmānuja, he held that God is a perfect personality endowed with all good qualities, and quite independent of everything in this universe. He is unique, supreme and second to none. God is the influencer and supporter of everything around him. Although in the created world there are different things, they are all permeated by the spirit of God. In other words, God's connexion with the things in the universe is perfectly natural. The supreme being in addition to his spirit permeating every thing, has also a special divine form called "*Nitya Vibhūti.*" In this peculiar state neither prakriti nor karma could touch him. Although the supreme being is immanent, He is not touched by the changes occurring in matter (prakriti) nor by the sufferings of the soul. All evil is the result of past wrong and it is due to the soul's embodied life, *i.e.*, life in samsāra. God is in no way responsible for it. He has made laws for guidance and he does not interfere with these regular laws. Souls and matter exist because of him and are subject to his will in spite of their being real and eternal.

In all his lectures Vedānta Dēśika deals with the characteristics of the tatvas including God: prominence is given to Prapatti and in his lectures collected together under the special name of "Rahasya trayasāram" he gives a detailed account of the character, power and qualities of God, and the qualifications necessary to attain to mōksha through the method of Prapatti. In all his lectures called "Rahasyams" he deals with the three tatvas and with the three mantrams or Rahasya mantras pertaining to Nārāyaṇa, the Supreme Being. In all these lectures he speaks of the same items, but from different points of view in each. As an example, the ideas expressed in one of these lectures (called Rahasyams) on tatvams are given below:—

The tatvas that ought to be clearly understood, by good and pious men initiated by good Āchāryas into the mūla mantras, are two, namely, Paratatva and Aparatatva.

Of these two the Paratatva is Śriyappati, the Purushōttama—(the Supreme Being). He is the seed or source of everything that can be thought of; he permeates everything and exists in them just as life exists in the body of living beings; he is unfathomable, the Great Light, the Great Dēva; he is the receptacle of wonderful qualities and possessor of the most exalted and unopposable good qualities; he is without an equal in goodness; he is capable of enjoyment without any hindrance from any source and is the possessor of all auspicious qualities; he, in order to prevent those who throw on his mercy from being born several times, assumes avatārs by being born in several forms; he does this to prevent those who believe in him fully from undergoing troubles by birth and in so doing he subjects himself seemingly to the sufferings incidental to such lives; he does good to the dēvas according to their merits; and evil to the asuras who think of doing evil; those who trust him as their innermost soul are trusted by him as his soul; he throws himself completely on those who surrender themselves to him unconditionally and entirely. He is also capable of existing in two Vibūtis, *i.e.*, both in Heaven and in this world, as stated by some Āzhvārs.—He is without a second as his equal; he is a wonderful being capable of existing in five forms, namely, Para, Vyūha, Vibhava, Antaryāmisvarūpa and Archāvatāram.

In Para rūpa he as a single form will be visible only to Muktas and Nityas;

"குழுமிற் றெவர் குழாங்கள் கைதொழச்
சோதிவெள் ளத்தினுள்ளே என்றும் ஆதியஞ்
சோதியுரு வென்றும் சொல்லுகிற படியே
வானுயரின்பம் மன்னு வீற்றிருந்த ரூபம்."

Translation:—"That form which remains high in the sky giving pleasure to all the beholders, the form remaining surrounded by the effulgent light emanating from it and the one in whose light emanations the worshipping men are standing with hands in a prayerful posture."

Vyūhas are rupas that have colours that are changing during Krita and Trēta yugams. The Rūpas Aniruddha, Pradyumna and Sankarshaṇa possessing the qualities, śakti, tējas, aiśwarya, vīrya, jñāna and balam. In disposing of and creating both these would be the qualities possessed by these.

In the four Vyūhas each is divided into three Vyūhāntaras and so there will be twelve Vyūhāntaras named Kēśava, Dāmōdara, etc. (twelve names).

Vibhavams are the avatārs of fish, tortoise, etc. These forms are the avatārs taken by God.

Antaryāmi Svarūpa is a form that can be seen only in the yōgic state (*i.e.*, when eyes become red).

Archāvatāram is a form that is conceived by men or devotees, form that is named by the men-devotee, that name—according to the views held by archakas, *i.e.*, Śēsha śēshibhāva established by him.

These rūpas will be śubha āśrayams. He who has seen Śrīman will not see one Being without Śrī.

That which is known as the Śarīra tatvam of one who is the highest spirit and named Aparatatvam may be divided into chētana and achētana tatvams.

12. The Tengalai Sri Vaishnavas.

Like the Vaḍagalai Sri Vaishnavas the Tengalai Sri Vaishnavas also have their own hierarchy of Āchāryas and they are represented in a tabular form below:—

Rāmānuja
|
Embār
|
(1024–1129 A.D.)
|
Bhaṭṭar
(Parāśara Bhaṭṭar)
(1062–1090 A.D.)
|
Nanjīyar
(1112–1213 A.D.)
|
Nampillai
(1207–1302 A.D.)

- Periyaāchchan Pillai (1226–1321)
  - Pillai Lōkācharya (1264–1327)
- Vaḍakku Tiruvīdippillai (1226– ?)

The Āchāryas usually recognized by the Tengalai Brahmans are all included in the above hierarchy. But when we take into consideration the dates of their birth and death, there arises some confusion. For instance in the table given above we find Embār as the successor of Rāmānuja. Rāmānuja and Embār are Tirumalai Nambi's sister's sons, and Tirumalai Nambi was the preceptor of both Rāmānuja and Embār. According to the tradition amongst Vaḍagalais, Embār could not have succeeded Rāmānuja, as Embār died seven years before Rāmānuja's death. Embār died in 1130 A.D. Both Embār and Rāmānuja were students studying under Yādavaprakāśa. After Embār comes Parāśara Bhaṭṭa, Kūrēśa's son. In this case also the succession is doubted. Parāśara Bhaṭṭa is said to be born in 1062 A.D. (4163 Kaliyuga) and to have lived only 28 years. So he must have died in 1090 A.D., *i.e.*, about 39 years before Embār and 49 years before the death of Rāmānuja. Under these circumstances it is considered impossible that Parāśara Bhaṭṭa succeeded Embār. Both Parāśara Bhaṭṭa and his younger brother Vedavyāsa Bhaṭṭa were the disciples of their father Kūrēśa.

The successors of Rāmānuja, Embār and Parāśara Bhaṭṭa were never celebrated as being well-versed in Prabandhams. On the other hand they were good Sanskrit scholars and their works in Sanskrit are free from partisan spirit and are accepted by all (*i.e.*, both by Vaḍagalais and Tengalais).

Here it should be remarked that Bhaṭṭa was the name given to more than one person. The younger Bhaṭṭa (Vedavyāsa Bhaṭṭa) was really a cleverer person than his brother, Parāśara Bhaṭṭa.

Nanjīyar who succeeded Bhaṭṭa (Parāśara Bhaṭṭa) is said to be a Madhva by caste and he was converted into Vaishnavism by Bhaṭṭa (Parāśara Bhaṭṭa). The name Nanjīyar was adopted only after becoming a Vaishnavite sanyāsi.

Nampillai succeeded Nanjīyar. He wrote the 9,000 again (ஒன்பதாயிரப்படி) after the loss of the same in the Cauvery. His period was an epoch-making one for the Tengalais, because it was he who paved the way for sectarianism amongst the Vaishnavites. The Ubhaya Simhāsanādhipati Varadāchāriar left finally Srirangam and went back to Conjeeveram. This enabled Nampillai to freely promulgate his views with energy, as there was no one to oppose him.

Just as in the case of Bhaṭṭa there were two persons known by the name Nanjīyar. The person who wrote commentaries on the 9,000 (ஒன்பதாயிரப்படி) on the Prabandhas was a disciple of Kaḍāmbi Āchchan. There was also another sanyāsi known as Nanjīyar, a disciple of Vedavyāsa Bhaṭṭa. Evidently the author of the Tengalai guruparamparai, Pinbalagiya Jīyar, confounded this person with the Nanjīyar of the 9,000 of the Prabandhic fame and thus confusion arose.

Nampillai's lectures drew to him several learned men and Periya Āchchān Pillai was one of his disciples. " Periya Āchchān attended the lectures of his master Nampillai and published the lectures on Prabandham as the 24,000 (இருபத்திநாலாயிரப்படி). In spite of the popularity of his lectures and views, it was absolutely necessary to show that these views were based upon the traditional account, based upon the teachings of the Āchāryas.

Without this basis people may not accept the views and follow the tenets without demur. As Nampillai made much of the fact that caste was nothing before creed and as he taught that Prabandhams in Tamil were superior to Sanskrit writings, his teachings appealed to the masses very much. An Āchāryic hierarchy had to be prepared to show to the people that there was really a continuity of teaching through the Āchāryas. Consequently a Guruparamparā was prepared and written by Pinbalagiya Perumāḷ Jīyar.

The Tengalai Guruparamparai did not fully follow the tradition. Some facts were ignored and certain facts were suppressed, as they were not found necessary for the purpose.

As already stated Rāmānuja strove hard to establish Vaishnavism by harmonizing and co-ordinating all the previous works. No distinction was made between the Sanskrit teachings and the Tamil Prabandhams. He considered the Tamil Prabandhams and the Sanskrit Vedas to be equal in every respect. Soon after Rāmānuja's death this balance of judgment gradually weakened and finally disappeared. One set of Āchāryas began to propound the Prabandhams to be all important, ignoring the study of Sanskrit writings. As a reaction, in opposition to this view, some Āchāryas insisted upon Sanskrit being studied more than the Prabandhams, though they did not ignore the Prabandhams completely.

Gradually the attachment to the Tamil Prabandhams became so great that Sanskrit was completely neglected. This was both good and bad at the same time. It was good because this movement enabled everybody to become acquainted with religious truths irrespective of caste. The religious truths and culture were till now the monopoly of the people who naturally read Sanskrit, and these were confined to the higher castes. The lower castes who constituted the mass being unable to follow the culture in Sanskrit, read and understood very well all the truths contained in the Tamil writings. The Prabhandic movement of the Tengalais thus led to the rapid spread of Vaishnavism among all grades of people and it became a popular creed. As a logical result of this movement several Non-Brahman castes, such as the Vanniyans, began to claim superiority, or at any rate, equality with the Sri Vaishnava Brahmans. This view was carried to such an extreme that certain Vanniyans took to the sacred thread, to the study of the Vedas and even to the establishment of temples and temple worship. Such a group of Vanniyans exists in Kumilam village in South Arcot District. (See "Castes and Tribes" under Pallis.) These people call themselves Kovilar. (See plate XII-A & B.) So far, they have remained isolated and no mixture with Sri Vaishnava Brahmans has been effected. In spite of the theoretical views expressed by the Tengalai Brahmans, they have not mixed with them in any way. Like the Vaḍagalais they have kept aloof from the Kovilar.

Along with the linguistic separation into Prabandhic school and Sanskrit school with Bhāshya and Vedas, some doctrinal differences also came in. They relate chiefly to Śrī or Lakshmī and Prapatti.

Śrī or Lakshmī is, as already explained, believed by Vaḍagalais to be with God in all states and endowed with all the powers possessed by God. So she has

" Vibhutvam ", *i.e.*, she is equal to God in every respect, inasmuch as she possesses the same powers as God. But according to the views of the Tengalais Śrī or Lakshmī is only one of the Jīvakōṭis and cannot be considered as possessing Vibhutvam. In other words she is like a finite being, but she is at the head of all. She is only a servant of God though her soul is superior to the souls of others. She is even superior to Vishvaksēna, but only of his class, *i.e.*, " Aparam " only. She can and may plead with God on our behalf, but she has no power to give mōksha to anybody.

Vaḍagalais consider Śrī or Lakshmī to be equal to God in every respect and she possesses Vibhutvam as stated above. They consider her to be always one with the Lord and to co-operate with him in the maintenance and preservation of this universe. Therefore she is as important as God in the determination and regulation of everything in our life.

Both the Vaḍagalais and Tengalais believe in " Bhakti " and " Śaraṇāgati ". But however, most of the Tengalais, especially those who belong to the Prabandhic school, hold that the Āzhvārs gave prominence to Śaraṇāgati (prapatti) in preference to Bhakti preceded by the strict performance of duties and by the acquisition of the knowledge of God (Jñāna). Śaraṇāgati or prapatti, according to the Āhzvārs, depends only upon the Grace of God and no preliminary effort is needed. The Vaḍagalais and a few Tengalais also hold that Rāmānuja showed that both bhakti and Śaraṇāgati were methods of obtaining salvation according to the Upanishads and Vedānta. While Rāmānuja was alive, and until some time after his death no difference of opinion as regards the method of preparation of a prapanna and the circumstances under which he could practise prapatti was held. Both the Vaḍagalais and Tengalais are agreed as to the need for prapatti, but the Tengalais say that mere surrender to God is enough. Self-effort or other kinds of preparation are considered unnecessary for self-surrender. God's love is spontaneous and so previous preparation is not needed. This theory of Śaraṇāgati logically leads to the idea of " Dōsha bhōgya " by God. The Vaḍagalais, on the other hand, hold that self-effort and a great deal of preliminary effort is needed to create a feeling of complete helplessness and unalloyed faith in God's grace. So, as a preliminary to prapatti (Śaraṇāgati) a great deal of preparation is necessary. Vedānta Dēśika in all his lectures shows the importance and the necessity of the previous preparation. No doubt that God's love is always available and he is also generous enough to ignore the soul's taints when prayed for.

In accordance with the above views the Tengalais do not submit themselves to the ceremony of prapatti after Panchasamskāra, whilst the Vaḍagalais seek an Āchārya and request him to help them to perform the prapatti (Śaraṇāgati) as a separate item, after the Panchasamskāra. The Panchasamskāra ceremony may be performed even when the candidate has not passed through the Upanayanam. When the candidate is in a precarious state of health, or is very eager on account of some other reason, this ceremony may be performed.

Both the Vaḍagalais and the Tengalais hold that for prapatti any person of any caste is qualified. If a person of a non-Brahman caste becomes a prapanna, he is considered to be equal to an orthodox Brahman prapanna in every respect by the Tengalai Brahmans. "A prapanna is, therefore, above the ordinary run of humanity, and in consequence he need not observe the rules of the caste (Varṇāśramadharma). He may, if he chooses, observe these dharmas for the sake of convention." But the Vaḍagalais say that in the case of a non-Brahman prapanna respect must be shown as a prapanna Sri Vaishnava, but socially creed cannot supersede caste and caste can be extinguished only with death. However holy and pious a man may be, he cannot free himself, during his life-time from the duties of his caste. Caste, however, does not stand in his way of getting mōksha, which he obtains from his dependence on God. The observance of Varṇāśrama-dharma is an absolute necessity. Non-observance leads to social degradation and spiritual bankruptcy.

During the initiation and prapatti the Vadagalais hold that in the case of women and Non-Brahmans the "Praṇava" of the "Mūlamantra" should not be pronounced and that in its stead the syllable "Am" is to be substituted. The Tengalais, on the other hand, hold that the Praṇava may be pronounced by all irrespective of caste. In accordance with this view of equality spiritual knowledge can be obtained even from a teacher of a lower caste. This, however, is not followed by the Vaḍagalais under any circumstances. It is not known if the Tengalai Brahmans have ever adopted the teachings from a non-Brahman Tengalai. As far as Tengalais are concerned, they have not as yet sought upadeśa from any non-Brahman Tengalai Vaishnavite.

A sanyāsi of the Vaḍagalai sect has to lead a life which is more rigorous than that of a householder. He is considered to be more holy than an ordinary grihastha. So he cannot do obeisance to a grihastha, unless he happens to be the Sanyāsi's own Āchārya. He is not to touch any metallic vessel and he is expected to live only by accepting meals offered to him by orthodox Sri Vaishnava Brahmans. He should not take food from the hands of anybody indiscriminately.

According to the Tengalais a Tengalai sanyāsi pays and receives obeisance even from a householder. He need not beg his food, and he is allowed the use of metallic vessels of all kinds.

Between these two communities there are other small differences in their rituals and ceremonies and also in their social customs. They are discussed below.

In the domestic worship of God, Vaḍagalais make use of a bell, while the Tengalais do not use it. During worship, prayers both in Tamil and Sanskrit are freely used, but Sanskrit predominates amongst the Vaḍagalais and Tamil predominates in the case of Tengalais.

In the matter of the performance of the annual śrāddha ceremony of any person, if it falls on an Ēkādaśi day, Tengalais do not perform it on that day. It is done on the next day. Vaḍagalais, on the other hand, hold that the postponement of the day of death is not permissible and so it is celebrated on the Ēkādaśi day only, if it falls on that day. When a person is under pollution of any kind, the ceremony of śrāddha is performed only on the day on which the pollution ceases.

On the day of the śrāddha food is offered to God in the first place and to the Nityas and Āchāryas in the second place, and then to the Brahmans representing the pitṛ-dēvatas, etc., by the Tengalais. On the other hand, the Vaḍagalais offer the food to God only and not the Nityas and Āchāryas.

Water touched even accidentally by the feet of the Bhāgavatas becomes holy and it is purificatory according to the Tengalais. The Vaḍagalais maintain that the Śrīpādatīrtha to be purificatory should be secured from the Bhāgavatas with the proper ceremonial. One necessary condition is the securing of the will of the Bhāgavatas.

Coming to the social custom there are several differences. The Tengalai women do not shave their heads when they become widows. But the Vaḍagalai widows, like the Smārta Brahman widows, remove the hair from their heads. Some Tengalai women tie their sarīs so as to have the one end passing over the right shoulder and covering it, whilst the Vaḍagalai women throw it on their left shoulder.

In the matter of obeisance the Tengalais do it only once. Mutual prostrations, irrespective of age is allowed. Both the disciple and the guru prostrate. They prostrate even to a woman. But among the Vaḍagalais prostrating to men older than themselves alone is observed. Only very old people observe the returning of prostration and it is never done in the case of young people when they prostrate adopting the prapatti. Reference may be made to Anga panchaka as developed by Vedānta Dēśika for the views held by the Vaḍagalais (cf. Anga panchaka of the Tengalais by—Maṇavāḷa Mahā-munigaḷ—see Govindachariar's translation).

Tengalais hold that the hearing of the divya mantra during Panchasamskāra, may be considered to be prapatti, and so prapatti need not be done later. Further, they hold that Rāmānuja did Śaraṇāgati for all Vaishnavas connected with him and as we are all his followers no prapatti need separately be adopted.

Vaḍagalais contend that what Rāmānuja did could apply only to those wno were living with him during his life-time; but those who came into this world after Rāmānuja cannot be brought under the Śaraṇāgati done by Rāmānuja. Every Jīva must do prapatti before or after Panchasamskāra, when he becomes fit for Prapatti or Saraṇāgati He must be an akinchana and this is an essential condition for prapatti.

Tengalais hold that jñānōpadēśa can be obtained from a teacher of any caste. The Vaḍagalais do not deny the fact. When a disciple prostrates before his guru, the guru should not return it by prostrating himself. In temples God alone is entitled for it and neither a Sanyāsi nor a grihastha is entitled for it so long as he stays in the temple Śishyas do not prostrate before God when they go with their Āchārya to a temple.

Amongst the Vaḍagalais, in the case of women, only mothers, elder sisters and Āchārya's wives may be shown respect by prostration. In the case of other women respect need not be shown by prostration amongst the Vaḍagalais.

Prapatti, the Tengalais say, is only a knowledge of śēshatvam. The Vaḍagalais hold that a mere knowledge of śēshatvam does not constitute prapatti. Along with this knowledge bhārasamarpaṇam is essential for Prapatti or Śaraṇāgati.

Effort and previous preparation is unnecessary as God's grace is "*Nirhētuka*" (one without cause). But the Vaḍagalais contend that although grace is "Nirhētuka" and that they should also do something to obtain it and this something is prapatti.

Tengalais think that no angas are needed for prapatti, although they may adopt it. According to the Vaḍagalais angas are particularly necessary and for that teachers of any caste can be engaged, but only for ordinary lore. For initiation into Brahma Vidyā and mantras, only a Brahman teacher is empowered to do it. For example, when Rāmānuja tried to get spiritual knowledge from Tirukacchinambi of Conjeeveram, he refused to be his Āchārya or preceptor on the ground that he was not a Brahman. Tengalais often say that Nāthamunigal was initiated by a Non-Brahman Āchārya Saṭhakōpa. But the Vaḍagalais contend that the initiation was done in yōga daśai in which state no question of caste can arise. It is only when initiation is done by a human being directly that it is objectionable. Madura Kavi is quoted by the Tengalais as having adopted as his master a Śūdra and so caste must go. But the Vaḍagalais hold that mantras with Vidyā were not given to Madura Kavi and so the knowledge obtained from his non-Brahman priest was only ordinary knowledge.

The Tengalais consider theoretically that a Vaishnavite of non-Brahman caste also is qualified to initiate a Brahman. But in practice amongst the Tengalai Brahmans there is not even a single instance of a Brahman being initiated by a non-Brahman Vaishnavite. Both Vadagalais and Tengalais are being initiated only by Brahman Vaishnavites at the present day.

Amongst the Tengalais some are swayamāchāryapurushas, while others are followers of Maṭhādhipatis. Vānamāmalai maṭham is one of the most important of the maṭhams and it is under the management of "Vānamāmalai Jīyar." The Jīyar is selected by the śishyas (see Plates-I-B, II-A). The plate II-B shows the successors to the priesthood from the earliest to the present time. The present Jīyarswāmi is seen in plate III-A and B. In plate IV-B is shown a Tengalai Sri Vāishnava who does not belong to Vānamāmalai maṭham.

13. The Daily Observances of Orthodox Sri Vaishnava Brahmans.

Every Sri Vaishnava Brahman should bear in mind that the end and aim of a man's life is to attain mōksha. During one's life one must devote most of one's time to the service of God. Every moment one should be thinking of his entire dependence on God. This dependence of a human being on God and God's condescension on the human being are referred to by the use of the terms "Śesha and Śēshi" bhāvams. To be able to worship God one should be pure in body and in mind. This can be attained only by the performance of certain rites. To get purified the daily rites such as sandhyā-vandanam, snānam, etc., ought to be performed regularly by one.

A day is usually divided into five periods by an orthodox person and during each period the rites fixed for that period are carried out. Full details are given in "Pancha kāla prakāśikā" and "Āhnikams" published by various people. But of all these the one called "Nityam" written by Rāmānuja is the oldest. Most of the details about the observances are taken from Nityam. The following account is based entirely upon Nityam of Śrī Bhāshyakāra, edited by Śrīman Mahāmahōpādhyāya Setlur Narasimhacharyaswami now living at Purasawakam, Madras.

A day is usually divided into the five following divisions for the performance of the various rites. They are—1. Abhigamanam, 2. Upādānam, 3. Ijyai, 4. Svādhyāyam and 5. Yōgam.

The *abhigamanam* period of the day is intended for bathing and for performance of the sandhyāvandanam. A prayer to God to enable the person to carry out the duties during this period successfully is also included. The next period of time is called the *Upādānakālam* and it is one in which the materials for the worship of God is secured. The securing of the materials such as flowers, sandal paste, the securing of peace of mind and goodness of mind by means of Kālakshēpams (spending the time by reading or hearing others about God) are also included under this heading. *Ijyai* is the period of the day devoted to the mādhyāhnikam and the Bhagavadārādhanam (worshipping God). The next period is *Svādhyāya* during which period Vedas, Itihāsapurāṇas, prabandhams and dwaya mantras are read and understood, with a view to increase the knowledge of God and His bhakti (or devotion) daily. Then *sāyamabhigamana* or *sandhyāvandana* for the evening and prayer to God are performed. *Yōga,* the last item of the daily performance, is the thought of God's good actions and his glories until he gets sleep. When he goes to sleep he is expected to imagine that his head is lying at the feet of his Lord.

GETTING UP FROM SLEEP.

The first thing that one does every day during the early part of the day is the getting up from his bed. He is expected, under ordinary circumstances, to wake up at least half an hour before sunrise and then he is to pronounce the name of God as Hari! Hari! at least six times. Then the person is expected to repeat the ślōkas describing the coming of God as Hari and destroying the distress of Gajēndra, the chief of the elephants. God is expected to remove all the sins and since he came out as Hari and destroyed the sorrows of Gajēndra, this fact is clearly pointed out in the ślōkas repeated. If the person getting up from his bed is strong enough and capable of commanding his time he may repeat the dhyāna ślōkas of the 108 tirupathis, the daśāvatāra stōtras, the larger gadya, other stōtras of God loudly and in a manner pleasant to be heard by others.

Then sitting in the same bed he thinks of the days that have passed without doing him any good and feels sorry for his not obtaining the mōksha so much expected by him. If the man is one who has not gone through the prapatti ceremony, he should feel for his present position of being an akinchana, a sinner incapable of getting rid of his sins. Seeing his inability to get rid of his sins and realising his low and incapable position, he feels very sorry. In the case of a prapanna, he should feel for his bondage, but as he is sure of his salvation having surrendered himself to God, he should feel glad of it. Though he may feel dissatisfaction of not having attained mōksha he should not be over-powered by that feeling so as to prevent him from attending to his other legitimate duties such as doing service to God. So he must think of his future duties to God as stated in the pāsuram "Gatattirku sōkiyādē varugira nīrukku aṇaikōlum kaṇakkile". This means "not feeling much for what is past, preparing for the future by proper means." He must spend his time by worshipping God. "Tarittezudi vāsittum kēṭṭum vaṇaṅgi vazipaṭṭum pūjittum pōkkinēn pōdu." When translated this means "I spent my time by writing, reading, hearing, praying and worshipping God."

The person then does 'Śrōtrāchamana' touching his right ear with his right hand and repeats the mantra for 'sātvīkatyāga', and is believed to become a dependent of God and so prays to Him that his kainkaryas (works to God) may be properly done and then he repeats some stōtras (praises) of God well and loudly. If time permits he may repeat portions of his Vedas, such as tiruvais of the same.

On getting from his bed he is to repeat the mantra "Om namaḥ kshitidharāya". This means "Oh I pray to you the supporter of this earth." He then prays to Varāha-mūrti who is supporting the world. He then places his right foot on the floor repeating a prayer to Bhūdēvī. He then prays to Trivikrama thus:—"Vishnōḥkramōsi" and walks on.

Evacuation of the Urine and the Faeces.

Taking the materials necessary for his bath such as fresh clothes, darbha, rice and sesamum and holding in his hand a bamboo stick and repeating "Śrī Kēśavāya namaḥ" (I am praying to Kēśava the name of God) he leaves his house. After going a certain distance, he places the materials he takes with him in a place which is clean and determined by him. The place he chooses for taking mud must be one in which no worms are found, not ploughed by a plough, not found mixed with fine 'alar' (soft mud), not mixed up with unholy things, not mingled with soil used by others and free from ant-hills. From such a place he takes enough mud and places this mud close to the place where he is to wash himself. Leaving his sandals he is to slap his palms thrice and then wrap round his head his upper or other cloth. He next winds round his right-ear his sacred thread so that it may not be dangling. His face and mouth are covered with his upper cloth, and then he sits for defaecation. Before sitting for this he should strew the ground with leaves that are dried and those not useful for sacrificial purposes. If the time is twilight or morning he should sit facing north and if the time is night he is expected to sit facing south. While sitting for this he should not speak with any person. He is not expected to sit for defæcation and be seeing temples, rivers, cows, brahmans, fire, sun, moon, air and *Ficus religiosa* tree. For this purpose he should avoid using the places such as the following:—"Flower garden, groves, tulsi gardens, crops, smaśānam (burning ground), alkaline land, hill, ant-hill, pits, unclean spot, sand, shade, ways and paths, water, ploughed land, cowsheds, foot of trees, darbha grown spot, rivers, tanks, sea shore, places where cow dung is stored, yajñabhūmi (place where yajña is performed), grassy-plot, spaces in front of dwelling houses, crevices of rocks or stones and places where insects abound. He should not see the leavings. During defæcation he is not to use wet clothes. During the time he sits for this process he is not to spit. As a matter of fact spitting is prohibited during the process of defæcation.

WASHING (ŚAUCHAM).

After defaecation he goes to a place where he has to wash himself taking the mud already secured in his right hand. He divides this mud into four parts and water is to be poured for use by a servant. If, on the other hand, washing is to be done in a pond, mud need not be brought. Rivers and watering places that are near temples or near God should never be used for purposes of washing after passing the faeces. While washing in ponds mud should not be brought from any other place. From a place under water, which is as deep as the hand up to the wrists upper limit (a depth of 9 to 10 inches), mud must be taken and it should be placed on the ground about 9 to 10 inches away from the edge of the water, after sprinkling that space with water. Then this mud is used for washing along with water. The left hand is used for washing. It is to be placed between the knees of the two legs and the right hand is kept outside the knees to the right. With his right hand he takes the mud and puts it into his left hand. If passing of the urine and faeces had been done at the same time, cleaning for the faeces has to be done first, and then for urination. If the process of urination and defaecation are at different times, the cleaning has to be done according to the process which has taken place earlier. The cleaning for urination is done by using the mud for cleaning six times and for the passing of the faeces it has to be used twelve or fifteen times. Between one cleaning and another the left hand has to be cleaned five or six times with mud and water. While doing the cleaning for urination, mud about the size of a nellikai (fruit of *Phyllanthus emblica*) has to be used. For cleaning for defaecation for the first time a handful of mud, for the second and the third time half of this quantity and for the remaining or subsequent washings mud about the size of two nelli fruits should be used. After using the hand for doing the washing once, it has to be washed with mud and water to clean it, and then it is again used for the purpose of washing. During the process of washing the hand enough water should be used, so that all the mud may be well removed from the hand. If the thigh and other parts are soiled they should be cleaned seven times.

Then getting up he should clean his left hand ten times with mud and water and his legs seven times with water similarly. Both his hands have to be cleaned ten or seven times with clean water. If it is only after urination, three or five washings with mud and water are enough. The left hand has to be washed five times using mud and water, and then both the hands, three times only, with pure water. Then the finger nails have to be cleaned and washed properly. The place used for washing has also to be cleaned. If sperm has come out without one's knowledge along with the urine all the processes have to be done twice as much as for urination. During the day time the processes have thus to be calculated. During night time half of this has to be done. While travelling only one-fourth of the above may be done. As far as women are concerned they have to do only half of the number of times that a male has to do. Brahmachāris have to do twice as many times; Vānaprasthas and monks have to do four times as much. For people who are not well in health the cleanings have to be done according to their strength, *i.e.*, as many times as they can stand. The point to be observed in such cases is only removal of bad things, smell and in cases of piles pain is to be avoided during the cleaning. After the washings he proceeds and on reaching water side he washes his hand and feet well. He also washes his mouth by means of water four or six times if after urination and eight to twelve times if after defaecation. After washing his mouth he puts on his sacred thread (Yajñōpavītam) properly and does āchamanam twice or thrice.

SIPPING OF THE WATER (ĀCHAMANAM).

The sipping of the water or āchamanam with the proper mentality and mantras is enjoined on all occasions as a purificatory thing. So when the ceremonies or the usual daily observances of any kind are to be begun āchamanam has to be performed. For doing āchamanam one should sit in a clean place, not squatting, but on feet and knees facing east or north. Both the hands are to be kept inside the knees. Touching the hand with the left hand he takes in his right hand as much water as would just be sufficient to drown a seed of black-gram. Then repeating the mantram "Om achyutāya namaḥ" (I bow to Achyuta) he sips water; this process of sipping water is repeated twice more repeating each time the mantrams "Om anantāya namaḥ" (I bow to Ananta) and "Om Gōvindāya namaḥ" (I bow to Gōvinda) respectively. After sipping three times with the base of the right thumb he wipes his lips twice and then touches the various parts of the body one after the other repeating the appropriate mantras again, after washing the base of the thumb and wiping, as detailed below:—

First with the tip of the right thumb of his right hand he touches the right and left cheeks repeating the mantras "Om kēśavāya namaḥ" (I bow to Kēśava) and "Om Nārāyaṇāya namaḥ" (I bow to Nārāyaṇa). Then touching the ring-finger at its base with the tip of the thumb bring the tip of the ring finger in contact with the right eye repeating the mantra "Om Mādhavāya namaḥ" (I bow to Mādhava) and touching the left eye repeat "Om Gōvindāya namaḥ" (I bow to Gōvinda). With the tip of the fore finger, whilst the thumb is at its base he touches the right and left sides of the nose repeating the mantras "Om Vishnavē namaḥ" (I bow to Vishnu) and "Om Madhusūdanāya namaḥ" (I bow to Madhusūdana). With the little finger and the thumb at its base he touches the two ears saying the mantras "Om Trivikramāya namaḥ" (I bow to Trivikrama) and "Om Vāmanāya namaḥ" (I bow to Vāmana). With the middle finger and with the thumb at its base he touches the right and the left shoulders repeating "Om Śrīdharāya namaḥ" (I bow to Śrīdhara) and "Om Hṛshīkēśāya namaḥ" (I bow to Hṛshīkēśa). With the right palm touch the navel repeating "Om Padmanābhāya namaḥ" (I bow to Padmanābha) and with all the fingers united the head is touched pronouncing the words "Om Dāmōdarāya namaḥ" (I bow to Dāmōdara).

CLEANING OF THE TEETH.

The cleaning of the teeth is next begun. For this he washes his feet and does āchamanam twice. Facing east or north and covering his head with his upper cloth he secures from one of the plants mentioned below a piece of stick six to eight inches long, one and a quarter to one-third of an inch thick, straight, free from nodes, worms and empty hollow portions. The piece he plucks for use must be from one of the following plants :— *Calotropis,* banyan, *Acacia arabica, Achyranthes,* margosa, mango, and others with juice and prickles The sticks of Bombax, *Ficus religiosa, Prosopis spicigera,* Areca palm, *Butea frondosa,* plantain, cotton, darbha grass, cocoanut and nānal grass should not be used. While plucking the stick for use as tooth-brush he is expected to repeat the following mantram:—"Āyurbalam yaśō varchaḥ prajām paśuvasūni cha | brahma prajñām cha mēdhām cha tvannō dēhi Vanaspatē." This when translated into English reads thus "Oh! king of the wood give us life, strength, fame, brilliance, children, cows, riches or property, knowledge of God, intelligence or wisdom."

While cleaning the teeth with the stick of any one of the plants mentioned above the mantra given above may be repeated. If sticks are not available, and if cleaning with sticks is prohibited as on some days, then leaves alone are used.

Beginning with the left side of the lower row of teeth, the leaf or the stick is taken round in the pradakshina way by polishing the teeth and then in the end the tongue is cleaned with it. Beginning with the lower teeth on the left side he should go round the teeth upwards and finish with the wiping of the tongue with the split stick. The stick is cleaned and then it is thrown on a clean ground towards the south-west corner. The mouth has to be rinsed with water sixteen times. On ceremonial days such as prathamā, full-moon day, shashṭi, chaturdaśī, ekādaśī, ashṭamī, janmanakshatra (star under which one is born) of three kinds one should not use the sticks. On amāvāsya day and ēkādaśī day he should use for cleaning the teeth only *Eugenia jambolana* (nāval) and mango leaves. On the śrāddha day, nothing is to be used, only rinsing of the mouth with water is allowed. Cleaning of the teeth must not be done in a cow-shed, temple, sacred river, burning ground (smaśānam), in a clean place, water and sacrificing grounds. Water used for the rinsing of the mouth should not be swallowed. After the rinsing of the mouth two āchamanams are to be done.

BATHING OR SNĀNAM.

One who intends bathing in a tank or river should go to a place where God is usually brought or where Bhāgavatās bathe. Selecting such a place he should clean with water the place he intends sitting, wash his legs and hands and then sit on this space facing east or north. While sitting he should wear on his ring-finger of the right-hand the pavitra, usually of darbha grass twisted, and do prāṇāyāmam three times.

The method of doing prāṇāyāmam is described below:—The prāṇāyāmam i; an important item and it is resorted to in almost every ceremony and at frequent intervals in each.

The left nostril is pressed down by the little and ring-fingers of the right-hand and the air inside the lungs is expired through the right nostril. The right nostril is then pressed by the thumb of the right hand so that the right nostril is closed and the two fingers on the left nose are released. As much air as can be taken in is drawn in by the left nostril and then both the nostrils are pressed and the eyes and the mouth are closed. In this condition, think of God, and the sapta Vyāṅṛtis, Gāyatrī and Gāyatrī's head are then pronounced thrice. After this all the air taken in is expired out through the right nostril and the right ear is touched pronouncing the praṇavam "Om."

Then with his hands in the posture of prayer he repeats the usual hierarchy of his Āchāryas. Next he repeats the tithi, vāram, and nakshatra after repeating "Śrī Gōvinda" and performs the usual sankalpam for snānam (bath). Repeating of "The bala mantra" and of the "Sātvikatyāga mantra" follows. He may also repeat ślōkas about "Sacred water" if he knows them and also about Achāryas.

The person who wants to perform these rites should think of service to God and nothing else. He is to repeat the following :—

"Svaśēsha bhūtēnamayā svakīyaiścha dēhēndriyāntahkaraṇaiḥ svakīyairēva kalyāṇatamaiḥ aupacharikasāmsparśikābhyavahārikaiḥ bhōgairakhilaparijanapariççhadānvitam svātmānam prītam kārayitumupakramatē"—In English this means "God with all his attendants and paraphernalia begins to make Himself pleased with the most auspicious materials which are His own and some of which are intended for doing honour, some for creating pleasure by touch and some for eating, supplied by me who is His servant through my body, senses and mind all of which are given by Him."

Next he goes to the side of the water and washes his hands and feet in a clean place, does āchamanam and then cleans a space on the shore. He then takes a quantity of mud from a clean place repeating the ashṭāksharam and places it on the spot already cleaned, dividing it into two parts. Taking mud from the larger part he wipes with it his body to remove the dirt from his body and bathes in water. After bathing he sits on the bank, thinks of God and performs the prāṇāyāmam thrice. He then takes the other portion of the mud into his left-hand, divides it into three parts and sprinkles water over them separately. Repeating the mūla mantra he takes one part from three parts in his hand and does digbandhanam by repeating the astramantram. With another part of this mud a pīṭham is made intended for the water which is to be sprinkled later on. The third part of the mud is used for smearing over the body. He then washes his hands and taking water in both of his hands pours or sprinkles it over the pīṭha made with one part of the mud. The water thus poured or sprinkled is considered to be the holy water of the Ganges coming from the right foot of God. While pouring the water ashṭākshara is pronounced and again taking water with both his hands and repeating the mūlamantra seven times he sprinkles over his head this water three or five times. Next he takes a small quantity of water in his right hand and takes in the same quantity of water repeating the ashṭāksharam. After this he performs an āchamanam and sprinkling over himself some water, he immerses himself in the water. While under water he should imagine that his head is below the feet of God and he should be repeating the ashṭaksharam as many times as he can possibly do. Then he comes out of the water, places his right leg in water and the left leg on the land and then sits. In this posture he does āchamanam once. He then stands on the shore and repeats ślōkas about Āchāryas and God and cleans with two cloths his body—with one his head and with another the other parts of his body. Afterwards he sprinkles water thrice repeating the three vyāhṛti mantras over the cloths placed in the "Tiruppakkūdai". Then repeating "Dēvasya tva savituḥ prasavēśvinōr bāhubhyām pūshnō hastābhyāmādadē." This when translated into English runs: "By the direction of the deity who directs all I take you by the hands of Aśvins and by the hands of Pūshā." The cloths are taken and then repeating "Udutyam jātavēdasam dēvam vahanti kētavaḥ dṛśē viśvāya sūryam" which means "The rays support that sun who knows all that are born, so that people may see him" they are shown to the sun. Then repeating the mantram "Avadhūtam rakshō avadhūtā arātayaḥ" which means "Let the enemies be destroyed and let those who do not give money perish." The cloths are shaken; with the words "Āvahantī vitanvāna kurvāṇā chīra mātmānaḥ | vāsāmsi mamagāvaśçha annapānēcha sarvadā | tatōmē śriyam āvaha", which means "First give me wisdom and then bring me prosperity very soon; bring me clothes, cows, food and drink, make them increased and make them remain with me." He wraps the cloth round his head, and then taking his yajñōpavītam (sacred thread) and making it nivīti winds it round his right ear and then wears his kaupīnam (piece of under cloth). Then he washes his hands and knees with mud and water and wears his lower and upper cloth. After this he washes his feet, does āchamanam twice and one prāṇāyāmam. He then does sankalpam saying "Śrībhagavadājñayā Śrīmannārāyaṇapprītyartham mantrasnānam karishyē" (By God's order and with a view to please Śrīmannārāyaṇa I am doing this both by repeating the mantras). Next repeating "Āpōhisṭhā mayōbhuvaḥ | tāna ūrjē dadhātana | mahēraṇāya chakshasē | yōvassivatamō rasaḥ | tasya bhājayate hanaḥ | uśatīriva mātaraḥ | tasmā aranga māmavaḥ | yasyakshayāya jinvatha | āpō janayatha chanaḥ |" (for the meaning of this see page 61) he sprinkles water over legs, head and sky, then over head, sky and legs and finally over sky, head and legs. Then he meditates on bathing and imagines of having bathed. He then thinks of God as existing with the effulgence of a crore of suns, as carrying śankham, chakra and gada in his four hands, and as having a kirīṭa on his head and bracelets and other ornaments. He should think of the feet of God who is holding śankham and chakra, and also think of Ganges falling from the feet on his head and entering his head through the brahmarandhra and cleaning both externally and internally. The wet cloths which he used before while actually bathing must not be placed in front of him but by his side. If he is a weak person he may use hot water for the bath. If, however, he is unclean due to death, etc., he ought not to use hot water. If a person is too weak to bathe the head, he can bathe up to the neck or up to the navel and clean the upper part with a wet cloth. If he is not strong enough even to do this he may adopt any method mentioned in the śāstras as suiting his capacity.

PUTTING ON THE ŪRDHVA PUṆḌRAM.

The person who is about to put on the ūrdhvapunḍram (marks made on the forehead and parts of his body with a kind of white clay and turmeric powder) takes water in a coconut-shell or "Tīrthahāri." From this coconut-shell he takes a little water and pours it into his left hand by means of an uddharaṇī (a spoon) made of gold, silver or wood. With this water he cleans his left hand repeating the astrāmantra "Vīryāya astrāyaphaṭ." Then repeating the praṇavam he places the tirumaṇ (white clay or mud) in his left hand in his palm. Then repeating the mantram "Gandhadvārām durādharshām nityapushṭām karīshiṇīm | īsvarīm sarva bhūtanām tvāmiha upahvayē śriyam" [this when translated runs thus "I invite here the deity of Earth who is resorted to by all, who is perceived by smell, who is not overcome by enemies, who is always full of plenty, who is full of cattle (cows, buffaloes, etc.,) and who creates and directs all the objects of creation] the tirumaṇ is rubbed in and dissolved in a small quantity of water. Then with astra mantra ashṭadigbandhanam is done. (The eight directions are closed by the repetition of the mantras). Then by repeating the praṇava the tirumaṇ is dissolved in water by rubbing it in the palm, the mūla mantra is repeated over it, then Nṛsimha bījākshara is written on it and it is then dissolved and mixed well by using the fore finger. Then over this he repeats the mantra "Vishnōr-nukam Vīryāṇi pravōcham yaḥ pārthivāni vimamē rajāmsi yōaskabhāyaduttaram sadhastam vichakramāṇastrēdhōrugāyah." This when translated runs thus "I shall fully describe the powerful deeds of Vishnu who is extolled by great men, who created the three lights, namely, fire, lightning and the sun on Earth, the intermediate region and the sky or heaven and who created the very extensions, the antariksha which supports the three worlds by walking over them with a stride in each (or who has firmly established heaven which is above all worlds and where yōgis dwell)." He also repeats the dwādaśākshara mantra. After this he repeats the following mantra "Vishṇōrarāṭamasi vishṇōḥ pṛshṭhamasi Vishṇōḥ snaptrēsthō vishṇōssyūrasi Vishṇōr dhruvamasi Vaishṇavamasi visṇavētvā | uddhṛtāsi varāhēṇa kṛshnēna śata bāhunā | bhūmir dhēnūr dharaṇībhūtadhārinī | mṛttikē hanamēpāpam yan mayā dushkṛtam kṛtam | tvayā hatēna pāpēna jīvāmi śaradaśśatam | mṛttikē dēhī mē pushṭim tvayi sarvam pratishṭhitam." This when translated runs thus "You are the forehead of Vishnu, you are the back of Vishnu, you are the joints of the lips of Vishnu, you are one that connects us with Vishnu, you are as firm as Vishnu, you have Vishnu as the presiding deity, and you are Vishnu himself. Oh Earth! you have been brought back by the thousand hands of Vishnu in his boar incarnation; you are like the milch cow always giving us what we require; you are the bearer of truth and support all objects of life. Oh Earth! destroy my sins and destroy all bad acts that I have done. Having been relieved of my sins let me live one hundred years. Oh Earth! give me comfort, for all the objects capable of giving comfort are stationed in you."

He then takes with the index finger a small quantity of tirumaṇ dissolved in the hand and smears it over the head repeating the praṇavam at the same time. With the fourth finger pavitra finger) he makes marks of tirumaṇ on the face and other parts of the body in regular order as detailed below. After putting on the nāmam in the face, it is put on the following places in the order given :—central place in the abdomen, centre of the chest, neck in front, right side of the abdomen, right shoulder, right side of the neck, left side of the abdomen, left shoulder, left side of the neck, lower portion in the centre at the back of the body and back of the neck. While making the marks of nāmam in each of these places mentioned above, the twelve names of God are repeated beginning with "Om Kēśavāya namaḥ." The names of God repeated in definite order are as follows :—Kēśavāya namaḥ, Nārāyaṇāya namaḥ, Mādhavāya namaḥ, Gōvindāya namaḥ, Vishṇavē namaḥ, Madhusūdanāya namaḥ, Trivikramāya namaḥ, Vāmanāya namaḥ, Śrīdharāya namaḥ, Hṛshīkēśāya namaḥ, Padmanābhāya namaḥ and Dāmōdarāya namaḥ."

After putting on the twelve nāmams if there should remain any quantity of tirumaṇ it is smeared over the head repeating the dvādaśākshara mantram. He then makes marks of śrīchūrṇa in the middle of the nāmams. For making the marks with śrīchūrṇam Lakshmī's turmeric must be mixed with it.

While marking with śrīchūrṇa the following mantras must be repeated, one for each mark made :—face—Śriyai namaḥ ; middle of the abdomen just above the navel—Amṛtōd bhavāyai namaḥ ; middle of the chest—Kamalāyai namaḥ ; front of the neck—Chandrasōdaryai namaḥ ; right side of the abdomen—Vishṇupatnyai namaḥ ; right shoulder—Vaishṇavyai namaḥ ; right side of the neck—Varārōhāyai namaḥ ; left side of the abdomen—Harivallabhāyai namaḥ ; left shoulder--Sārnginyai namaḥ ; left side of the neck--Dēvadēvyai namaḥ ; back at the lower portion just above the waist—Mahā Lakshmyai namaḥ ; neck at the back—Lōkasundaryai namaḥ ; and top of the head—Sarvābhīshṭa phalappradāyai namaḥ."

The nāmams in order are then touched repeating the mantras "Kēśavāya namaḥ", etc., one after the other. Then with folded hands the following mantra must be repeated :—"Chatuschakram namasyāmi kēśavam kanakapprabham|Nārāyaṇam ghanaśyāmam chatus śankham namāmyaham||Mādhavam maṇibhangābham chintayāmi chatur gadam | chandrahāsam chatuśśārngam Gōvindam ahamāśrayē || Vishnum chaturhalam vandē padma kinjalka sannibham | caturmusalamabjābham samśrayē Madhusūdanam | agnivarṇam catuḥ khaḍgam bhāvayāmi trivikramam || Vāmanam bāla sūryābham chaturvajram vibhāvayē | Śrīdharam puṇḍarīkābham chatuppaṭṭasam āśrayē | chaturmudgaramabhyēmi Hṛshīkēsam taṭit prabham | panchāyudham Padmanābham praṇamāmyarkarōchisham | Dāmōdaram chatushpāśam indragōpanibham bhajē || Vāsudēvamupāsēham pūrnēndvayuta sannibham." This when translated into English runs thus :—"I worship Kēśava of the lustre of gold and who is in possession of four chakras or discs. I worship Nārāyaṇa of deep black colour and possessing four śankhas or conches. I meditate on Mādhava of the lustre of the cut surface of a diamond and possessing four gadas or maces. I take refuge in Gōvinda of the lustre of the moon and possessing four *saranga* or bows. I bow to Vishnu who is as beautiful as the filament of a lotus and possesses four *halas* or ploughs. I take refuge in Madhusūdana of the lustre of a lotus and possessing four *musala* or wooden pestles. I contemplate on Trivikrama of the colour of agni or fire and who is in possession of four *khaḍgas* or swords. I worship Vāmana of the lustre of the dawning of sun and possessing four *Vajras* or thunderbolts. I take refuge in Śrīdhara of the colour of lotus and possessing four *paṭiasa* or spears with sharp edges. I meditate on Hrishīkēśa of the colour of lightning and possessing four *mudgaras* or hammers. I salute Padmanābha of the brilliance of the sun and possessing the five weapons of Vishnu. I take refuge in Dāmōdara of the lustre of fire flies and possessing four *pāśa* or nooses. I meditate on Vāsudēva who is as beautiful as ten thousand moons put together."

While repeating the above the hands which are pressed together should be moved towards the correct nāmam at the repetition of the suitable mantram. Afterwards the twelve Tamil stanzas of Śrīman Dēśika is repeated praising each deity in one stanza.

After making the punḍrams on the various parts of the body as detailed above the palms of the hands should not be cleaned with water. If the time at one's disposal is short, or if the person is weak, instead of the twelve nāmams, two may be put on, one in the face and the other at the back of the neck. These two nāmams should always be put on and one should not fail to do this. Now-a-days almost all Śrīvaishnavas who are not Vaidikas put on only two nāmams on all ordinary days. They put on the twelve nāmams only on ceremonial days.

Then the following ślōkas and pasuram should be repeated in the order given :—

"Asmad gurubhyō namaḥ | asmad parama gurubhyō namah | asmad sarva gurubhyō namaḥ | Śrīmatē Vēdānta guravē namaḥ | Śrīmatē Rāmānujāya namaḥ | Śrīmatē Mahā Pūrṇāya namaḥ | Śrī Rāma Miśrāya namaḥ | Śrī Punḍarīkākshāya namaḥ | Śrīman Nāthamunayē namaḥ | Śrīmaté Śaṭhakōpāya namaḥ | Śrīmatē Vishvaksēnāya namaḥ | Śriyai namaḥ | Srīdharāya namaḥ |

Asmad Dēśika masmadīya paramāchāryānaśēshān gurūn śrīman Lakshmana yōgi pungava mahā pūrṇau munim Yāmunam | Rāmam padmavilōchanam muni-varam nātham śaṭhadvēshiṇam śēnēsam sriyamindirā sahacharam Nārāyaṇam samśrayē ||."

The Tamil stanza quoted here of Śrīman Vēdanta Dēsika is also repeated. The names of āchāryas are mentioned in this stanza.

"என்னுயிர் தந்தளித்தவரைச் சரணம்புக்கி
யானடைவே அவர்குருக்கள் நிரைவணங்கி
பின்னருளால் பெரும்பூதூர் வந்தவள்ளல்
பெரியநம்பி ஆளவந்தார் மணக்கால்நம்பி
நன்னெறியை யவர்க்குரைத்த உய்யகொண்டார்
நாதமுனி சடகோபன் சேனைநாதன்
இன்னமுதத்திரு மகளென்றி வர்களைமுன்னிட்டு
எம்பெருமான் திருவடிக ளடைகின்றேனே."

—See page 8.

In the above Sanskrit and Tamil stanzas only the prominent Āzhvārs and Āchāryas are mentioned. He should in addition to this repeat the ślōkas in praise of his own Āchārya. During the time of repeating the above he should be wearing round his neck garlands made of tulsi beads, lotus fruits, and must wear in his right hand a pavitra on the pavitra finger.

Offerings of Water and Rice to Dēvarshis and Forefathers (Dēvarshi Pitṛ Tarpaṇam).

The performer cleans his hand and feet with water and then does āchamanam and sankalpam to perform the Dēvaṛshi and Pitṛ tarpaṇams as follows:—"Śrīman Nārāyaṇa pprītyartham snānāngam dēvaṛshi pitṛ tarpaṇam karishyē." He performs the tarpaṇam believing that devatas, ṛshis and pitṛs have in them the amśam of God. That is to say he should believe that the spirit of God is in all these.

Then repeating the following mantras he does tarpaṇam, *i.e.*, leaves water mixed with rice and sesamum in his hands as described below:—

"Brahmādayō yēdēvāstān dēvāmstarpayāmi | sarvān dēvāmstarpayāmi | sarvadēva gaṇāmstarpayāmi | sarva dēva patnīstarpayāmi | sarvadēva gaṇapatnīstarpayāmi."

This in English means "I please all Dēvas from Brahma downwards by the libations of water. I please all Dēvas by these libations of water. I please all troops of Dēvas by these libations of water. I please all the wives of the Dēvas by these libations of water. I please all the wives of the troops of Dēvas by these libations of water."

Repeating the above he does his tarpaṇam through the tips of his fingers. Now he has his sacred thread in the usual way, *i.e.*, in the proper way.

He then puts on his sacred thread round his neck with both the hands outside the thread (i.e. as nivītī) and holding with both the thumbs the sacred thread does tarpaṇam repeating the following. That is he pours water mixed with rice and sesamum while repeating the mantras.

"Om Krishṇa dvaipāyanādayō yē ṛshayaḥ tān ṛshīmstarpayāmi | sarvān ṛshīms-tarpayāmi | sarva ṛshi gaṇāmstarpayāmi | sarva ṛshipatnīstarpayāmi | sarva ṛshi gaṇa patnīstarpayāmi | ".

This when translated runs thus:--

"I please all sages from Vyāsa onwards by these libations of water. I please all sages or hymn singers by these libations of water. I please the whole host of patriarchal sages by these libations of water. I please all the wives of the sages by these libations of water. I please all the wives of the whole host of patriarchal sages by these libations of water."

Then with the sacred thread (yajñōpavīta) as prāchīnāvīti (*i.e.*, putting on the sacred thread on the right shoulder and placing the left hand through so that the sacred thread passes round the right shoulder above and the lower portion of the thread passes on the left side below the left shoulder) he proceeds with the tarpaṇam as detailed below. He repeats the following mantra while doing the tarpaṇam:—

"Sōmaḥpitṛmān yamōngirasvān agnikavya vāhanādayō yē pitaraḥ tān pitṛms-tarpayāmi | sarvān pitṛmstarpayāmi | sarvapitṛgaṇāmstarpayāmi | sarvapitṛpatnīstar-payāmi | sarva pitṛgaṇapatnīstarpayāmi | ." This means "I please all the Manes commencing from Soma, pitṛmān, yama, Angirasvān, agni, kavyavāhana and others by these libations of water. I please all the Manes by these libations of water. I please the whole class of Manes by these libations of water. I please the wives of the Manes by these libations of water. I please the wives of the whole class of Manes by these libations of water."

The above tarpaṇam is performed by pouring water mixed with rice and sesamum between the thumb and the index finger.

Then repeating the following mantra "Ūrjam vahantīramṛtam ghṛtam payaḥ kīlalam pariśṛtam svadhāsta tarpayatamē pitṛn" water is thrown three times after taking the water round in a pradakshina manner on the left side. This water must be thrown thrice on the bank saying each time "Tṛpyata, tṛpyata and tṛpyata." The meaning of the above passage is "May these waters please my Manes, those waters which contain the essence, issuing from flowers, which may be classed as essence of food, ghee and milk which are capable of curing all diseases, preventing death and relieving the bondage of man."

Then putting on the yajñōpavīta in the proper way he does āchamanam.

This dēva-ṛshi-pitṛ-tarpaṇam should not be performed when one does not bathe fully immersing wholly under water or when he is under pollution due to the death of some near relation.

MORNING PRAYERS (MORNING SANDHYĀVANDANAM).

The Sandhyāvandanam is performed by the very orthodox Brahmans as detailed in Ahannikams (books describing the various rites usually observed by the orthodox Sri Vaishnava Brahmans). Sri Vaishnava Brahmans who are not orthodox perform this Sandhyāvandanam using only some of the mantras, leaving out many as of secondary importance.

The ceremony of Sandhyāvandanam is begun by doing āchamanam twice. After doing the āchamanam the performer repeats "Srībhagavadājñyayā śrīmannārāyaṇa prītyartham prātassandhyāmupasishyē." This when translated runs thus:—

"I am now engaged in the prayer during the morning of twilight under the orders of the divine Lord for propitiating the Lord Nārāyaṇa who is associated with Lakshmī."

After repeating the above mantra the performer repeats "Kritanchakarishyāmi." Then he repeats "Prātassandhyāvandanākhyēna bhagavatkarmaṇā bhagavantam archayishyāmi." This when translated runs as follows:—"I worship the divine Lord by this divine action known by the name of prayer during the morning twilight." Next he repeats the mantra beginning with "Bhagavatō balēna" and repeats the bala mantra to its end which is "Bhagavatō Vāsudēvasya." This when translated runs thus:—"By the strength given by God . . . of the Divine Lord Vāsudēva. He then begins by repeating "Bhagavānēva" and does sātvīkatyāga by repeating "Prātassandhyōpāsanākhyam karmasvasmai svaprītyae svayamēva kārayati." This when translated runs thus:—"God himself makes me do the action of morning prayer for his own gratification."

If one does not put on the nāmams as already described he should make the marks of nāmam using water with the right pavitra finger at the right place and repeat the proper mantras. Then repeating the mantra "Āpōhishṭhēti mantrasya sindhudvīpa ṛshiḥ dēvīgāyatrīçhandaḥ āpō dēvatā" he touches the head, nose and the chest with the four fingers except the thumb. This means sindhudvīpar is the ṛshi of the mantra. The chandas for this is "Dēvīgāyatrī" and the dēvatā is "Ap." Then repeating the words "Prōkshaṇē viniyōgaḥ." he should touch the water with his right hand. He should then place his fingers with their tip outward and scatter over himself water by repeating certain mantras detailed below. Repeating the praṇava he scatters over himself water once, then with the three vyāhṛti mantras, with gāyatri and repeating the mantra beginning with "Āpōhishṭhā" he should scatter water over himself. Repeating all these mantras he should sprinkle water over his head only, but while repeating "Yasyakshayāya jinvatha" he should sprinkle water over his knees. The mantra repeated is "Āpōhishṭhā ma yōbhuvaḥ | tāna ūrjē dadhātana mahēraṇāya chakshasē yōvaśśivatamōrasaḥ tasya bhājayatēhanaḥ uśatīriva mātaraḥ tasmā aranga māmavaḥ yasya kshayāya jinvatha āpōjanayathā chanaḥ Om bhūr bhuvassuvaḥ." This when translated reads as follows :— "Oh! waters that are in this form representing Paramātmā! you are responsible for our happiness. Bestow cooked rice (or food) to us for use with our beautiful indriyas (such as sight, etc.). That which you consider as an auspicious rasa, make us have that rasa just like mothers. That rasa which resides in you and makes you loving, for that rasa we are likely to trouble you incessantly. Oh! waters make us to be born ones?"

Towards the end he says "Om bhūr bhuvassuvaḥ." This represents the praṇava coupled with Vyāhṛti—traya and while repeating this he should sprinkle water around himself.

Afterwards repeating the words "Sūryaschētyanuvākasya agniṛshiḥ | dēvīgāyatrī çhandaḥ | sūryōdēvatā" he should touch his head, nose and chest. (This touching is called nyāsam.)

For the above anuvāka "Sūryascha" ṛshi is agni, chandas (metre) is dēvī gāyatrī and sun is dēvatā. (For the sake of ātmaśuddhi he drinks this water after repeating the following mantra.) Repeating "Apām prāsanē viniyōgaḥ" water is taken as if for āchamanam. The Sanskrit words when rendered into English mean : "This water is intended for drinking" Taking water in the hand as for āchamanam the following mantra is repeated. "Sūryascha māmanyuscha manyupatayascha manyukṛtēbhyaḥ | pāpēbhyō rakshantām | yadrātryā pāpamakārisham | manasā vāchā hastābhyām padbhyā mudarēṇa śiśnā rātristadavalumpatu | yatkinchā duritam mayi | idaṃ maham māmamṛta yōnau | sūryē-jyōtishi juhōmi svāhā" | and he drinks the water by sipping. The above passage when translated reads as follows :— "Sun, anger and the raga, etc., which are gods to anger protect me from the sins caused by anger. Any sin that might have been committed by me during the night by my mind, voice, hands, feet, belly and male organs be destroyed by 'rātri' (the night). If there is any other sin in me let that also be destroyed. Let me offer as a sacrifice my ātmā or life principle to the Sūrya who is brilliant with effulgence. This is the hōma mantra."

Then āchamanam is done. Then repeating the following mantra "Dadhikrāviṇṇēti mantrasya Vāmadēvarṣhiḥ | anushṭupchandaḥ | Dadhikrāva dēvatā," he touches his head, nose and chest. (This is doing nyāsam.) This means the ṛshi for the mantra "Dadhikrāviṇṇō" is Vāmadēva ṛshi and the çhandas (metre) is anusṭup and Dadhikrāva is the dēvatā." Water is sprinkled over repeating the mantra "Apām prōkshaṇē viniyōgaḥ." and then the following mantra is repeated and water is sprinkled over the head during the recital. "Dadhikrāviṇṇō akārisham | jishnō raśvasya vājinaḥā | surabhinō mukhākarat | praṇāyūmshitārishat | āpōḥishtāmayōbhuva . . . Om bhūr bhuvassuvaḥ." This when translated means: "I am only praising Dadhikrāva who is the successful person, who is permeating everything and who is the protector of all. May our faces be made to appear bright. May our 'āyus' (period of life) be free from troubles . . ."

Repeating "Om bhūrbhuvassuvaḥ" he surrounds himself with water by sprinkling it around.

He then does prāṇāyāmam and does sankalpam as follows:— "Śrī Bhagavadājñayā Srīmannārāyaṇapprītyartham prātassandhyārghyapradānamkarishyē." Some people omit this sankalpam. The performer standing repeats "Arghya pradāna mantrasya viśvāmitra ṛshiḥ dēvīgāyatrīçhandaḥ | savitā dēvatā" and does "nyāsa." He then says: "Arghya pradānē viniyōgaḥ" and spreads out his hands and bring them together. He then takes water in his hands keeping all his fingers close together, his thumbs far apart and then repeating the praṇava, Vyāhṛtitraya and gāyatrī and thinking of God who is residing in the centre of the sun, raise the hands as high as the brows and throws the water down. If while doing this, the sun is visible, prāṇāyāmam and sankalpam are done as follows:—"Śrī Bhagavadājñayā Śrīmannārāyaṇaprītyartham prātassandhyā kālātīta prāyaschittārtham turīyārghya pradānam karishyē." ("By the order of God and with a view to please Nārāyaṇa I am pouring this water as a prāyaschitta for doing it after the proper time" is the translation of the above.) Then repeating the seven vyāhṛtis and the gāyatrī he gives one arghya. Then repeating "Asāvādityō Brahmā" along with praṇavam and vyāhṛti trayam he sprinkles water round himself in a pradakshina manner. Afterwards he does āchamanam and taking water in both his hands, having the palms together and the thumbs apart, pours it down twelve times repeating each time one of Kesava's names. The first is "Kēśavam tarpayāmi"; the second throwing of water is done repeating "Nārāyaṇam tarpayāmi"; the third "Mādhavam tarpayāmi"; the fourth "Gōvindam tarpayāmi"; the fifth "Vishṇum tarpayāmi"; the sixth "Madhusūdanam tarpayāmi"; the seventh is "Trivikramam tarpayāmi"; the eighth is "Vāmanam tarpayāmi"; the ninth is "Śrīdharam tarpayāmi"; the tenth is "Hṛshīkesam tarpayāmi"; the eleventh is "Padmanābham tarpayāmi"; and the twelfth is "Dāmōdaram tarpayāmi. Then one āchamanam is done.

If the japam is to be performed standing in water, he should stand in knee-deep water. In case he wants to do on the shore, he has to place one leg in water and the other above on land and in a sitting posture he has to do the ceremony. One should not perform sandyhā with wet clothes on. In case he has to do with wet clothes on he has to stand in water knee-deep and do japams of the Sandhyāvandana. In this case he cannot do pradakshina and namaskārams. Strictly speaking the performer of Sandhyā is expected to go to a temple or other clean spots and do the japam there.

The place intended for the japam is sprinkled with water after the repetition of the praṇavam and vyāhṛtitrayam and darbha grass is spread and on it he sits for doing japam.

During japam he sits facing east. Thus sitting on the darbha grass, facing east, he does "nyāsa" repeating the mantra "Āsana mantrasya pṛthivyā mēru pṛshṭa ṛshiḥ sutalam çhandaḥ | Śríkūrmo dēvatā." This when translated runs thus :—"For the mantra intended for sitting, Pṛthivyā mērupṛshṭa is the seer or sage, the meter is sutalam, and the presiding deity is Kūrma." Then repeating "Āsane viniyōgaḥ" with hands together and up in a saluting posture prayer is offered to the earth thus:—"Pṛthvi tvayā dhritā lōkāḥ dēvi tvam vishṇunā dhṛtā | tvam cha dhāraya mām dēvi pavitram kuruchāsanam. |" This when translated runs thus "Oh! Earth the whole world consisting of the movable and immovables is borne by you. You are borne by Vishṇu. Oh Goddess! You please hold me. Make my seat pure."

He afterwards does nyāsa repeating the following mantra :—"Praṇavasya ṛshiḥ brahma | dēvī gāyatrīchandaḥ | paramātmā dēvatā." For praṇava the ṛshi is Brahma dēvīgāyatrī is chandas (metre) and paramātmā is the dēvatā. Then he repeats "Bhūrādi saptavyāhṛtīnām Atri Bhrigu Kutsa Vasishṭa Gautama Kāśyapāngirasaṛshayaḥ | gāyatryushniganushṭup brihatī panktiḥ trishṭup jagatyaḥchandāmsi agniç vāyu arka vāgīśa Varuṇēndra viśvēdēva dēvatāḥ." This when translated means "The seven vyāhṛtis are bhūḥ, bhuvaḥ, suvaḥ, mahaḥ, janaḥ, tapaḥ, and satyam." (In front of each of these the praṇava "Om" should be added). For the Vyāhṛti Bhūḥ Atri is ṛshi gāyatrī is chandas and agni is dēvatā; for the vyāhṛti "Bhuvaḥ" Bhrigu is ṛshi, ushnik is the çhandas and Vāyu is dēvtā; for the vyāhṛti "Suvaḥ" Kutsa is ṛshi, anushṭap is the çhandas (metre) and sūrya is dēvatā; for the vyāhṛti "Mahaḥ" Vasisṭha is ṛshi, brihatī is çhandas (metre) and Bṛhaspati is dēvatā; for the Vyāhṛti "Janah" Gautama is ṛshi, panktī is çhandas (metre) and Varuṇan is the dēvatā; for the Vyāhṛti "Tapah" Kāśyapa is ṛshi, trishṭap is çhandas (metre) and Indra is dēvatā"; for the vyāhṛti "Satyam" Angiras is ṛshi, jagatī is chandas (metre) and Viśvēdēva is the dēvatā."

Savitrīya ṛshi Viśvāmitraḥ | dēvīgāyatrīchandāḥ | savita dēvatā |." This when translated runs thus: "For Savitṛ Viśvāmitra is ṛshī, gāyatri is çhandas (metre) and Savitā is the dēvatā."

"Śirasō Brahma ṛshiḥ anushṭup çhandaḥ paramātmā dēvatā |." When translated this is as follows:—"For the head of the gāyatri the ṛshi is Brahma, anushṭup is çhandas (metre) and paramātma is dēvatā."

Repeating the above, nyāsam is done and then repeating "Sarvēshām prāṇāyāmg viniyōgaḥ" he says "Om bhūḥ" and touches the legs; he repeats "Om bhuvaḥ" and touches the knees; repeating "Om suvaḥ" he touches the thighs; repeating

"Om mahaḥ" he touches the belly; he touches the chest repeating "Om janaḥ"; he touches the nose repeating "Om tapaḥ"; he touches the head repeating "Om satyam"; then repeating "Om tatsavituḥ jñānāya hṛdayāya namaḥ". touches the heart with the thumb and the index finger; repeating "Om Varēnyam aiśvaryāya śirasē svāhā" touches the head with the four fingers except the thumb; repeating "Om bhargō dēvasya śaktyai sikhāyai vaushaṭ" touches the tuft of hair (hair-knot) with the thumb (by the middle of the thumb); repeating "Om dhīmahi balāya kavachāya hūm" touches from the neck to the waist in the body; repeating "Om dhiyō yōnaḥ tējasē nētrābhyām vaushaṭ" touches both the eyes simultaneously with the index finger and the middle one; then repeating "Om prachōdayāt vīryāya astrāyaphaṭ" slaps the two hands together, snaps the fingers and does "Digbandhanam" round the head. Then he thinks of the deity by repeating "Muktāvidruma hēma nīla dhavalacchāyair mukhai stīkshanaiḥ yuktāmindukalānibaddhamakuṭām tatvārtha varṇātmikām | gāyatrīm varadābhayāmkuśakaśāḥśubhram kapālam guṇam śankham chakra mathāravinda yugalam hastair vahantīmbhajē." This when translated runs "In the kīriṭa we may see the moon and in the body five faces, three eyes in each face; faces have the colour of pearl, coral, gold blue and white; there are ten hands and in them are found varadāna mudra, abhaya mudra, amkuśa, Kaśai (Korada—stick with a rope tied), white kapālam, rope, śankam and chakram; she has two lotuses and she is "Sarva tatva svarūpiṇī (one knowing and in the form of tatvam) "Sarvārtha svarūpiṇī" (embodiment of all wealth or money) "Sarvākshara rūpiṇī" (having all the letters). I am saluting such a gāyatrī." So saying he salutes and with the chief part of the gāyatrī (*i.e.*, repetition of "Om") touches the body from the head to the feet.

Repeating the above, and repeating the gāyatrī portion "Om | āpōjyōtīraso amṛtam brahma bhūrbhuvassuvarōm" he smears the whole of his body with both his hands. He at the same time thinks of God by repeating "Arkamanḍala madhyastham sūryakōṭi Samaprabham! brahmādi sēvya pādābjam noumi brahmaramāsakham". This when translated runs as follows:—"I am thinking of Śriyappati by praising Him who resides in the centre of sūryamandala, who is as brilliant as a crore of sūryas, whose feet are served by Brahmans and others and who is the Para Brahma rupi". After praying to God as above he does prāṇāyamam three times. Then touching the right ear he repeats the following as sankalpam:—"Śrī bhagavadājñayā śrīmannārāyaṇaprītyartham ashṭottara sahasram (or ashṭottara śatam, or daśavāram) prātassandhyā gāyatrī mantra japam karishyē." Then he says "Āyātvityanuvākasya, Vāma dēva ṛshiḥ | anusṭup çhandaḥ | gāyatrī dēvatā" and touches the head, nose and heart (does nyāsa). This is followed by saying "Gāyatrī āvāhanē viniyōgaḥ." The above when translated runs thus:—"For the anuvāka beginning with "Āyātu" the ṛshi is Vāmadēva, anusṭup is chandas (metre) and gāyatrī is dēvatā." The gāyatrī is āvahanamed in the heart by the anuvāka "Āyātu." The performer then repeats "Āyātu varadādēvyaksharam brahma samhitam | gāyatrīm çhandasām mātēdambrahma jushasva nah! ōjōsi sahōsi balamasi bhrājōsi dēvānām dhāma nāmāsi viśvamasi viśvāyuḥ sarvamasi sarvāyurabhi bhūrōm gāyatrīm āvāhayāmi" and does āvāhanam. This when rendered in English runs thus:—"The dēvatā gāyatrī, who is capable of satisfying all the wishes of those who pray to her, who is ever present, who is equal to the praṇava and who is the mother of all the chandās has to come here and accept our praises in Veda ślōkas; you are the power holding the indriyas, you are rapid in your motions, you are the power, you are bright, you possess the tējas of the dēvatās, you are everything and you are capable of increasing the age of everything; you are supporting the things yourself that are dear to you; you are the person causing changes in time; you are the person capable of destroying all sins; I am requesting the presence of such gāyatrī in the form of praṇavam."

After this he contemplates repeating the following:—

"Prātardhyāyāmi gāyatrīm ravimanḍala madhyagām! ṛg vedamuchchārayantīm raktavarṇām kumārikām! akshamālākarām brahmadaivatyām hamsavāhanām." This when rendered into English runs thus:—"It is called gayatrī in the morning. That dēvatā remains in sūryamanḍala. It is repeated by ṛgvēda and the colour is red; when age is considered it is young. It has in its hands "Akshamālā" and its vāhanam is "Hamsam". Its dēvatā is "Brahma".

Then Nyāsa is done repeating the following mantra:—"Praṇavasya rishi brahmaḥ, dēvīgāyatrī çhandaḥ paramātmā dēvatā ‖ bhūrādi sapta vyāhṛtīnām vyāhṛtitrayasya atri bhṛgu kutsā ṛshayaḥ gāyatryushniganusṭup çhandāmsi agnivāyvarkā dēvatāḥ | savitriya ṛshiḥ Viśvāmitraḥ dēvīgāyatrīçhandaḥ savitā dēvatā."

The translation for the above is as follows:—"The ṛshi of the Praṇavamantra is Brahma; the metre of the mantra is the holy Gāyatrī; the deity that has been contemplated by the mantra is the Paramātmā (God). Atri, Bhṛgu and Kutsa are the ṛshis of the three vyāhṛtis beginning with Bhū. Their metres are Gāyatrī, Ushnik, and Anushṭup. Agni (fire), Vāyu (wind) and the Sun are the deities contemplated by these mantras. Viśvāmitra is the ṛshi of Savitṛ mantra; its metre is the holy Gāyatrī and Savitā is the deity contemplated by this mantra."

He then says "Japē viniyōgaḥ" and touches the various parts of the body by repeating the following mantra:—He smears the outside and inside of both his hands saying "Vīryāya astrāyaphaṭ"; he touches and smears from base upwards the thumbs by his index fingers repeating "Om bhūḥ angushṭābhyām namaḥ"; he smears with his thumb the index finger repeating "Om bhuvah tarjanībhyām namaḥ"; he smears with the thumb the middle finger saying "Om suvaḥ madhyamābhyām namaḥ"; he smears the nameless (4th finger) saying "Om tatsaviturvarēṇyam anāmikābhyām namaḥ"; he smears the last and the little finger saying "Om bhargōdēvasya dhīmahi kanishṭhikābhyām namaḥ by the thumb. Repeating "Dhiyō yōnaḥ praçhōdayāt karatala karaprishṭhābhyām namaḥ" smear both the hands inside and outside.

Then he does anganyāsam as follows:—Repeating "Om bhūḥ jñānāya hṛdayāya namaḥ" he places his right hand on his chest touching it with the thumb and index-fingers; repeating "Om bhuvaḥ aiśvaryāya śirasēsvāhā" he places the four fingers, except the thumb, on the head; repeating "Om śvaḥ śaktyai sikḥāyai vaushaṭ" he touches his tuft of hair with the lower part of his thumb; repeating "Om tatsavitur varēṇyam balāya kavachāya hūm" smear the body from the neck to the waist; repeating "Om bhargō dēvasya dhīmahi tējasē nētrābhyām vaushaṭ" with the tips of the index finger and the middle finger he touches both the eyes at the same time; repeating "Om dhiyō yōnaḥ praçhōdayāt vīryāya astrāyaphaṭ" presses the knuckles of the hand so as to produce a noise (snaps the fingers) on the right side and does "Digbandhanam"

After doing the anganyāsa he repeats the ślōka "yōdēvassavitāsmākam dhiyō dharmādi gōcharaḥ prērayēt tasya yadbhargastadvarēṇyamupāsmahe |". This passage when translated runs thus :—"We contemplate over that very high tējas (light) which is emanating from the sun and that is the dēva giving us the knowledge of dharmam, etc. (Here is sūrya in the maṇḍala in which Śrīman Nārāyaṇa is residing)."

Then he contemplates on God repeating :—"Āditya maṇḍalē dhyāyēt paramātmānamavyayam | vishṇum chaturbhujam raktapankajāsana madhyagam | kirīṭahāra kēyūra kaṭakādivibhūshitam Srī Vatsavanamālā Srī tulasī kaustubhōjvalam | harim pītāmbaradharam Śankhachakragadādharam | prasannavadanam ratnakuṇḍalair maṇḍitānanam | sarvaratna samāyuktasarvābharaṇabhūshitam |." This passage when rendered into English runs thus :—We should meditate on Vishṇu who is eternal and the soul of the universe or the Lord of all as living in the disc of the sun. He should be meditated as possessing four arms, as seated in the middle of red lotus, as having been ornamented by a crown, garland, bracelets in the arms and zones, etc., as having been more resplendent by the mole called Srīvatsa on the chest, by wearing the garland Vanamālā, a garland of tulasī leaves and wearing the jewel kaustubha in his breast as wearing a golden coloured silk cloth, as holding the Śankha (conch) the chakra (discus) and gada, as having a very clear face, as having his ears ornamented by diamond ear-rings, as having been adorned with several jewels set with all kinds of precious gems."

He places both the hands, under the upper cloth, closing them and then does the gāyatrī japam repeating the gāyatrī and counting them from the lowest lines of the last finger, the upper lines of the same finger, then the top lines of the next two fingers, the three marks of the index finger and the two lowest marks in the middle and the fourth finger. These ten marks of the right hand are counted in the direction of the clock. One is expected to do 1,008 gāyatrīs or 108, or 18 if he finds no time for doing 1,008 times. While doing gāyatrī japam, it should not be pronounced by the mouth, but it should only be thought of in the mind. In the gāyatri those who follow the Yajurveda should pronounce while repeating the gāyatrī "Varēṇyam." Brahmachāris should stop at the words at the end of the praṇavam, at the end of the Vyāhṛtis, at the end of the words "Varēṇyam, dhīmahi and prachōdayāt." Grihasthas (married men) should not stop the repetition at the end of the praṇava but may stop at the other four places mentioned above.

Then gāyatrīs are finished in one pradakshina and then this is counted as one ten in the left hand. During japam he should not talk with any person. He should not see wicked men, śūdras, and dēvatāntarabhaktas (outcastes, that is those who worship others than true God). If it so happens that he has to see them while doing the japa, he should see the sun after seeing them. If he has to talk to them he should think of his old Āchāryas, or puṇyapurushas. If while doing japam Āchāryas and Bhagavatars (elderly men of the same persuasion) come he should get up, do namaskāram and with their permission finish the japam afterwards.

As soon as the japam is finished, he does the prāṇāyamam and the sankalpam repeating "Prātassandhyā gāyatrī upāsthānam karishyē." Then he does nyāsa repeating "Uttamētyanuvākasya Vāmadēva ṛshiḥ | anushṭup çhandaḥ | gāyatri dēvatā" and says "gāyatrī udvāsanē viniyōgaḥ." Translation :—"For the anuvaka beginning with 'uttamē sikharē dēvi' the ṛshi is Vāmadēva, anusṭup is çhandas and gāyatrī is dēvatā." It is used in removing the gāyatrī dēvatā from its place.

Then he repeats the following standing, with hands in a praying posture "Uttamē śikharē dēvi bhūmyām parvatamūrdhani | brāhmanēbhyōbhyanujñānam gaccha dēvi yathā sukham" and continues "Mitrasyēti trichasya viśvāmitra ṛshiḥ ādyasya bīrūṭ çhandaḥ | parayōr gāyatrī trishṭūbhau chandasī mitrō dēvatā ||" and does nyāsa and says "Prātassandhyōpasthānē viniyōgaḥ."

Translation :—"Oh dēvi! After being given leave by Brahmans you may proceed to the holy top of the mountain where you were beforehand with pleasure." The mantra "Mitrasya" consists of three riks. The ṛshi for this is Viśvāmitra; for the first rik bīrūṭ is çhandas, for the second rik gāyātri is çhandas and for the third trishṭubhī is çhandas; dēvatā is Mitra. For all the three it should be done as upasthānam in the morning sandhyā ceremony.

Then upasthāna is done by repeating the following mantra :—"Mitrasya charshiṇī dhṛtaḥ sravōdēvasya śānasim | satyam chitrasravastamam | mitrōjanānyātayati prajānan | mitrō dādhāra prithivīmutadyām | mitraḥkrishṭīranimishābhichashṭē | satyāya hayyam ghṛtavad vidhēma | prasamitra martto astu prayasvān | yasta āditya sikshatir vratena | nahanyatē najīyatétvōtō naiyna magam ḥō aśnōt yantitōna dūrāt |." This when rendered into English runs thus: "I am praising the kīrti or good name of Sūrya (Sun) who is the dēvāta supporting so many beings and this good name is truthful, capable of being well attained and it is very wonderful to hear. This Mitra knowing the karmas of every human being treats him according to his karma. This Mitra is the supporter of this earth and svarga. This sun looks after the human beings without closing his eyes. To him we offer food with ghee for obtaining full strength. Oh Mitra Sūrya Nārāyaṇa the cause of everything, who worships you with interest becomes united with the result of his actions; he, who is protected by you will never be worried by any disease. He will not be conquered by his enemies. Further, sins will not approach him, either from near or far, who is protected by you."

The above upasthāna refers to God who is supposed to be in sūrya maṇḍala. After repeating the above the worshipper holds up his hands together in the posture of prayer and turns round clockwise (pradakshina) the four corners of the compass saying "Om Sandhyāyai namaḥ." Om sāvitryai namaḥ. Om gāyatryai namaḥ. Om sarasvatyai namaḥ. Then he says "Sarvābhyō dēvatābhyō namō namaḥ, kāmōkārshīt manyurakarshīt" and salutes by prostrating on the floor and does abhivādanam. Then again he salutes the directions saying "Om prāchyaidiśēnamaḥ" (I am saluting the east), "Om dakshiṇāyai diśēnamaḥ (I am saluting the south), "Om pratīchyai diśēnamaḥ. (I am saluting the west). "Om udīchyai diśēnamaḥ." (I am saluting the north). Then lifting his hands over his head he repeats "Om ūrdhvāya namaḥ" and then turning his hands towards the earth he repeats "Om adharāya namaḥ"; again lifting his hands upwards in a prayerful posture he says "Antarikshāya namaḥ" and then turning his hands towards the earth repeats "Om bhūmyai namaḥ"; finally he prostrates saying "Om Vishṇavēnamaḥ." Then holding up his hands he says "Dhyeyassadā savitṛ manḍala madhya vartī nārāyaṇaḥ sarasijāsana sannivishṭaḥ kēyūravān makarakunḍalavān kirīṭa hārīhiraṇmayavapuḥ dhṛtaśankhachakraḥ || śankhachakragadā pāṇe dwārakānilayacchyuta gōvinda puṇḍarīkāksha rakshamām śaraṇāgatam | namō brahmaṇyadēvāya gōbrāhmaṇa hitāya cha, jagaddhitāya kṛshṇāya gōvindāya namō namaḥ." This is a prayer offered to God in the sūryamaṇḍala. After this prayer the man does abhivādanam. The above prayer when rendered into English runs thus:--"Śrīmannārāyaṇa always staying on a padmāsana with bracelets for upper arms, makarakuṇḍalas in his ears, kirīṭa on his head, hāra (garland) and other ornaments and with a body brilliant with yellow gold colour is one to be thought of at all times. He must be contemplated thus as one abiding in the orb of the sun, as one sitting on a lotus flower, as wearing bracelets in the arms, makarakunḍalas in ears, a crown on his head, garlands and other ornaments, with a body of golden colour and as holding śankha and chakra in his arms. 'Save me, Oh God, who lives in Dwāraka, who does not desert one who believes in you. Oh Gōvinda, with eyes as beautiful as the lotus. (At this he prostrates himself for absolution from his sins). I am saluting the feet of Kṛshṇa who is the dēvatā of the Brahmans, who is always doing good to the cows and the Brahmans, who always thinks of the good of the world and who always protects the cows as his."

If the japam is finished before sunrise, the upasthānam should be done only after sunrise. So till the rise of the sun he should be repeating ashṭākshara. If sandhyā is performed after sunrise the upasthānam may be done and the sandhyā concluded. In the morning the japam may be performed either standing or sitting. In the midday he should stand and in the evening he should sit during japam.

Repetition of the Ashṭāksharam.

This japam is performed only by those who have been initiated fully and by those who have passed through the ceremony of prapatti (See Pl. I-A).

The japa is begun by repeating the taniyans (stanzas in praise) of his own Āchārya who initiated the performer and taught the vākya guruparamparā, Ślōka guruparamparā, mantra, mantrārtha, and then he should repeat the mūla mantra twenty-five times and do prāṇāyāmam. Then he performs the sankalpam repeating the following mantra :—" Śrī bhagavadājñayā śrimannārāyaṇaprītyartham prātāssandhyāyām ashṭōttara śatakritvaḥ (or daśakritvaḥ) ashṭāksharamahāmantrajapam karishyē."

He does nyāsam repeating as follows :—" Asya śrīmad ashṭākshara mahā mantrasya badarikāśramavāsinārāyaṇa ṛshiḥ | dēvī gāyatrīçhandaḥ | paramātmā śrīman-nārāyaṇō dēvatā," and then contemplates about Nārāyaṇa. The translation in English of the above is " Nārāyaṇa ṛshi is the seer of the divine, eight syllabled mantra, the metre is the divine gāyatrī, the presiding deity is Nārāyaṇa associated with Lakshmī and the Lord of all." The contemplation of Nārāyaṇa is done by repeating the following :— " Aum bījam, āyaśaktiḥ, mām kīlakam, hrīm kavacham, buddhistatvam, udāttādisvaraḥ | Śrī Vaikuṇṭham Kshētram jīvaparamātmanōḥ svasvāmibhāvassambandhaḥ | śrīman-nārāyaṇaprītyarthe japē viniyōgaḥ "||.

Then repeating the tirumantra he smears the inside and outside of his hands and does anganyāsas and karanyāsas.

He does aksharanyāsa as is usually done. Then he does nyāsa as in the gāyatrī japam repeating "om om angushṭhābhyām namaḥ | om nārāyaṇa madhyamābhyām namaḥ | om om anāmikābhyām namaḥ | om kanishṭhikābhyām namaḥ | om nārāyaṇāya karatalakara pṛshṭhābhyām namaḥ||."

Then he does anganyāsa repeating "Om om jñānāya hṛdayāya namaḥ om namaḥ aiśvaryāya śirasēsvāhā | om nārāyaṇa śaktyai śikhāyai vaushaṭ | om om balāya kavachāya hūm | om namaḥ tējasē nētrābhyām vaushaṭ | om nārāyaṇa vīryāya astrāya phaṭ|| ".

Folding his hands and saluting he repeats the following dhyāna ślōka :—"Savyam pādam prasārya śritaduritaharam dakshiṇam kunchayitvā jānunyādāya savyētaramitara-bhujam nāga bhōgē nidhāya | paśchāt bāhudvayēna pratibhaṭaśamanē dhārayan śankhachakrē dēvī bhūshādi jushṭō janayatu jagatām śarma vaikunṭha nāṭhaḥ." The translation of the above is as follows :—" May the Lord of Vaikunṭha give happiness to all the world, who is seated on the serpent couch with his left leg hanging down, with his right leg which removes the distress of its refugees bent and kept erect over the couch, with his right arms placed over the right knee and with his left hand resting on the couch and who is holding the śankha and chakra which are used in quelling his enemies by his two backarms and who is in company with his wife and adorned by several ornaments and other things."

He thinks of Para Vāsudēva after repeating the above ślōkas. Then he thinks of God by repeating the following ślōkas and then does japa of " Tiru ashṭākshara." " Iha sangra-hataḥ śrīmān gōptā śeshī samādhika daridraḥ | śaraṇam sarvaśarīri sēvyaḥ prāpyaścha sādhubhirbhāvyaḥ "|| and " Padatrayētra samkshēpāt bhāvyānanyārhasēshatā | ananyōpāyatā svasya tathānanyapumarthatā "|| The above passages when translated are as follows :—" In short the Lord of the Universe has to be conceived by Sri Vaishna-vas as having Lakshmī as his consort, as the protector of all, as the master of all, as having poverty, as not having an equal or superior, as the only refuge, as having the whole universe as his body. and as the only one to be served and reached." "In brief the purport that should be conceived from the three words are that no other than Nārāyaṇa associated with Lakshmī is the master, the means to attain him, and the end or aim to reach."

Then with hands raised together he contemplates on God repeating:—"Kshīrāmbhonidhiratnamaṇḍapamahāsauvarṇasimhāsane vāmānkē sthitayā prasannavadanās ī-kāntayālingitam | dōrdanḍānkitaśankhapankajagadāchakrairudāra śriyam tvām nityam kalayāmi janma vimukhō Lakshmīśa Nārāyaṇa"||. This passage when rendered into English runs as follows:—"Oh Nārāyaṇa, Lord of Lakshmī, feeling a deep aversion to births, I daily contemplate on You, as having been seated on a golden throne supported by lions, placed in a temple of diamonds in the centre of the milky ocean, as having been embraced by Lakshmī of pleasant face sitting on Your left thigh, and as appearing more beautiful by holding Śankha, lotus, gadā and chakra in Your hands."

ĀDHĀRAŚAKTI TARPANAM.

Afterwards he does dvayam, charama ślōkam, dvādaśākshara and Shadākshara according to the time available and means.

This is begun by āchamanam and then Prāṇāyāmam. The ceremony is begun by repeating the following sankalpam:—"Srī Bhagavadājñaya Śrīmannārāyaṇa prītyartham ādhāra śaktyāditarpaṇam karishyē." Repeating the above he takes water with both the hands, as in kēśavādi tarpaṇam during sandhyā. Then he does tarpaṇam with this water repeating the following mantras:—"Om ādhāraśaktai namaḥ Om prakṛtyai namaḥ | Om akhila jagadhādhārāya kūrma rūpiṇē Nārāyaṇāya namaḥ | Om anantāya Nāgarājaya namaḥ | Om bhūm Bhumyai namaḥ | Om Srī Vaīkuṇṭhāya divya lokāya namaḥ | Om Srī Vaikuṇṭhāya divya jana pādāya namaḥ | Om Śrī Vaikuṇṭhāya divya Nāgarājāya namaḥ | Om Srī Vaikuṇṭhāya divya vimānāya namaḥ | Om ānandamayāya divya manḍapa ratnāya namaḥ | Om āstaraṇa rūpāyānantāya Nāgarājāya namaḥ | Om dharmāya pīṭha pādāya namaḥ | Om jnānāya pīṭha pādāya namaḥ | Om vairāgyāya pīṭha pādāya namaḥ | Om aiśvaryāya pīṭha pādāya namaḥ | Om adharmāya pīṭha gātrāya namaḥ | Om ajñānāya pīṭhagātrāya namaḥ | Om avairāgyāya pīṭhagātrāya namaḥ | Om anaiśvaryāya pīṭhagātrāya namaḥ | Om abhiḥr parichinnatanavē pīṭhabhṛte saḍātmanē anantāya -nāgarājāya namaḥ | Om ashṭadala padmāya namaḥ | Om vimalāyai chāmarahastāyai namaḥ | Om utkarshiṇyai chāmarahastāyaī namaḥ | Om jnānāyai hasthāyai namaḥ | Om kriyāyai cāhmarahastāyai namaḥ | Om yōgāyai chāmarahastāyai namaḥ | Om prabhvai chāmarahastāyai namaḥ | Om satyāyai chāmara hastāyai namaḥ—Om Īśānāyai chamarahastāyai namaḥ | Om anugrahāyai chāmara hastāyai namaḥ | Om Īagatprakṛtayē divyayōga pīṭhāya namaḥ—Om divya yōga paryankāya namaḥ | Om sahasraphaṇāmaṇi manḍitāya anāntāyanāgarājāya namaḥ | Om pāda pīṭhātmanē anantāya Nāgarājāya namaḥ | Om sarva parivārānām padmāsanē bhyō namaḥ | Om anantagaruḍa Vishvaksēnānām sapīṭhaka padmāsanēbhyō namaḥ | Om asmadgurubhyō namaḥ | Om Śrīmatē Nārāyaṇāya namaḥ | Mūlamantrē namaḥ | Om Śrīm Śriyai namaḥ | Om bhūm Bhūmyai namaḥ | Om nīm nīlāyai namaḥ | Sarvābhyō bhagavad divya mahishībhyō namaḥ | Om kirīṭāyamakuṭadhipatayē namaḥ | Om kirīṭa mālāyai apīḍātmanē namaḥ | Om dakshiṇa kunḍalāya makarātmanē namaḥ | Om Vāmakunḍalāya makarātmanē namaḥ | Om Vaijayantyai Vanamālāyai namaḥ | Om Śrīmad tulasyai namaḥ | Om Śrīvatsāya Śrīnivāsāya namaḥ | Om hārāya sarvābharaṇādhipatayē namaḥ | Om kānchī guṇōjvalāya divyapītāmbarāya namaḥ | Om sarvēbhyō bhagavad divya bhūshaṇēbhyō namaḥ | Om sudarśanāya hētirājāya namaḥ | Om nandakāya khaḍgādhipatayē namaḥ | Om Padmāya namaḥ | Om Pānchajanyāya śankhādhipatayē namaḥ | Om kaumōdakyai gadādhipatyai namaḥ | Om Sārngāya chāpādhīpatayē namaḥ | Om sarvābhyō bhagavaddivyāyudhēbhyō namaḥ | Om Sarvābhyō bhagavatpādāravinda samvāhinībhyō namaḥ | Om anantāya nāgarajāya namaḥ | Om Sarvēbhyō bhagavat parijanēbhyō namaḥ | Om Bhagavat pādukābhyām namaḥ | Om Sarvēbhyō bhagavat paricchadēbhyō namaḥ | agrataḥ Om Vam vainatēyāya namaḥ | Om Bhagavatē Vishvaksēnāya namaḥ | Om gam gajānanāya namaḥ | Om jam jayatsēnāya namaḥ | Om ham harivaktrāya namaḥ | Om kam kālaprakṛtisamjñakāya namaḥ | Om Sarvēbhyō bhagavadvishvaksēna parijanēbhyō namaḥ | Om chandāya dvārapālaya namaḥ | Om prachandāya dvārāpālāya namaḥ | Om bhadrāya dvārāpalaya namaḥ | Om subhadrāyadvāra pālāya namaḥ | Om jayāya dvārapālaya namaḥ | Om vijayāya dvārapālāya namaḥ | Om dhātrē dvārapālāya namaḥ | Om vidhātrē dvārapālāya namaḥ | Om sarvēbhyō Bhagavaddvārapālēbhyō namaḥ | Om kumudāya janādhipatayē savāhana parivāra praharaṇāyą namaḥ | Om kumudākshāya gaṇādhipatayē savāhana parivāra praharaṇāya namaḥ | Om punḍarīkāya gaṇādhipatayē savāhana parivāra praharaṇāya namaḥ | om vāmanāya gaṇādhipatayē savāhana parivāra praharaṇāya namaḥ | Om śankukarṇāya ganādhipatayē savāhana parivāra praharanāya namaḥ | Om sarvanētrāya gaṇādhipatayē savāhana parivāra praharaṇāya namaḥ | Om sumukhāya gaṇādhipatayē savāhana parivāra praharaṇaya namaḥ | om supratishṭhitāya gaṇādhipatayē savāhana parivāra praharaṇāya namah | om sarvēbhyō bhagavat pārshadēbhyō namaḥ | Iti santarpya dēvarshi kānḍa ṛshi pitṛ tarpaṇam karishyē."

The above when translated runs thus:—"Om salutation to the support which supports the Vaikuṇṭha loka. Om salutation to primordial matter Om salutation to Nārāyaṇa in the form of tortoise who is the supporter of the whole universe. Om salutation to the serpent king Ananta. Om salutation to the earth. Om salutation to Vaikuṇṭha, the divine world. Om salutation to the population of Vaikuṇṭha. Om salutation to the divine city of Vaikuṇṭha. Om salutation to the dome of the divine world. Om salutation to the divine manḍapa which is blissfull. Om salutation to the king of Nāgas who is in the form of bed to Vishnu. Om salutation to Dharma which supports the seat of Vishnu. Om salutation to Aiśwarya which supports the seat of Vishnu. Om salutation to adharma which embodies the seat of Vishnu. Om salutation to ignorance which embodies the seat of Vishnu. Om salutation to Avairāgya which embodies the seat of Vishnu. Om salutation to Anaiśwarya which embodies the seat of Vishnu. Om salutation to Ananta who is the king of Nāgās or serpents, who is of good soul, and who is supporting the seat embodied by these dēvatās. Om salutation to the lotus of eight petals. Om salutation to vimala, chamara holder. Om salutation to Utkarshiṇi, another chāmara holder. Om salutation to Jnāna another chāmara holder. Om salutation to Kriyā another chāmara holder. Om salutation to Yōga another chāmara holder. Om salutation to Prabhu, another chāmara holder. Om salutation to Satya another chamara holder. Om salutation to Īśāna, another chāmara holder. Om salutation to Anugraha, another chāmara holder. Om salutation to the divine Yōga-seat which is the embodiment of primordial matter of the universe. Om salutation to the divine Yōgi-bed. Om salutation to Ananta, the naga-king ornamented by the diamonds of his thousand hoods. Om salutation to Ananta, the naga-king who embodies the support on which Vishnu rests his foot. Om salutation to the lotus seat of the several followers of Vishṇu. Om salutation to the lotus seats with bases of Ananta, Garuḍa and Vishvaksēna. Om salutation to my preceptors. Om salutation to Nārāyaṇa associated with Lakshmī (This may be done even with the ashtākshara mantra). Om Śrīm salutation to Goddess Lakshmī. Om bhūm salutation to Earth. Om Nīm salutation to Nīlā. Salutation to all the divine Consorts of Vishnu. Om salutation to the presiding deity of the crown of Vishnu. Om salutation to the chaplet tied round the crown of the head. Om salutation to the makara kunḍala in the right ear of Vishnu. Om salutation to the makara kunḍala in the left ear of Vishnu. Om salutation to the garlands known by the name of Vaijayantī and Vanamāla. Om salutation to the tulasī plant or leaves. Om salutation to Śrīnivāsa the abode of Lakshmī. Om salutation to the garland and to the lord of several ornaments. Om salutation to the divine pitāmbara which is made more resplendent by the zone worn over it. Om salutation to all the various divine ornaments. Om salutation to Sudarśana the lord of missiles. Om salutation to Nandaka the lord of swords. Om salutation to the lotus. Om salutation to Pānchajanya the lord of śankhas or conches. Om salutation to Kaumōdakī the lord of all gadas. Om salutation to the Śārnga the lord of all bows. Om salutation to all the various divine weapons. Om salutation to all the shampooers of the lotus feet of Vishnu. Om salutation to Ananta the Naga-king. Om salutation to all the attendants of Vishnu. Om salutation to the sandals of the divine Vishnu. Om salutation to all the paraphernalia of Vishnu. Firstly om salutation to Garuḍa. Om salutation to the holy Vishvaksēna. Om gam salutation to the elephant-faced. Om jam salutation to Jayatsēna. Om ham salutation to Hari Vaktra. Om kam salutation to the kāla prakṛti. Om salutation to all the attendants such as Vishvaksēna and others. Om salutation to the door-keeper Chanḍa. Om salutation to the door-keeper Prachanḍa. Om salutation to the door-keeper Bhadra. Om salutation to the door-keeper Subhadra. Om salutation to the door-keeper Jaya. Om salutation to the door-keeper Vijaya. Om salutation to the door-keeper Dhātri. Om salutation to the door-keeper Vidhātri. Om salutation to all the door-keepers of Vishnu. Om salutation to Kumuda, a lord of all attendants, with his vehicle, attendants, weapons, etc. Om salutation to Kumudāksha, a lord of all attendants, with his vehicle, attendants, weapons, etc. Om salutation to Puṇḍarīka, a lord of all attendants, with his vehicle, his attendants and weapons. Om salutation to Vāmana, a lord of all attendants, with his vehicle, attendants and weapons. Om salutation to Śankukarṇa, a lord of attendants, with his vehicle, attendants and weapons. Om salutation to Sarvanētra, a lord of attendants, with his vehicle, attendants and weapons. Om salutation to Sumukha, a lord of attendants, with his vehicle, attendants and weapons. Om salutation to Supratīshṭhita, a lord of attendants with his vehicle, attendants and weapons. Om salutation to all the various leaders or lords of attendants. Having pleased all the above deities by offering libations of water by uttering the mantras whose meanings are given above I shall then please the Dēvas, Ṛshis, Kāṇḍa Ṛshis and Pitṛs by libations of water."

After repeating the above he does tarpanam repeating the mantra ending with "Sarva rshigaṇapatnīstarpayāmi" and then repeats the following:—"Om prajāpatim kāṇḍa ṛshim tarpayāmi. Om Sōmam Kāṇḍa ṛshim tarpayāmi Om agnim kāṇḍa rshim tarpayāmi. Om viśvāndēvān kāṇḍa rshīmśtarpayāmi. Om sāmhitīṛ dēvatā upanishadastarpayāmi. Om yājñakīr dēvatā upanishadastarpayāmi. Om brahmānam svayambhuvamstarpayāmi; sadasaspatimtarpayāmi." This when translated runs thus:—"I please Prajāpati a rshi of a particular kānda of the Veda by this libation of water. I please Soma, a rshi of a particular kānda of the Veda by this libation of water. I please Agni, a rshi of a particular kānda of the Veda by this libation of water. I please Viśvēdēvās, ṛshis of particular kāṇḍas of the Veda by this libation of water. I please the deity of the Upanishads known by the name of Samhita by this libation of water. I please the deity of Upanishads by the name of Yajña by this libation of water. I please Brahma, who was self-born, by this libation of water. I please Sadasaspati by this libation of water." Repeating the above mantra he does tarpanam by pouring water after each mantra. Then the other tarpanams are done repeating the appropriate mantras.

Then āchamanam is done. He puts on the sacred thread as "nivīti" and the wet upper cloth folded in four and repeats the following mantra:—"Yēkē chāsmat kulē jātā aputrā gōtrajā mrtāḥ tē grhnantu mayādattam vastranishpīdanōdakam." The meaning of this passage is as follows:—"Those who were born in our lineage and are dead without sons and those who were born in our gōtra and are dead without sons let them receive these libations of water given by me, got by squeezing out this cloth." After repeating the above mantra he takes the wet cloth folded into four in an apradakshina manner and twists it so as to make the water flow out. Then the cloth thus treated is placed on his left wrist and he puts on the sacred thread properly and then does āchamanam twice. The āvāhanams of tīrthas that were done during the snānam must now be done so as to do āvāhanam within himself. The "Vastranishpīḍana" (ceremony of pressing out the water from the cloth described above) should not be done on dvādaśi and pournami days. On amāvāsya days, sankramana days and śrāddha days the Vastranishpīḍanam is done after the tarpaṇa srāddhas. If one's father is alive the Vastranishpīḍanam should not be performed.

Then sātvikatyagām is done by repeating the mantra beginning with "Bhagavānēva" and ending with "Prātassandhyōpāsanākhyam karma svasmai svaprītayē svayamēva kāritavān." This when rendered into English runs thus:—"The divine Lord . . . has done this act, viz., the prayer at the morning twilight, himself, for his own sake and for his own gratification." Then he finishes the prātassandhyā by repeating "Prātassandhyōpāsanākhyēna bhagavatkarmaṇā bhagavān prīyatām Vāsudēvah." This in English runs thus:—"May the divine Lord Vāsudēva become pleased by this divine act of prayer at the morning twilight."

BRAHMA YAJÑAM.

This part of the ceremony is begun by the performer doing āchamanam and prāṇāyāmam and then sankalpam is done as follows:—"Śrī Bhagavadājñayā Śrīman Nārāyaṇaprītyartham brahmayajñēna yakshyē." Afterwards he repeats "Kritamcha karishyāmi . . . brahma yajñēna bhagavantam Vāsudēvamarchayishyāmi." The above in English runs thus:—"I am doing what has been done. I shall worship the divine Vāsudēva by brahmayajña. By the power of our Lord, etc. . . . The divine Lord makes me do this brahmayajña himself for his own sake and for his own gratification." After the above he repeats the bala mantra thus:—"Bhagavatō balēna", etc. He then does sātvikatyāga by repeating thus:—"Bhagavanēva . . . brahmayajñākhyam karmasva . . . Kārayati" After this he repeats the mantra "Vidyudasi Vidyamē pāpmānamṛtāt satyamupaimi," "Oh deity you are the cause of separation. Make my sins go away from me. From this water I reach satya or Paramātmā." He then takes water with the right hand and cleans his left hand with it. Then without uttering the mantras he performs āchamanam three times. He then cleans his hand with water, wipes his mouth, touches his head with all his fingers, with the fourth finger he touches his eyes, his nose he touches with his forefinger or the second one, his ears are touched by his fifth finger and his chest he touches with the palm of his hand. Every time he touches the above parts he also touches the water and wipes his hand without uttering any mantra. Finally he washes his hands, places darbha or spreads it as āsana and sits on it. Then he puts on pavitras on both the hands and does prāṇāyāmam three times. He next places his right leg on the left leg, keeps his two hands joined together on the knee of the right leg and, says "Om bhūḥ, om bhuvaḥ, om suvaḥ, om tatsavitur varēṇyam, om bhargō dēvasyadhīmahi, om dhyōyōnaḥ prachdayāt ¦ om tatsavitur varēṇyam bhargō dēvasya dhīmahi om dhiyōyōnaḥ prachōdayāt, om tatsavitur varēṇyam bhargō dēvasya dhīmahi dhiyōyōnaḥ prachōdayāt." Instead of this the following may be substituted:—Om bhūḥ tatsaviturvarēṇyam, om bhuvaḥ bhargō dēvasya dhīmahi, om suvaḥ dhiyō yōnaḥ prachōdayāt ¦ om bhūḥ tatsaviturvarēṇyam bhargōdēvasya dhīmahi om bhuvaḥ dhiyōyōnāḥ prachōdayāt, om suvaḥ tatsaviturvarēṇyam bhargōdēvasya dhīmahi dhiyō yōnaḥ prachōdayāt, om bhūrbhuvassuvaḥ tatsaviturvarēṇyam bhargō dēvasya dhīmahi dhiyōyōnaḥ prachōdayāt." If the performer is a sāmavēdī instead of the above he has to repeat the following: "Tatsaviturvarēṇyam om, bhargōdēvasya dhimahī om, dhiyōyōnaḥ prachōdayāt om tatsaviturvarēṇyam bhargō dēvasya dhīmahi om dhiyōyōnaḥ prachōdayāt, om tatsaviturvarēṇyam bhargō dēvasya dhīmahi dhiyōyōnaḥ prachōdayāt om, bhūḥ bhuvaḥ suvaḥ purushaḥ satyam om." He should also repeat after the above, gāyatrī sāma and vyahṛti sāma.

Then the performer repeats the following:—"Hariḥ om agnimīḍē purōhitam yajñasya dēvamṛtvijam hōtāram ratnadhātamam | Hariḥ om Hariḥ ōm | Ishētvōrjētva vāyavasthō pāyavastha dēvōvassavitā prārpayatu śrēshṭhatamāya karmaṇē Hariḥ om Hariḥ om | Agna āyāhi vītayē gṛṇānō havyadātayē nihō tā satsi barhishi." This passage runs in English thus:—I praise Agni (fire god) who secures hōma or oblations for sacrifice or who is in front of me, who is endowed with the quality of giving gifts, who is the hōtā (one of the four kinds of officiating priests) of the sacrifice and who is the giver of enormous wealth.

"Oh Palāśa branch! I am cutting you in order to use you as an offering to Dēvas (in order to give food and strength to the dēvas). Oh calves! go away from your mothers to the forest to eat grass and again return to your master's house in the evening. Oh cows! the Supreme Lord that is within you prompts you to go to the forest to eat grass so that your milk may be used in sacrifices.

"Come Agni! to eat the sacrificial offering and to carry the sacrificial offerings to the Dēvas. Sit on the holy grass as Hōtā being praised by us."

If the performer is a Sāmavēdī he should repeat the following instead of the above:—"The sāma beginning with "Om agnāyi."

Then he should say "Hariḥ Om Hariḥ Om śannōdēvīrabhishṭaya āpōbhavantu pītayē samyōrabhiśravantunaḥ | Hariḥ Om".—The English version of the above is:—"Oh waters! be of comfort to us by removing our sins, be of use to our sacrifice, be of use to our drink. Remove all our diseases that have already afflicted us and kept us away from diseases that have not begun to afflict us. Sprinkle over us to purify us." Some say that the performer should repeat the beginning or the characteristic portion of his own Veda. Then he is to repeat a śākhā or some part of his Veda daily. If he does not know Vedas he must at least repeat the purusha sūkta. In case he is not acquainted with this, he is expected to say his gāyatrī ten times. After this he says "Om bhūr bhuvas suvaḥ | satyam tapaḥ sraddhāyām juhōmi" once. This is followed by the repetition of "Om namō brahmaṇē namōastvagnayē namaḥ pṛthivyai nama ōshadhībhyaḥ | namōvāchē namōvāchaspatayē namō Vishṇavē / bṛhatē karōmi" three times. This in English is as follows:—"Salutation to Brahma, salutation to Agni, salutation to Earth, salutation to the woods, salutation to Speech, salutation to the Lord of Speech, salutation to Vishṇu. I do this for the Vedas."

Then he repeats the following:—"Vishṭirasi vriśchamēpāpmānamṛtāt satyamupāgām" and takes water in the right hand and cleans the left palm and then does āchamanam. The above passage when translated into English runs as follows:—"Oh deity! you are the cause of separation, remove all my sins. From the water I have reached satya or paramātmā." Then sātvikatyāgam is done repeating the usual mantra as follows:—"Bhagavānēva . . . brahmayajñākhyam karma kāritavān." This in English would run thus:—The

Divine Lord . . . has himself done the act, *viz.*, brahma yajña. Then samarpaṇam (finishing offering) is done by repeating the following :—"Kṛtamcha . . . brahmayajñēna Vāsudēvaḥ." This in English runs thus:—I am doing what has been done. May Vāsudēva become pleased by the Brahma yajña. If one fails to perform the brahma yajñam, while doing the morning sandhyāvandanam, he may perform this ceremony after the mādhyāhnikam or Vaiśvadēva ceremony.

After performing brahma yajña the performer proceeds to a temple to pray to God. While proceeding to the temple on his way he should show respect to the following doing pradakshiṇa round them :— God's temple, Āchārya, a scholar who is proficient in pāncharātra śāstra, a ficus tree, a banyan tree, cow, a meeting of big men and house of his Āchārya. On reaching the temple he should prostrate, at least twice for each, before Vishvaksēna and Dvārapālakas and with their permission he enters the temple. On entering the temple he must prostrate as many times as he can before God and after the prostrations he should stand on the right side of the God. Then he should feel that he is to be a servant of God, and he should repeat guruparamparā before this. On account of seeing God who is pure and capable of attracting one's mind, one feels very much pleased. He begins to repeat stōtras of God (praises of God) capable of attracting God's attention. There he should obtain sacred water, tulasi and other prasādams after prostrating. He should use them with proper obeisance and feeling of respect to God. He should think that he is purified by thus worshipping God and taking permission from God he should sit within the temple in a place and do japam by repeating "Tirumantrams." Then he comes out from inside the temple. He should not turn round his body while leaving the temple. He should not show his back portion of the body to God. He should leave the temple facing God. On leaving the temple thus without any apachārams, he is to show respect to Vishvaksēna and take his permission to leave the temple. On coming out he is to take water in a vessel of gold, silver or copper and go to his house. There he is to wash his hands and legs with this water and sprinkle water all over within the house. On his way to his house he should not see any pāshaṇḍis (men who do not worship Vishnu and who worship only Śiva) nor can he talk to them.

Persons who go to the temple to worship God should avoid the following apachārams *i.e.*, they are not to do the prohibited things. The apachārams are detailed below :—

(1) Those who cause disturbance by loud noise to music, to dancing and to the reading of sacred writings enter into 21 kinds of naraka. Then they are born as donkeys.

(2) Those who pray to God with the upper cloth covering the body will be born three times with white leprosy.

(3) Persons who come to God to pray to Him with woollen clothing on will be born as chaṇḍāḷas for fourteen janmas.

(4) Men who with oil smeared over them and with their shoes or foot-wear come to pray to God and enter the temple with these are born as dogs for three generations.

(5) Those who throw nails, hair and bones into God's sannidhi are to be born as flies for seven times.

(6) He who spits the betel and nut from his mouth in the precincts within God's temple will be in naraka as long as pancha bhūtas exist.

(7) One who spits in God's temple has to remain in the hall where worms are abundant and he will be born as trees.

(8) One who goes to smaśānam and does pūja to God without bathing, loses the good that he secured during seven births.

(9) A person passing urine in God's temple precincts, falls head downwards into a hell called urinal "mūtra gartam".

(10) He who passes fæces in the temple of God suffers in 21 narakams and is born as a worm in the fæces.

(11) He who has seen at close quarters of a dead body and comes to the temple without bathing and tries to worship God is sure to be born as a crow.

(12) He who carries a dead body and enters the temple without bathing is bound to be born as a chaṇḍāḷa.

(13) One who worships God after taking food in nimantraṇam is sure to be born as a sparrow (house sparrow).

(14) One who stays in the shade of a Vimāna except during pradakshiṇa will be born as a thorny tree in an open space.

(15) He who passes urine or fæces near the temple gets into the hell called "Rau ravādi" naraka.

(16) Those who talk in God's temple about ordinary matters, and not about God, are sure to be born as "Tittiri" birds.

(17) Those who take the light away from the presence of God to any other place, are sure to be born as blind people.

(18) Those who do not care to listen to the words spoken about God's capabilities and who mock at these words are sure to be born either as deaf or dumb people.

(19) Persons who remain within the temple with their legs stretched and picking out insects from their body and sleep are likely to be born as trees in water-less deserts.

(20) Those who worship God with flowers that are set apart for other dēvatās are born as frogs.

(21) Those who go to the temples of dēvatās and then come to the temple of God without a bath are likely to be born as beggars going from house to house and yet not securing enough to be happy.

(22) He who considers God as only a dēvatā and equal to them is born as a Chaṇḍāḷa.

(23) Those who smell the flowers intended for the worship of God are born as lepers emitting bad smell.

(24) Persons who are not generally allowed to come near such as Chaṇḍāḷas, patitas outside a temple, should not be treated as untouchables when they come to pray to God. One should not bathe if they happen to touch them during God's procession.

(25) Any one suspecting that he is defiled during an utsava and who bathes to get rid of this defilement will fall into Naraka from Swarga with his pitrs.

(26) After taking Srīpāda tīrtha of Vaishnavas or the tīrtha (sacred water) of God āchamanam should not be done.

The following are considered sins against God in a temple: so these should be avoided as far as possible :—

Entering a temple on a vāhana or with shoes on his feet; avoiding to see the procession of God during an utsavam; not doing obeisance (praṇāmam) to God on meeting God; saluting God with one hand; turning round and round in the presence of God; prostrating to God while unclean or under pollution; stretching legs in front of God; sitting on a plank in front of God; sleeping, eating, talking secretly, bawling loudly in the temple, crying in the presence of God, fighting before God, abusing one before God, blessing a person in the presence of God; talking to women with evil intention, and talking badly in the presence of God; leaving gas through the anus while in the presence of God; covering one's body with a woollen clothing; abusing or praising others in God's presence; doing only formal things when one is strong; eating things not offered to God; not offering to God fruits grown in the season; offering to God portions of food already used; sitting with the back turned to God; prostrating to men in temples; remaining quiet without talking to his guru in the temple; praising himself; decrying God; insulting a Vaishnava if he touches blood unknowingly and lying down within the temple just as he pleases; talking idly and repeating the Vedas at times not prescribed by the śāstras; sitting within the temple on an āsana or plank. Any one who thinks that God is only an idol made of metal and that his Āchārya is only a mortal being falls into hell.

Another set of things that are to be avoided in the temple are the following :—

Entering the temple to salute God after eating things that have been prohibited; going near God without cleaning one's teeth; touching God without bathing after cohabitation with women; coming close to God without bathing after seeing a corpse; coming near God without bathing after touching a woman in menses; touching a dead body and coming to salute God directly after burning the corpse and without bathing; while doing pūja to God passing gas through the anus; passing fæces and urine in the temple precints; bawling loudly when worship to God is being performed; saluting and seeing God with a black cloth covering the upper part of his body; saluting God with a single cloth in his waist; doing service to God with anger; offering flowers to God not fit for pūja; worshipping God wearing a cloth coloured red; touching God in the dark; doing service to God without bathing after touching dogs and such other unclean animals; saluting God after eating the flesh of animals; touching God immediately after touching the lamp; coming to God's presence directly from the smaśāna without bathing; saluting God after neglecting the bhāgavatās; saluting God with one hand; coming to God's temple for the sake of meeting and bringing strangers; not offering new grains to God; offering to God dhūpa only without flowers; rousing God from sleep without sounḍing the bhēri.

AUPĀSANAM.

The worshipper approaches the fire which he used the previous day, after washing his legs and doing two āchamanams. For use he takes fire from this by using darbha or samit and mixes it with fire in the place where he intends doing the ceremony and he repeats the following mantra while burning the samit or the darbha in the fire:—"Upāvarōha jātavedaḥ punastvam dēvēbhyō havyam vahanaḥ prajānān āyuḥ prajāmrayimasmāsudhēhi ajasrōdīdihinō durōṇē" The meaning of the passage is as follows:—"Oh Agni, again come down to earth from aranai (*Ficus religiosa*). Knowing well that this havis or offering has been given to the Dēvas, carry this offering to them. Give us life, children and wealth. You who are always living shine forth in our houses."

If the fire is in the samit he has to repeat the following mantra "Ājuhvānassupratīkaḥ purastādagnē svāmyōnimāsīdasādhyā | asmin sadhastē adhyuttarasmin viśvēdēvā yajamānaścha sīdata" and do "Avarōhanam" (removal) to it. The translation of the above is:—Oh Agni! having been invited with great favour, with grace, reach your own good place in the eastern direction. Oh! Viśvēdēva, you and the sacrificer sit on the best seat provided in front of us, where you can very well sit with Agni. Then he does sankalpam repeating "Śrī Bhagavadājñayā śrīman Nārāyaṇaprītyartham prātaraupāsanahōmam hōshyāmi" and then repeats the bala mantra as follows:—"Kritancha karishyāmi prātaraupāsanēna bhagavat karmaṇā . . . bhagavatō balēna." Then he does the sātvīkatyāga by repeating the following mantra:—"Bhagavānēva . . . prātaraupāsanākhyam karma . . . kārayati."

In a place in front of the worshipper where he is sitting he has to draw three lines, west to east, and three lines north to south, with the help of darbhas and then he has to throw the darbhas on the ground, sprinkle water over them and then they are thrown towards the nirṛti corner. Then he touches water and pronouncing three times the Vyāhṛtis along with the praṇavam takes the fire and keeps it in the place where hōmam is to be done. Afterwards he pours the water down, that was used for sprinkling, either towards the east or north and fills the empty vessel with fresh water and places it either to the north or east of the fire-place. Round the fire-place he places sixteen darbhas, four on each side, beginning with the east and going round in a pradakshiṇa manner, that is to say, four darbhas to the east first with the sharp points or apex of the darbhas towards the north, then on the south with the tips of darbhas to the east, then on the west with the tips towards the north and lastly on the northern side with the tips towards the east. The darbhas placed to the south should be above the darbhas placed towards the east and the west and the darbhas placed towards the north with the tip to the east should be below the darbhas placed towards the west and the east. After placing the darbhas round the fire as described above, he places the hands in a praying posture (hands together with the palms touching) and repeats the following mantra:—"Chatvāri śṛngā trayōasyapādā dvēśīrshē sapta hastāsō asya | tridhābaddhō | vṛshabhō rōravīti mahōdēvō martyān āvivēśa | ēshahi dēvaḥ pradiśōnu sarvāḥ | pūrvōhi jātaḥ sa u gaṛbhē antaḥ | savijāyamānaḥ sajanishyamāṇāḥ pratyangmukhāstisṭhati viśvatō mukhaḥ." Translation of the above passage is :--" The great deity Agni has come down to men and he is attended to by sacrifices. He has four Vedas as his four horns, the three svaras are his three feet, Brahmōdana and Pravargya are his two heads, the seven vedic metres are his seven heads; He is regulated by the Mantra, Kalpa and Brāhmaṇa; He is the bestower of fortunes. He is sung with and without music with the hymns of the Rg., Yajus and Sāma by the sacrificial priests such as Hōta. Self-resplendent Paramātmā realised by wise men having been present in all quarters was born Hiraṇya-garbha in the beginning of creation. He is the same Paramātmā. He has been born as Dēvas, beasts, etc., and is going to be born as such hereafter too. He is living in the hearts of all beings, is seeing all and is inciting them to do their action." Then he prays repeating ." Prāngmukhō dēva agnē abhimukhō bhava" which in English runs thus "Oh Agni of divine splendour, please be seated in the eastern direction and be disposed friendly towards me". He takes some akshata in the left hand and taking small quantities with the right hand places it in the directions mentioned, beginning with the east and ending with the Īśanyam the north-east or the eighth corner. While placing the rice he repeats in order the following mantras beginning with the east :—" Omagnayēṇamaḥ. jāta vēdasē namaḥ. Om sahōjasē namaḥ Om ajirāprabhavē namaḥ Om Vaiśvānarāya namaḥ Om naryāpasē namaḥ. Om panktirāthasē namaḥ Om visarpiṇē namaḥ!"

This when rendered into English is " Om salutation to Agni. Om salutation to jāta-vēdas. Om salutation to sahōjas. Om salutation to Ajirāprabhava. Om salutation to Vaiśvānara. Om salutation to Naryāpasa. Om salutation to Panktirathas. Om salutation to Visarpiṇ. "

After placing the turmeric dyed rice all round the fire in eight places, he takes some white rice and repeating the following mantra "Om yajñapurushāya namaḥ" puts the rice in fire. Then repeating "Sarvēbhyaḥ Śrī Vaishṇavēybhyō namaḥ" he scatters the akshata close to the bhāgavatas on the ground. The above Sanskrit passages mean "Salutation to the all-powerful Lord who is pleased by this sacrifice" and "Salutation to all the Sri Vishnavas." Then he pours water with the hand round the fire repeating "Aditēnu manyasva | anumatēnu manyasva | sarasvatēnu manyasva | deva savitaḥ prasūva." This when rendered into English is as follows :—"Oh Earth, please allow me to get the kingdom. Oh wife of the Dēva, who willingly supports all actions, please allow me to attain what I wish. Oh Sarasvati, please allow me to attain what I wish. Oh Sun that impels all beings, incite me to do the Vājapēya sacrifice." After repeating the above he places one samit (piece of palāśa stick) in the fire. Then he takes a handful of rice in the left hand, sprinkles water over it with the right hand and taking half the quantity of rice offers it to Agni through the fingers repeating "Sūryā-ya svāḥā." Repeating "Sūryāyēdam na mama" he takes the remaining quantity of rice from the left hand and repeating the mantra "Om agnayē svishṭakṛtē svāha" offers it to Agni. Afterwards he repeats "Agnayē svishṭa kṛta idam na mama." This when rendered into Englishwould be "I give this oblation to Svishṭakṛt (Agni). This oblation belongs to Svishṭakṛt and it is not mine." If it is evening instead of using the term "Sūrya" "Agnayēsvāhā" is used and the rest of the mantra may be repeated as those mantras are common. He puts another samit in the fire.

Followers of Sāma veda do not repeat the mantra beginning with "Chatvāri sṛngā." They do parishēchanam repeating the mantra "Dēva savitaḥ prasuva, yajñam prasuva, yajñapatim bhagāya divyō gandharvaḥ, ketapūḥ kētam naḥ punātu vāchaspatir vāchām naḥ svadātu." This in English runs thus:—"Oh Sun lord! Incite me to do the sacrifice. Make this sacrifice go on without impediment. Incite the sacrificer also so that he may get fortunes. The gandharva that is in swarga cleanses the knowledge that is in the minds of others. Let him cleanse our knowledge so that it may be without confusion. Let vāchaspati correct our words (mantra) used in this act, *i.e.*, sacrifice." Paristaraṇa should be placed east, south, north and west. In the morning while doing hōmam he says "Sūryāya svāhā sūryāya idam na mama, prajāpatayē idam na mama" and in the evening repeats the following while doing hōmam:—"Agnayē svāhā agnayē idam na mama, prajāpatayēsvāhā prajāpataya idam na mama." This means "I give the oblation to Agni. This oblation is for Agni and it is not mine. I give the oblation to Prajāpati. This oblation is for Prajāpati and it is not mine." Then in the morning he repeats "Yadindra hām yāthā tvam" sāmam. In the evening he recites "Yādindrā haim yāthauhau hōvā-hāyi" sāmam. This in English runs thus "Just as Indra is the lord of wealth amongst the Dēvas so I should also become the lord of wealth." Afterwards he repeats Vāma-dēvyam and śāntijapa.

The āhutis put in fire should not touch one another. If they should mix he does sankalpam as follows:—"Āhuti samsarga prāyaśchittārtham vanaspatihōmam karishyē." This means "To expiate the sin arising out of the mixing of offered oblations in the sacrificial fire I am doing the vanaspati hōma." He places one samit in fire repeating "Yatra vēttha vanaspatē dēvānām guhyā nāmāni tatra havyāni gāmaya svāhā." This passage when rendered into English runs "Oh Vanaspati, you know the places where the secret names of the Dēvas are well known, hence make my oblations reach those places." After putting the samit in the fire he repeats:—"Vanaspataya idam na mama." This means "This oblation is offered to Vanaspati and it is not mine." Then the mantra:—"Om aditēnvamagam sthāḥ | Om anumatēnvamagmsthāḥ | Om sarasvatēnva-magmsthāḥ | dēva savitaḥ prāsāviḥ" is repeated.

This in English runs as follows:—"Oh Earth! you have allowed me to get the kingdom. Oh wife of the Dēva, willingly supporting all actions, you have permitted me to attain what I wished. Om oh Sarasvati! you have permitted me to attain what I wished. Oh Sun that impels all beings! you have incited me to do the Vājapēya sacrifice." Sāma Vedis should recite the mantra beginning with "savitaḥ prāsāviḥ yajñam prāsāvīḥ | " and ending with "Ketam napāvīt Vāchaspatir vācham nō svadīt." This when translated runs as follows:—Oh Sun that impels all beings! You have incited me to do the Vājapēya sacrifice. You have helped me in doing the Vājapēya sacrifice. "The gandharva who is in the dēvalōka perfects the knowledge of men, may he perfect our knowledge of this Vājapēya sacrifice. May Vāchaspati make us recite properly the mantras that are uttered by us in this sacrifice." The fire is then sprinkled with water. This is followed by the placing of a samit or two darbhas into the fire and repeating. "Śrī Vishṇavē svāhā, Śrī Vishṇavē paramātmanē idam na mama." This means "Om I offer this oblation to Śrī Vishṇu. This oblation is for Śrī Vishṇu the supreme Lord of all and it is not mine." As soon as the rice put in fire is burnt he gets up and with palms placed together and lifting them in a prayerful posture repeats the following:– "Agnēnaya supathā rāyē asmān viśvāni dēva vayunāni vidvān | yuyōdhyasmajjuhurāṇa mēnō bhūyishṭhām tē nama uktim vidhēma." This when rendered into English runs thus:—"Oh shining Agni you possess all kinds of knowledge and therefore you are wise; lead us in a good way to the wealth of swarga which we should attain. Therefore keep us away from the crooked sins which stand in the way of attaining our desires. We make huge praise of you."

If the performer is a Sāma Vedi he recites "Nāmastau hōgnāyi." This means "Oh Agni, I praise you."

The performer repeats the mantra "Om Agnayē namah | mantra hīnam kriyā hīnam bhakti hīnam hutāśana yaddhutamtu mayā dēva paripūrnam tadastutē prāyaśchittanyāśēshāṇi tāpaḥ karmātmakānīvai | yānitēshāmaśēshānām kṛshṇānusmaraṇam param." This in English runs thus:—"Om salutation to Agni. Oh resplendent Dēva! Let the offering or oblation given to you by me be a complete one though there may be deficiency in the mantras uttered, in the actions done, and in the devotion in the spirit it was offered. Of all the expiatory acts either in the form of penance or action, etc., the repeated recollection of Kṛshṇa is the best." After repeating the above mantra he repeats "Śrī Kṛshṇāya namaḥ", prostrates, and does abhivādanam (repeating his gōtra, pravara and name). Then by repeating "Bhagavānēva . . . prātaraupāsanākhyam karma . . . kāritavān" he does sātvikatyāgam. The above passage when rendered into English runs thus:—"God himself . . . has done the act, *viz.*, the morning aupāsana for his own pleasure, etc. . . . "

The morning aupāsana ceremony is concluded by repeating "Kṛtamçha karishyāmi . . . prātaraupāsanēna . . . Vāsudēvaḥ." This when translated runs thsu:—"I am doing what has been already done. May the divine Lord Vāsudēva become pleased by this morning aupāsana."

Then he utters "yātē agnē yajñiyātanūstayōhyārōhātmātmānam acchā vasūni kṛṇvan nasmē naryā purūṇi yajñō bhūtvā yajñamāsīda svām yōnim jātavēdō bhuva ājāyamānaḥ sakshaya ēhi." This rendered into English runs thus:—"Oh Agni! Come to me in the form suitable to sacrifices. Having come get over me being pleased to give us a large quantity of wealth which is useful to man. Having taken the form of yajña, get into my body, which is your own place and which is doing this yajña or sacrifice. Oh Agni! having been born in front of me from the earth, come to me along with your own house to dwell in me."

After uttering the above he places the darbha pavitra over the right ear, heats the palm by taking it near the fire and then does "Ātma samārōpaṇam."

ABHIGAMANA ĀRĀDHANAM.

The worshipper, before entering the temple, wears flowers, sandal and clothing, cleanses his mouth by means of water after chewing betel-leaf and nuts and cleans his hands and feet. As soon as he enters the temple, he stands at a distance and prostrates before God. Getting up and with the permission of the two dvārapālakās he enters the temple precincts to near God and while doing so he repeats the following:—"Kausalyā supraja Rāma Pūrvāsandhya pravartatē ūttishṭha naraśārdūla kartavyam daivamāhnikam|| Vīra saumya vibuddhyasva kausalyānandavardhana jagaddhi sarvam svapititvayi suptē parantapa|| Yāminyapaiti yadunātha vimuncha nidrām unmēshamṛcchati tavōnmishitē na viśvam | jātasvyam ḳhalu jagaddhitamēva kartum dharmapravartana dhiyā dharaṇītalēsmin||." This when translated runs thus:—"Oh Rāma! Kausalyā is very fortunate in having a good son. The morning twilight is dawning in the East. Rise up, Oh tiger among men. The divine daily routine has to be gone through. Oh Hero of benign qualities and who increases the happiness of Kausalyā, wake up. Oh destroyer of foes, when you sleep the whole world will go to sleep. Oh Lord of Yadu! the night is gone, wake up from your sleep. The whole universe wakes up when you wake up. You are indeed born yourself in this world with the intention of spreading dharma in order to do good to the whole world." Instead of this other ślōkas which rouse God may be repeated. Then he does ārādhana offering tulasi flowers and fruits. He prostrates freely on the floor with bhakti and stands with the hands in a prayerful posture. While thus standing he repeats the dwaya mantra and then recites the gadya in which the meanings of dwaya are included. Then he prays to God that all things that have to be done should be properly performed and ended well and does śaraṇāgati. In the end he looks at auspicious things such as mirror, etc. Afterwards repeating "Saurabhēyās-sarvahitāḥ pavitrāḥ puṇyaraśayaḥ | pratigṛhṇantvimam grāsam gāvastrailōkya mātaraḥ ||" he gives a handful of grass to the cow of others. The above passage when translated into English runs thus:—"Let the cows accept the handful of grass, the cows who are the mothers of the three worlds, who have descended from Surabhi or Kāmadhēnu, who are good to all, who are pure and who are a heap of virtue." Afterwards obeisance is to be done to Āchāryas and other elderly men.

If one is not able to do "Abhigamanam" as stated above he may do obeisance to his Āchārya and do bharanyāsam. If he is unable to do even this, then he may repeat "Tirumantra" and think of God. If he is under any pollution he must think of these things in his mind. He should not repeat the usual things then, but he may repeat ordinary Tamil verses or Sanskrit ślōkas other than the above and think of God. From a distance he has to do anjali to God.

Towards the end he repeats the following:—"Bhagavānēva . . . Kṛtancha abhigamākhyam kāritavān" and does sātvikatyāgam and then concludes as follows:—" . . . abhigamanēna . . . . Vāsudēvaḥ ||."

UPĀDĀNAM.

During the second yāmam he does sankalpa repeating "Kṛtancha . . . upādānena . . . archayishyāmi." Then he repeats the Balamantra "Bhagavānēva . . . upādānākhyam . . . kārayati" and does sātvikatyagām. The person who wants to perform this part of the ceremony is expected to secure flowers, fruits, and other things needed for the worship of God. Only flowers that are clean and found on plants growing in clean situations and those accepted as fit by older Āchāryas are to be secured for use. Flowers having good smell, and are beautiful to look at, ghee, milk and curds are to be secured for use. They are to be cleaned properly and kept for use. Flowers that are grown by the activity of a person are superior. Those flowers that are secured from plants growing in a wild state are not very good and they have only a medium value. Those purchased in the bazaar are about the worst in value. Flowers secured stealthily or by begging are very bad. Flowers white in colour belong to the class sātvika. Red flowers are put under rājasa and blue and black belong to the tāmasa class. One should avoid flowers growing on plants found in unclean places; those flowers that are faded, those that are not full, unripe buds, old flowers are also to be avoided; flowers used by any body, flowers smelt, flowers touched by unclean animals, flowers with worms in them are also to be avoided. Flowers of oleander should never be used in houses for God's archana. All flowers should be secured by repeating "Vīryāya astrāyaphaṭ." The leaves of the plants, *Achyranthes aspera, Ocimum sanctum*, the Bael tree, *Ficus religiosa*, black tulasi, and vanhi tree may be secured for use. Water flowers such as lotus cannot be accepted two days after plucking. For dhūpam the wood of sandal, dēvadaru and ahil are to be used. Things obtained from animals should not be used. But kastūri and gōrōjana, though obtained from animals, may be used for God. With the exception of red lotus, red "Sengashanir," red flowers should not be used for doing pūja to God. Flowers and other things meant for the use of God should never be obtained from women of ill-fame, a wicked fellow who is doing things against caste, a napumsaka and from one who hates God. Things should not be brought and used from any house where no bhagavadarādhana is performed.

Repeating "Samidhaḥ pāvanāḥ pūjyāścharmayuktāḥ paruṭ parāḥ | yushmān harāmi hōmārtham asmān rakshantu sarvadā" he secures samit-sticks of *Butea frondosa*. This means "Oh palāsa sticks, you are pure, worthy of adoration, causing happiness to others, endowed with knots. I cut you for the sake of offering to Agni. Protect us always." Darbha is secured by repeating the mantra that follows:—"Virinchēna sahōtpanna parameshṭhiparigraha | nuda sarvāṇi pāpāni dharbha svastikarō mama (bhava)." This passage when rendered into English runs thus:—"Born along with Brahma, accepted of him, oh Darbha, remove all (my) sins and give me peace and happiness." Tulasi (sacred basil) is secured by plucking small pieces, so that each may have four leaves and all round young bud of leaves in the centre. While plucking the tulasi the following mantra is repeated:—"Tuḷasyamṛta janmāsi sadātvam kēśavapriyē | kēśavārtham lunāmitvām varadā bhava śōbhanē || mōkshaikahētōḥ dharaṇiprasūtē vishṇōssamastasya gurōḥ priyētā | ārādhanārtham purushōttamasya lūnami patram tuḷasi kshamasva." This when translated means:—" Oh Tulasi! you have been born from nectar. You are always fond of Keśava or Vishnu. I cut you for the sake of Keśava. Oh brilliant one! be a granter of boons. Oh one born from Earth! you are very dear to Vishṇu who is the perceptor for all, and through Whom only one can attain moksha or release from bondage. I cut your leaf for the propitiation of purushōttama. Oh Tulasi forgive me." Tulasi should not be plucked on Sundays, Fridays, New Year Days at any time, in the afternoons, nights, evening times and on Sankarānti days every month. New moon day, fullmoon day, dvādaśi are also days on which the plant should not be touched on any account. If secured, it must be considered tantamount to plucking God's head from the body. For use on these prohibited days, tulasi secured the previous day should be used.

When money or other substances are received for ārādhana of God both the giver and receiver repeat " Achyutaḥ prīyatām." For the worshipper of God, mercy to all living-beings including man, keeping completely under control one's indriyas, mercy without himsā to all living creatures, patience, knowledge, contemplation and truthfulness are essential features to be possessed. These qualities are essential for every one who worships God and so a worshipper should do his best to increase the possessions of these characteristics by association with good āchāryas, talking and associating with them and reading good sacred books during the "Upādānakāla." Those who are not required to secure all these things during the time may spend their time by reading and listening to good things only. In case one has to do ārādhana soon on special occasions, he may shorten the ceremonies abhigamanam and upādānam. Then he may do the sātvika-tyāgam and pray to God.

MĀDHYĀHNIKA SNĀNAM.

For this snānam also some mantras are repeated as for bathing in the morning. Just before the bath he repeats the following:—" Āvāhayāmi tvām dēvi snānārthamiha sundari | ēhigangē namaṣtubhyam sarvatīrthasamanvite." This when translated runs thus:—" Oh beautiful Goddess! I invite you here for my bathing. Oh Gangā! salutation to thee, who possess all the sacred waters of the world." The usual sankalpa, bala mantra and sātvikatyāga mantra are repeated before the above mantra. Repeating the above āvāhana mantra he takes water in both his hands and invokes Gangā to come over there. Then arghyam is given repeating "Vishnu vāmā padāngushṭha nakhaśrōtō vinisrutē | tadbhakti vighna rūpāt tvam gangē mām mōchayāinasaḥ ||." This in English runs thus:—"Oh Gangā that came out from the nail of the left great toe of Vishnu! Please release me from the sins which stand as obstacles to his devotions." He then bathes for the midday as for the morning and dresses himself as usual after the bath. Ūrdhvapunḍram, etc., are put on the face and various parts of the body.

MĀDHYĀHNIKAM.

He does āchamanams as for the morning Sandhyā Vandanam, but in the Sankalpam instead of "Prātassandhyām" he has to say "Mādhyāhnika sandhyām." After prāṇāyāmam he repeats the following:—" Āpaḥpunantvityanuvākasya āparshiḥ anushṭup cchandaḥ brāhmaṇaspatirdēvatā | apām prāśanē viniyōgaḥ." Translation:—For the anuvāka " Āpaḥpunantu " Āpas are Ṛshi, and Anushṭup is chandas and the Dēvatā is Brahmaṇaspati."

Then taking water in the right hand he repeats " Āpaḥpunantu prithivīm prithivī pūtā punātumām, punantu brahmaṇaspatiḥ brahmapūtā punātumām, yaducchishṭam abhōjyam yadvā duścharitam mama | sarvam punantumāmāpaḥ astāmcha pratigraham svāhā " and drinks it.

Translation: " Let waters purify the earth; let the world (earth) which is purified make me pure; Nārāyaṇa who is superior (the master of) to the Chaturmukha, let him purify water; let waters purified by Paramātmā purify me; let the waters remove the evils and purify me who by eating the remains that should not be eaten have become consequently a sinner and who has received sins from bad people. "

Afterwards all the mantras are the same as in the morning Sandhyā Vandanam. The " Arghyam " is given twice instead of thrice.

In the case of japam also mantras are similar to those which were used in the morning up to upasthānam. After upasthānam the following mantra is repeated:— " Āsatyēnēti shaḍṛchasya hiraṇyastūpa ṛshiḥ | ādyayōḥ trishṭup chatasṛṇam gāyatrī jagatyushniktrisṭubhaḥ cchandāmsi | savitā dēvatā | mādhyāhnika sandhyōpasthānē viniyōgaḥ."

Translation:—Āsatyēna form six riks, Ṛshi is Hiraṇyastūpa, Cchandas are tṛishṭup, tṛishṭup gāyatrī, jagati tṛishṭup and anushṭup; savitā is the Dēvatā."

Then he repeats the following mantra:—" Āsatyēna rajasāvartamānō nivēsayan amṛtam martyamcha, hiranyayēna savitā rathēnā dēvōyāti bhuvanāvipaśyan | udvayam tamasaspari paśyantōjyōtiruttaram | dēvam dēvatrā sūryam aganmajyōtiruttamam | udutyam jātavēdasam dēvam vahantikētavaḥ driśē viśvāyasūryam | chitram dēvānāmudagādanīkam chakshur mitrasya Varuṇasyāgnēḥ | āprādyāvā prithivī antariksham sūryaātmā jagatastasthushaścha | tat chakshurdēvahitam purastāt śukra muccharat | paśyēma śaradasśatam | jīvēma śaradaśśatam | nandāma śaradaśśatam | mōdāma śaradaśśatam | bhavāma śaradaśśatam | śṛṇavāma śaradaśśatam | prabravāma śaradaśśatam | ajītāsyāma śaradaśśatam | jyōkchasūryam driśē | ya udagān mahatōrṇavāt vibhrājamānassarirasya madhyāt samā vṛshabhlōhitākshāḥ sūryo vipaśchinmanasāpunātu."

Translation:—" Sun, the dēva enveloped in glory and shining in good places, moves in his golden car seeing the doings (Karmas) of every human being as a witness and also influencing the dēvatās and men to do their duties. We, who see the sun that destroys darkness that is full of effulgent light, that is a good dēvatā, that is an excellent being and one that protects dēvatās, shall obtain superior brilliance or tējas. The dēvatā who knows all the karmas that are done and who is well known as the sun bears one thousand rays to enable men to see him. There arose the manḍala which is a wonderful sight to dēvatās and which is like an eye to the dēvatās mitra, varuṇa and agni. The sun existing in that maṇḍalam is the soul of the living and he is permeating the sky, earth and svarga. We shall see for a hundred years the maṇḍalam which is good to dēvatās, which is like an eye to them, which is white at sunrise and which rises early. (This means that we shall worship all our lifetime.) May we live a hundred years; may we have sons and grand children; may we be happy; may we become prosperous in our own place; may we hear only speech that is dear to us; may we speak only dear and good words; may we not be overcome by our enemies; we pray that we may see the sun that is shining forth. Let me be protected with proper support by that sun who has arisen from the big ocean, who shines in the midst of water, who grants the wishes of everyone, who is red in colour and who knows everything." Then the person is expected to do the Japa of ashṭākshara and then Vastranishpīḍanam, etc.

Ārādhanam or Worship.

The person who intends to do worship to God, at first attends to his personal cleanliness. He cleans his feet and hands and then selects a suitable place for him. This place is cleaned by repeating the śōshaṇa, dāhana and plāvana mantras. Sitting on the place thus selected he meditates on the parampara of his gurus and God. He is to think that the end and aim of his is only to attain God's presence and the only way to attain Him is His grace. He should also think that God is the only person who can remove unpleasant things and think of the svarūpa, rūpa, character and vibhūtis of God. He should try to approach God's feet by repeating the stōtra ślōkās beginning with "Akhilahēyapratyanīka."

After attaining the feet of God and with mind strengthened by his favour, he should think of God only as one dear to him and as one whom he is always thinking as being before him. Then with the grace arising from such a devotion he is to begin the worship of God. Repeating "Bhagavānēva . . . upakramatē" he does nyāsam with panchōpanishad mantras in samhāra order and then does one prāṇāyāmam. With his right hand he touches his navel repeating the mūla mantra and afterwards says "Mantrōdbhūta chanḍa vāyvāpyāyita nābhi dēśastha vayunā śarīramantarbahiścha tatvakramēṇa śōshayāmi." This in English is as follows:—"I dry up the body both internally and externally in the order of tatvas by which it is constituted, by the wind situated in the navel being spread up by the chandra vayu proceeding from the mantra uttered." After repeating the above mantra he thinks that his whole body has been dried up (śōshaṇam). Again he does prāṇāyāmam and with his right hand he touches his heart repeating the mūla mantra and then repeats the following mantra:—"Mantrōdbhūta chakrāgni jvālōpa bṛhmita jāṭharāgninā tattat samashṭi pralīna sarvatatva sarva kilbisha sarvājñāna tad vāsanam śarīram dāhayāmi." This when translated runs thus:—"I burn the body with the several tatvas, all sins, all ignorance together with vāsanā, so that the several tatvas may merge in the samashṭi śṛshṭi by the fire in the abdomen spread up by the flames of the Jāṭharāgni proceeding from the mantra uttered." After repeating the above he thinks that his whole body was burnt and he should place his scul so as to rest below the thumb of the right foot of God. Then doing another prāṇāyāmam he imagines that by

God's grace he has become an object fit to do service to God and then he thinks that his soul has come out from the foot of God. He is expected to think that he is standing below the toe of the feet of God, that water in the form of amṛta flowing from the feet of God is washing him and that he has secured his body capable of doing service of every kind to God. Finally he should do nyāsa on his body repeating the panchōpanishad mantras in the order of creation. He should then touch his head repeating "Om shaum namaḥparāya paramēshṭhyātmanē;" touch his nose repeating "Om yām namaḥparāya purushātmanē," touch his chest repeating "Om rām namaḥparāya viśvātmanē" and touch his guhya repeating "Om v m namaḥparāya nivrityātmanē" and touch his legs repeating "Om lām namaḥparāya sarvātmanē." (The meaning can be learnt only by Upadēśa!) He is to imagine that he has obtained his body according to the śaktis. He does another prāṇāyāma and thinks that he has bathed in the water of Ganges flowing from God's toe and then puts on the twelve nāmams and begins the ārādhanam of God.

Then he does sātvikatyāga repeating "Bhagavānēva . . . upakramatē" and then does hrittyāgam as usual. Then he has to place on his right side all the materials required for worshipping God and on his left side the "Tirukkāveri" vessel filled with water. Taking flowers, sandal paste in his hand he repeats the ashṭākshara seven times, does śōshaṇa, dāhana and plāvana to these materials. Next he repeats again the astramantra and waves his hand all round the eight directions. He places on his right side all the other materials needed for worship and in his front in a seat he places the arghya, pādya, āchamanīya and snānīya vessels. Afterwards he cleans them by repeating the astramantra, does śōshaṇa, dāhana and plāvana and then he fills these vessels with some water. Into the vessel containing arghya water he puts in siddhārtakam, sandal paste, flowers, top pieces of darbha grass and rice grains (akshatai). He places into the pādya vessel cynodon grass, *Evolvulus alsinoides* (Vishnu kranthem), syāmākam, padmākam, etc. He puts into the āchamanīya vessel cardamoms, cloves, takkolam, khuskhus, and flowers. Into the snānīya vessel he puts turmeric, kastūrimanjal, murai, saileyam, takkolam, jatamanji, sandal paste and flower buds of *Michelia Champaca.* The vessel placed in the centre contains water and it is generally called "Sarvārthatōyam." Then touching the arghya pātra with his right hand he repeats the mūla mantra and then repeats the mantra "Om namō bhagavatē arghyam parikalpayāmi" (I am preparing the arghya for God). In the same manner he touches the other vessels repeating the mūla mantra and then repeats the mantra "Om namō bhagavatē pādyam parikalpayāmi." All the five vessels he touches repeating the mūla mantra and repeats the above mantra "Om . . . āchamanīyam . . . etc., only altering the name of the vessel.

Taking water in an uddharaṇi (spoon) from the arghya vessel he sprinkles it over the place where the ārādhana is to be done, over the vessels to be used during the worship (or ārādhana) and over himself separately.

In places where the above described "Ādhāraśaktyādipīṭha" is not established God is requested to come for ārādhana from paramapada (heaven), milk-ocean, sun, heart,

Mathura, Dvāraka, Ayodhya and Srirangam. The worshipper should imagine that God is associated with his wives, ornaments, arms, and with dvārapālakas and other men. He should think of God as possessing three kinds of chētana and achētana things with their svarupa (form) sthiti (existence) and pravṛtti (permeation) as being under His control. God is not touched by karma or thoughts about these things. The worshipper should also think that the characteristics, knowledge (Jñānam), power (balam), wealth (aiśvaryam), boldness (vīryam), strength (śakti) and light (tējas) are possessed by God. The worshipper should think of God as above described, and offer himself to God by repeating the ashṭākshara. Then he should begin the regular worshipping ceremony.

From the "Arghyapātra" (arghya vessel) he takes some water by means of the uddharaṇi (spoon) and lifting this with both the hands up to the nose of God repeats with due respect, "Bhagavannidam pratigṛhṇīshva." (Oh God kindly receive this). During this time the worshipper thinks of God and taking the water close to God's face and offering it pours some water on God's hands and then he pours the remaining water into the arghya or arghya pratigraha pātra. Then cleaning his hands he places flowers at the feet of God and with a spoon takes water from the pādya vessel and sprinkles it over the feet of God and thinks that he has washed the feet of God and pours the remaining water into the "Pādya pratigrahapātra" (vessel intended to receive the water taken out of a pādya vessel). Then cleaning his hands with a clean cloth folded he removes water from the feet of God by wiping them with the folded cloth and then offers to God sandal paste and flowers. Next he takes water from the āchamanīya vessel by means of the uddharaṇi (spoon) and pours it in the right hand of God and imagines that God has done the āchamanam. The remaining water in the uddharaṇi (spoon) is poured into the āchamana pratigrahapātra (vessel intended to receive the water taken out of the āchamana vessel). Then sandal paste, flowers, incense, light, āchamanam, betel leaves and nuts are offered. When prostrating before God he prays that God should accept him and everything near Him as objects fit for service. He also repeats "Ātmānam ātmīyam cha sarvam bhagavān nityakinkaratayā svīkuru" while praying. The translation of the above passage is as follows :—"Oh God, kindly accept me and all belonging to me as worthy of your service always." Then he offers to God Snānāsana. He places sandal paste and flowers over the āsana and decorates it. He then prostrates before God and then with God's permission offers to Him the sandals (pādukais of wood) and requests God to occupy the āsanam (snānāsanam). While in snānāsanam cloths, ornaments and garlands worn by God are removed and these are handed over to Vishvaksēna who is close by. Then the worshipper offers to God the Snāna Sāṭikā (cloth for bath) and afterwards the following things in order, *viz.*, arghya, pādya, āchamanīya, pādapīṭham (plank for the feet), dantakāshṭam, (toothbrush) jihvānirlēkhanam (tongue scraper), gaṇḍūsham (mouthful of water for rinsing), mukhaprakshāḷanam (cleaning the face), āchamanam (sipping water three times), ādarśa pradarśanam (showing of mirror), hastaprakshāḷanam (cleaning of the hands), mukhavāsatāmbūlam (betel leaves, etc., for beautifying the face), tailābhyanganam (smearing oil to some part of the body), udvartanam (rubbing and cleaning the body with fragrant unguents) āmalakatōyam (washing with water containing the essence of *Phyllanthus emblica*), kankajam (haircomb), plōta dēhaśōdhana śāṭikā (cloth for drying up the water on the body), haridrālēpanam (turmeric unguent) prakshāḷanam (washing), vastram (cloth), uttarīyam (upper cloth), yajñōpavītam (sacred thread), pādyam (water for washing feet), āchamanam (water sipping), pavitram (darbha grass) twisted for putting on the 4th finger, gandham (sandal paste), pushpam (flowers), dhūpadīpams (redhot fire and light), āchamanam (water sipping), dēhaśōdhanam (cleaning the body), vastram (cloth), uttarīyam (upper cloth) yajñōpavītam (sacred thread) and āchamanam (sipping of water).

Next the Alankārāsana is worshipped by pūja and God is requested to occupy this pīṭha by prostrating before him. Then taking God's permission the wooden shoes (pādukais) are presented to him. After God has occupied the seat presented to Him, he prepares as before and presents to him arghyam, pādyam, āchamanīyam and sarvārtha tōyam. Arghya, pādya, āchamanīya and the sandal paste, flowers and pāda-sammardanam (pressing of feet), vastra (cloth), uttarīyam (upper cloth), ornaments, sacred thread and āchamanīyam are also presented to Him. For the other attendants of God snānam (bath), vastram (cloth) and bhūshaṇams (ornaments) are given and sandal paste, etc., are served to them after offering them to God. Further, for the parivāras (servants) of God sandal paste alone is to be offered. (Arghyam, pādyam and āchamanīyam need not be offered). He does the various upachāras to God by offering sandal paste, flowers, alankāras, ūrdhvapuṇḍrams, anjanam, ādarśam, frankincense, light, āchamanam, dhvajam, umbrella, chāmaram, vāhanam, śankām, chihnam, kāhaḷī, bheri with dancing, songs and vādyas.

Repeating the "Ashṭākshara" he offers flowers for every syllable or letter. Similarly he repeats the dvādaśākshara, the shaḍākshara, Vishnu gāyatrī, panchōpanishanmantras and purushasūktam and offers as many flowers as he can. For the dēvi (Goddess) he does the same pūjās repeating the appropriate mantras. He does praṇāmams for the four corners and does pradakshiṇa and offers flowers. After doing praṇāmam in the front he repeats some stōtras that are pleasant to the ear. Then he should pray to God to accept him as His daily devotee and do the "Ashṭākshara japa" according to his capacity. Then he offers tīrtha to God as if finishing everything to be done to God. He next offers mukhavāsa tāmbulam, arghya and Bhōjyāsanam.

He does pūja to the Bhojyāsanam, does praṇāmam to God and with God's permission offers the wooden sandals (pādukais). Then imagining that God has occupied this seat, he offers to God pādyam, āchamanīyam and arghya and afterwards Madhuparkam is offered; that is to say jaggery, honey, ghee, curds and milk are secured and kept separately, after subjecting these to the usual śōshaṇa, dāhana and plāvana processes arghya water is sprinkled over these articles and then these articles are offered to God. Then if available a cow, gold, precious stones such as diamonds, etc., and grain are sprinkled with water and they are offered to God by placing them before Him. Then food that is properly and cleanly prepared (cooked rice), ghee, curds, milk, honey, fruits and roots of sorts are placed before God and are sprinkled with arghya water. Digbandhanam is done by repeating the "Astra" mantra and "Surabhi" mudra is shown. Then arghya tīrtham is taken saying the mantra "Atiprabhūtam . . . idam svīkuru." This when translated runs thus:—"Kindly accept the food, etc., which are prepared in large quantity, with the greatest affection, with all its completeness and with the greatest heart-felt devotion." He does pranāmam and with bent head prays to God and requests him to make use of the things offered to Him. Afterwards he should offer to God anupānam, tarpaṇam at first and then hastaprakshāḷanam, āchamanam, hastasammārjanam, sandalwood paste, and mukha vāsa tambūlam.

Then he does pranāmam to God and cleans the mantrāsana and requests God to occupy this, after taking his permission and after cleaning and doing pūja to the āsana. He offers the pādukais to God. As soon as God occupies the seat, he removes from His body the sandal paste, garlands, etc, and hands them over to Vishvaksēna. Afterwards he offers to God pādya, āchamanīya, sandal paste, flowers, dhūpa (smoke of incense), light, āchamana, bhakshyam, fruits, and āchamanīyam He goes round Him twice (two pradakshinas) and prostrates before Him

Then he cleans the paryankāsana (seat intended for bedding) and after getting God's permission offers Him the new seat. While He is in the new seat he offers him the pādukais (wooden sandals). He presents to God the usual pādyam, āchamanīyam, and then takes over from God His garlands, ornaments and cloth and hands them over to Vishvaksēna. Next he offers to God soft clothing, ornaments, garlands, upavītam (sacred thread) and water for āchamanam. Lastly he offers sandal paste, flowers, light, dhūpam, āchamanīyam and mukhavāsa tāmbūlam. Afterwards he repeats the mantra "Svanīyāmya . . . prativāditavan." The meaning of this passage is as follows:—"God himself for his own sake, for his own pleasure has brought into being all auspicious materials, intended for honour, bodily pleasure, eating and all other things, with all attendants and paraphernalia, which are his own and which are in large numbers, very dear to heart, which are in entirety and which are full of devotion, collected by my body, senses, etc, which are given by him alone and belonging to me whose body, existence and action are entirely governed by him and who is his sole servant and performs the sātvīkatyāga." He gets permission from God to take a small portion from the things offered to Him for Vishvaksēna and the remainder to offer to his Āchārya and other Vaishnavas. The person doing ārādhana to God now does pūja to Vishvaksēna and offers to him the things he has set apart for this purpose. Finally he prostrates before God and does to God śaranāgati. He is expected to prostrate properly and do the śaraṇāgati in the proper form. Out of the offerings made to God a part is taken and kept separately for Vishvaksēna and the remaining part is divided into three parts—one for himself, one for those who do service to God and one part for Āchāryas and Vaishnavas. The part offered to Vishvaksēna is put in water. Then the worshipper praying to God and dvārapālakas finishes the pūja. Next he begins to repeat some ślōkas from Dēśika's work if he is a Vaḍagalai Sri Vaishnava after repeating some Tamil pāsurams (stanzas) from Tiruvāimozhi. When the worshipper is a Tengalai Sri Vaishnava he omits Dēśika's stōtras and repeats only the Tamil Tiruvāimozhi. Sacred water is distributed to those present and while doing this Dēśika's stōtrapāṭhas are repeated amongst the Vaḍagalais.

VAIŚVADĒVAM.

This ceremony is usually done only by the very orthodox people. Persons who do this ceremony make use of the food taken by them from the food offered to God during the ārādhanam of God and towards the end of the ceremony. The performer cleans his feet, does two āchamanams and a prāṇāyāmam. Then he begins this ceremony of Vaisvadēvam by repeating "Śri bhagavadājñayā śrimannārāyaṇaprītyartham pratar Vāiśvadēvam karishye. He then repeats "Kṛtancha karishyāmi" and says "Prātar vaiśvadēvēna bhagavatkarmaṇā bhagavantam Vāsudēvamarchayishyāmi." After this he continues to repeat "Bhagavatō balēna" and then does sātvikatyāgam by repeating "Bhagavānēva . . . prātar vaisvadēvākhyam karma . . . kārayati." He makes use of agni in the pit which is either aupasanāgni or agni which was used for cooking the food. After putting the fire in the pit he draws lines and does agni pratishṭhai and paristaranam as is usually done for aupāsanam. His wife brings food cooked by her and set apart for vaiśvadēvam and gives it to him saying "Bhūtam." Saying "Tatsubhūtam Virāḍannam tanmā kshāyi" he takes the food and shows it to fire. The above when translated runs thus:—"The food is well completed and well embellished. Therefore it will not perish." He takes the food and shows it to fire. Then he places this food to the left and sprinkling water over it, divides it into two parts, one towards the south and the other towards the north. Then in the part of the food in the north he divides the food into three parts by drawing lines east to west. After thus separating the food, he sprinkles water round the fire saying "Om aditē . . . savitaḥ prasūva" and places in the fire one stick. He then takes out from the food a small quantity (about the size of the fruit of "Nellikāi") from the south-eastern part and touching with his left hand the vessel in which food is kept, he places this food in fire. Hōmam ought to be done according to the upadēśa the worshipper has received--that is to say—either Chakrākāram method or Vyajanākāram method.

PANCHAMAHĀYAJÑAM.

Immediately after Vaiśvadēva the person performs this ceremonial, Panchamahāyajñam. He begins this ceremonial by doing "śrōtrāchamanam" and prāṇāyāmam in the usual way. Then he does sankalpam repeating "Śrībhagavadājñayā . . . dēva yajñēna yakshyē." Taking water he washes his left hand repeating "Vidyudasi" and then repeating "Aditēnu manyasva . . . prasūva" does parishēchanam to agni (*i.e.*, take round water) and puts in fire a samit or darbha. After this he takes the food from the part in the east which is marked off as the northern part, and repeating "Om dēvēbhyasvāhā" puts in the fire, and then repeats "Dēvēbhya idam na mama" and places in the fire a darbha. Then once again he pours water round the fire repeating during the process "Om aditēnu . . . prāsāvīḥ" and smears the hands repeating "Vṛshṭirasi." The meanings of the above Sanskrit passages are given here seriatim:—"This food is offered to the dēvas. This offering belongs to the Dēvas and it is not mine or it does not belong to me. You are the cause of cutting."

Again he does śrōtrāchamanam and wearing the yajñōpavīta with the left hand through it and the string on the right shoulder (*i.e.*, prāchīnāvītī) repeats "Śrībhagavadājñayā . . . pitṛ yajñēna yakshyē" doing sankalpam. He smears the hands repeating "Vidyudasi." The above Sanskrit when rendered into English run thus:—"I make the sacrifice by pitṛ yajña. You are the cause of separation". He pours water and smears the earth to the south of the fire-pit and takes a small quantity of food from the cup again and repeating 'Om pitṛbhyassvadhā" places his hand on the ground. Then repeating "Pitṛbhya idam na mama" he pours water in the apradakshiṇa way round the fire and cleans his hands by wiping while repeating "Vṛshṭirasi." The meaning of the Sanskrit in the above runs thus: "I offer this ball of rice to Pitṛs. This offering belongs to Pitṛs and it does not belong to me. You are the cause of cutting."

Putting the yajñōpavīta in the right way he does śrōtrāchamanam and prāṇāyāmam. Then he does sankalpam repeating "Śrī bhagavadājñayā . . . bhūta yajñēna yakshyē." Repeating "Vidyudasi" (you are the cause of separation) he cleans his hands by smearing. He cleans the earth to the west of agradāna and takes from the cooked rice already used a small quantity of food and saying "Om bhūtēbhyō balim harāmi" (I offer a ball of rice to all created beings) places it on the ground. Then he does parishēchanam to it saying "Om bhūtēbhya idam na mama" (this offering is for all created beings and it does not belong to me) and smears his hands repeating "Vṛshṭirasi" (you are the cause of cutting).

Again he does śrōtrāchamanam and then praṇāyāmam. Afterwards he does sankalpam repeating "Śrī bhagavadājñayā . . . manushya yajñēna yakshyē." Then saying "Vidyudasi" (you are the cause of separation) he takes from the central portion of the food some quantity of food (annam) and places it between agradāna and bhūtabali saying "Manushyēbhyōhantā" and doing parishēchanam. Then he cleans his hands by wiping and at the same time repeating "Vṛshṭirasi".

Then he does Śrōtrāchamanam and repeating "Om Śrī Vishṇavē svāhā" puts in fire a darbha and then says "Om Śrī Vishṇavē idam na mama." Then he gets up and repeats the mantra beginning "Agnē naya" then does praṇāmam after repeating "Agnayē namaḥ . . . param" and then abhivādanam. The balis offered to pitṛs and dēvas are placed aside and the remaining part is retained and in it put in the other balis. The food used in agradānam and manushya yajña is taken and mixed with that part used for atithis.

He does āchamanam and repeating "Bhagavānēva . . . prātar Vaiśvadēvākhyam karma . . . kāritavān" the sātvikatyāga is done. Finally he repeats "Kṛtancha . . . Vāsudēvaḥ." Then the sacred water of God is taken and he waits sometime (till the milking of a good cow) for atithis and then he sits for his meal.

BHŌJANAM (TAKING ONE'S FOOD).

The person proposing to eat, washes his feet, does āchamanam twice and cleans a space in his front with water mixing with it a little of cow's urine. On the spot thus cleaned he places a plantain leaf after cleaning it well with water. A vessel filled with water is placed on his right side and he sits in front of the leaf. He should not sit at any time facing west but he may choose anyone of the remaining three. In his right hand he is expected to have a golden pavitram (a form of ring) on his ring finger and if he does not possess one he should make a pavitra out of darbha and put it on that finger. Then he sits and his wife or some other person serves the various things cooked on the leaf. After this service he keeps both his hands in a saluting posture ("Kūppikkoṇḍu") and prays saying "asmākam nityamastvētat." This means "Let this food be perpetual to us." He afterwards sprinkles water over his food saying "Om bhūrbhuvassuvaḥ" and does śōshaṇa, dāhana and plāvanam. By repeating astra mantra he does digbandhanam and offers the food to the antaryāmin (God who is inside his body). In case one eats in another's house, he should offer mentally to his archai everything and to his antaryāmin afterwards. Then he takes water in his right hand poured by his wife or some other person and with it and placing his legs so as to touch the ground he does parishēchanam twice. To obtain this water he should not hold his hand across his food and the water poured into his hand should not fall on any vessel. While doing parishēchanam he must repeat the mantra "Om bhūrbhuvassuvaḥ" (the names of lōkas) "Satyam tvartēna parishinchāmi" (I sprinkle Agni around you who is Sūrya.) If it is night he is expected to use the words "Om bhūrbhuvassuvaḥ" the names of lōkas "Ṛtam tvā satyēna parishinchāmi" (I sprinkle Sūrya around you who is Agni).

He should then in his right hand receive a small quantity of sacred water used in the worship of God and drink it saying "Amṛtōpastaraṇamasi," as he does during āchamanam. Then he should do prāṇāhuti. He should hold the leaf on the left side in one place with his left thumb and the first and second fingers (really second and third if thumb is counted as the first), and using his thumb, middle finger and ring finger he should lift the food and place it in his mouth and while doing so he should repeat the words "Prāṇāya svāhā" "Apānāya svāhā" "Vyānāya svāhā" "Udānāya svāhā" "Samānāya svāhā."

"I offer this (small quantity of cooked rice) to Prāṇa. I offer this (small quantity of cooked rice) to Apāna. I offer this (small quantity of cooked rice) to Vyāna. I offer this (small quantity of cooked rice) to Udāna. I offer this (small quantity of cooked rice) to Samāna and take as many handfuls of food (cooked rice with ghee)." After putting into his mouth the cooked food he repeats in the interval "Prāṇāyēdam na mama," "Apānāyēdam na mama," "Vyānāyēdam na mama," "Udānāyēdam na mama" "Samānāyēdam na mama."

This when translated runs thus:—"This is for Prāṇa and it does not belong to me. This is for Apāna and it does not belong to me. This is for Vyāna and it does not belong to me. This is for Udāna and it does not belong to me. This is for Samāna and it does not belong to me." While thus taking the food into his mouth, he should think of God in the jāṭharāgni and do hōmam mentally. It is only after fully swallowing one āhuti (quantity of food put in the mouth) another āhuti is taken into the mouth. The swallowing is so done that the food in the mouth does not come in contact with the teeth.

After taking five morsels and repeating the mantras stated above, he should repeat as the last mantra "Brahmaṇima ātma mṛtatvāya" (May my jīvātmā merge in Paramātmā for the sake of mōksha.)

Then he cleans his left hand which was holding the leaf by means of water poured over the fingers by his wife or some other person. Until this time he should be quiet without uttering anything except repeating the mantras already stated above. Then he begins to eat the various things served on the leaf and which were offered to God previously. He should not take anything that is prohibited by rules. During eating if he wants anything he may ask for it. He may also talk to persons eating with him, provided the talk is to show respect to them in serving things. If he is forced to speak about anything outside the food, he should repeat "Om bhūrbhuvassuvaḥ" (the lōkas Om bhūḥ, Bhuvaḥ and Suvaḥ) and then begin to eat again. Fruits, and bhakshyas should be broken into pieces by the fingers and while doing so the nails should not come in contact with these articles. For the Vaḍagalais things that should not be taken as food are described by Vēdānta Dēśika in a book called "Āhāraniyamam," which consists of twenty-one stanzas in Tamil.

While eating, he should not be standing or place his legs on the seat. He should always do āchamana before eating. He should not wear a single cloth, cover his body and head, touch another person, or be hearing the speeches of śūdras, and women in menses. While eating in a line with others he should not get up in the middle. If he is obliged to get up, he should draw a line by using water, fire, a pole, or darbha between himself and his neighbour and then get up. From the vessel containing water he may drink once and he should not use the same water again. In case he has to partake the same water he has to pour on the floor some quantity of water from it and then use the water for drinking. While eating after swallowing every morsel he should repeat the name of God as Gōvinda. After eating to his satisfaction he removes the pavitra of darbha and holding it between the pavitra finger and the next one and receives the water for "Uttarāpōśanam." While drinking this water poured into his right hand he has to repeat "Āmṛtāpidhānamasi." A small quantity of water must be left in the hand without sipping the whole quantity. This water which remains in the hand is poured on the left side of the leaf repeating "Rowravē puṇyanilayē padmārbuda nivāsinām—arthinām̄udakam datta makshayya mupatishṭhatu." This when translated runs as follows:—"This water is offered to those who have been longing for salvation by having been confined in Raurava Hell, the abode of sinners, for many many millions of years. May this undecaying offering please them." The darbha between the fingers is thrown below the leaf. After uttarāpōśanam the leaf should not be touched. After getting up from the place, he goes out, cleans his hand and washes his mouth thrice and spits out the water each time on the left side. He may use some powder to clean his mouth and while doing so he uses water to finally clean his mouth 13 times and uses stick to remove dirt. The water put in the mouth for cleaning the mouth should not be swallowed but should be spitted out. The teeth should not be touched and washed by using the fingers. He cleans his hands and legs and does āchamanam. Then sitting he repeats "Prāṇānām grandhirasi rudrōmā viśāntakastēnānnēnāpyāyasva" (oh Ahankara that is in my heart! you are inseparably united to my prāṇa. May your presiding deity that is known by the name of Rudra being a destroyer of miseries enter into my body. May the food taken by me grow my body.) and touches his chest. After this he repeats "Angushṭha mātraḥ purushōngushṭamcha samāśritaḥ | Īśaḥ sarvasya jagataḥ prabhūḥ prīṇāti viśvabhuk". This in English runs thus:—"Paramātmā of the size of one's own thumb lives in the space within the heart. He governs the whole world. He is the master. May he be pleased by this food". Taking water in the hand he pours it down in such a way that it trickles through the right hand on the right toe. Afterwards touching the belly he repeats the following mantra:—"Śraddhāyām prāṇēniviśyā mṛtagm hutam prāṇamannēnāpāyasva, apānē niviśyāmṛtam hutam apānamannē nāpyāyasva | vyānē niviśyāmṛtagm hutam vyānamannēnāpyāyasva | udānēniviśyāmṛtam hutam udānamannē nāpyāyasva | samānē niviśyāmṛtagm hutam samānamānnē nāpyāyasva | brahmaṇima ātmā amṛtatvāya." This runs in English thus:—"With due reverence to vaidic observances and with great respect to Prāṇavāyu this imperishable and sweet oblation has been offered. Oh presiding deity of Prāṇavāyu! may this food increase you.

With great respect to Apāna this imperishable and sweet oblation has been offered. Oh presiding deity of Apāna!. May this food increase you.

With great respect to Vyāna this imperishable and sweet oblation has been offered. Oh presiding deity of Vyāna! may this food increase you.

With great respect to Udāna this imperishable and sweet oblation has been offered. Oh presiding deity of Udāna! may this food increase you.

With great respect to Samāna this imperishable and sweet oblation has been offered. Oh presiding deity of Samāna! may this food increase you.

May my Jīvātmā merge in Paramātmā for the sake of mōksha." Next he sees the sun repeating "Udutyam . . . Viśvāyasūryam." This in English is as follows:—"The well-known and one who knows all beings that are born . . . so that the whole world may see the sun." After this he touches the stomach (belly) repeating the following:—"Vishṇurattā tathaivāham pariṇāmaścha vai sadā | satyēna tēna mē bhuktam jīryatvannamidam tataḥ". "The eater of the food is Vishnu. I too am Vishnu. The changes that are always going on are Vishnu. I have eaten according to this principle. Let the food be digested."

To those who take food with him, he presents betel leaves and nuts that were offered to God and then he takes the same for his own use. In chewing he must first put into his mouth the leaf and then only the nuts.

Then repeating "Bhagavānēva . . . ijyākhyam" he concludes by saying "Kṛtancha . . . Ijyākhyēna . . . Vāsudēvaḥ."

SVĀDHYĀYAM.

In tne fourth yāma he does sankalpam as follows:—"Kṛtancha . . . svādhyāyēna . . . archayishyāmi." Then he repeats the bala mantra "Bhagavānēva . . . svādhyāyākhyam karma . . . kārayati" and does sātvikatyāgam. He then goes on reading about upanishads, the meanings and applications of the meanings of mūlamantra, studying Śrībhāshya, reading of grandhas about God and his doings, Śrīmad Rāmāyaṇa, Bhagavadgītā, and Bhārata, and doing tatva nirṇayas with Brahmachāris and disciples.

SANDHYĀVANDANAM.

Towards evening one should change his cloths by wearing fresh ones and do the evening sandhyāvandanam. The performer is expected to clean his hands and feet and do prāṇāyāmam. Then he does sankalpam repeating "Śrībhagavadajñayā Śrīman Nārāyaṇaprītyartham sāyam sandhyāmupāsishyē". Prōkshaṇa, etc., are done as in the morning sandhyāvandanam. He does nyāsam by repeating "Agniśchētyanuvākasya Sūrya ṛshiḥ | dēvīgāyatrīcchandaḥ | agnirdēvatā." Then he takes water in his right hand as if for āchamana and says "Apām prāśanē viniyōgaḥ." He then says the mantra "Agniścha māmanyuaścha manyupatayaścha manyukṛtēbhyaḥ | pāpēbhyōrakshantām yadahnā pāpama kārsham | manasā vāchā hastābhyām padbhyā mudarēṇa śiśnā | ahastadavalumpatu | yat kincha duritam mayi | idamaham māmamṛtayōnau | satyējyōtishi juhōmi svāhā" and drinks the water in his hand. (Same meaning as the mantra Sūryaścha but some words are changed and they are "agniścha" = fire; "ahnā" = day time (in the day time); aha = day time, "satyē" = in the form of satyam. The arghya is done facing the west now. Other things are done as in the morning sandhyā.)

Then Japam is begun and the sankalpam should begin with the words usually repeated and it should refer to "Sāyam sandhyā" instead of "Prātassandhyā."

In this after repeating "Āyātu varadādēvī aksharam brahma sammitam | . . . Gāyatrīm āvāhayāmi" he does āvāhanam and repeats "Sāyam sarasvatīm śyāmām ravimaṇḍala madhyagām | sāmavēdam vyāharantīm chakrāyudha dharām śubhām || Dhyāyāmi Vishṇudaivatyām vṛddhām garuḍavāhanām |" (I contemplate on Sarasvati, as black in colour, repeating Sāma Vedam, with chakram in hand, as old, with garuda as vahanam, as Vishnu, devata.)

He repeats the usual upasthāna mantra until "Gaccha dēvi yathā sukham" and after this he does nyāsam repeating "Imammaīti pancharchasya Dēvarāta ṛshiḥ | gāyatrī trishtup, gāyatrī jagatī trishṭubhasçhandāmsi | savitā dēvatā." (For the five riks in the mantra Imam mē the Ṛshi is Dēvarātar; çhandas is Gāyatrī, etc. Dēvatā is the Sun.)

Then he does sankalpam for upasthānam and for it repeats the mantra "Imam mē varuṇa srudhīhavamadyācha mṛḍaya | tvāmavasyu rāchakē | tatvāyāmi brahmaṇā vanda māna stadāśāstē yajamānō havirbhiḥ |. Ahēḍamānō Varuṇēha bōdhyuruśagm samāna āyuḥpramōshiḥ || yacchiddhi tē viśōyathā pradēva varuṇavratam | minīmasidyavidyavi | yat kinchēdam varuṇadaivyē janē abhidrōham manushyāścharāmasi |

achittī yattava dharmāyuyōpima mānastasmā dēnasō dēvarīrishaḥ ‖ Kitavāsō yadripur nadīvi yadvāghā satya mutayanna vidma | sarvātā vishya śithirēva dēvāthātēsyāma varuṇa priyāsaḥ."

Translation:—Oh Varuṇa! Listen to this prayer of mine. You should make me a happy being now alone. Desiring my protection I am praying to you for my satisfaction. Therefore I am becoming your slave by praising you by means of Vedas. One who does yāga by the offering of purōḍāśa, etc., prays for what he wants. Oh Varuṇa! In this world you should listen and accept my prayers. One who has a big reputation, please do not destroy my life (āyus). Oh Varuṇadēva! That vrata which is done daily for you . . . daily like men we become destroyers. Oh dēvata! do not trouble us with those sins which we as human beings by ignorance may have done towards dēvatās and those sins by which we destroyed your dharmas (good things). Kindly destroy all those sins of ours that were done by us as hypocrites, those sins committed by us knowing them to be sins, and those committed by us without our knowledge. Let those sins be destroyed Then we become people well known to you and liked by you.

The remaining part is similar to that done in the morning.

After sandhyāvandanam he does the aupāsanam in the evening also as was done in the morning. If possible he does pūja to God as in the morning or day time. He does everything from alankārāsanam to śayanāsanam as already described. During "Bhōjyāsanam" all things prepared for the use in the night should be placed before God for nivēdanam. Then he does Vaiśvadēvam by doing only the six āhutis and the hōmam.

Then he eats the food observing all the rules and regulations already described. After food does Vēdādhyayanam, reads Purāṇas, etc. In the end he does Sātvikatyāgam as usual and prays as usual to God.

YŌGAM.

He cleans his legs and hands and does the usual āchamanam. Sitting in a clean spot facing east he does three prāṇāyāmams. Then he does sankalpam repeating "Krtancha . . . Yōgēna . . . Archayishyāmi." Next he does sātvikatyāga repeating "Bhagavānēva . . . yōgākhyam . . . kārayati." He repeats after this "Amalanādipirān, Śrī Vaikuṇṭha gadya, Bhagavaddhyāna Sōpānam, etc. and contemplates on God's greatness and his good doings. As soon as he feels sleepy he lies down believing that he is placing his head at the feet of God. If he wakes from sleep till he sleeps again he contemplates on God. Sleep is to be considered as rest to enable one to be able to do Bhagavad ārādhana, etc., during the day as usual.

For one who does Bhagavadārādhana during the five periods of the day, all duties become services to God. He does not waste even a second. All the good things one is enjoying becomes part of God's enjoyment only. An orthodox man is expected to spend his time in this manner.

14. The Archaka Sri Vaishnava Brahmans.

Amongst Sri Vaishnavas God is worshipped in two different ways. One way is worshipping God in one's own house and it is called Svārthayajanam. This domestic worship of God or Svārthayajanam has already been described under Panchakāla observances of an orthodox Sri Vaishnava Brahman. The other method of worship or Parārthayajanam is meant for all people. This is the form of worship that is usually adopted in all temples. All the temple rituals connected with the daily worship, worshipping on special occasions and the establishment of idols and invoking of God's spirit have all to be carried out by men specially trained or initiated for these purposes. These men constitute the Archakas or Bhaṭṭar Sri Vaishnavas. Generally only men who are qualified to do the work may carry on the work of Archakas.

Here it must be stated that the Archakas and Sri Vaishnavas do not freely intermingle with one another, though both of them are Sri Vaishnavas following the same rituals in most of their ceremonies. There is no intermarriage between these two sections. Cooked food offered to God within the temple by the Archakas are freely eaten by all Sri Vaishnavas, though things prepared in Archakas' houses are not accepted by Sri Vaishnavas. Similarly Archakas avoid taking things prepared by Sri Vaishnavas in their houses, though things cooked by them and offered to God in the temple are accepted and eaten by the Archakas. The Archakas do not usually cook the food in temples and it is always done by a Sri Vaishnava Brahman within the temple precincts. This person is really the cook within the temple.

The mode of worship carried out in the Vishnu temples falls into the two distinct classes or systems of worship. These two systems are called Pāncharātra system and Vaikhānasa system. A great number of temples in this presidency have adopted the Pāncharātra system of worship, while the Vaikhānasa system is the form adopted in a few temples. Strictly speaking the mode of worship should not be changed from one into the other, *i.e.*, Vaikhānasa into Pāncharātra and Pāncharātra into Vaikhānasa. But recently at Buthugur a temple in which the form of worship was Vaikhānasa was changed into Pāncharātra system.

The Pāncharātra system of worship is more popular because in the absence of the Archakas any gṛhastha (married man) can look after the worship of God temporarily. This change is possible only in ordinary temples. But in the case of well-known old temples such as those of Śrirangam or Conjeeveram the Archakas are never absent, and even when one who is doing pūja has to go, his work is undertaken only by another Archaka and not by an ordinary gṛhastha. The Vaikhānasa system of worship is not so easy. It can be done only by a Vaikhānasa Archaka and no other person is entitled to worship even temporarily.

The Pancharātra system of worship is based on the Pancharātra āgamas and these āgamas are derived from what they call "Rahasyāmnāyam." Some Archakas claim that even the four Vedas are to be considered as derived from Rahasyāmnāyam. Such Archakas say that since Rahasyāmnāyam was communicated to them directly by God it should be taken as the chief authority for everything. It is evident that these people give to the Vedas only a secondary place.

According to the view held by the Pancharātras God exists as Para Vāsudēva. He appears in Vyūha forms as Samkarshaṇa, Pradyumna and Aniruddha. The characteristics of the manifestations of God are already described under Rāmānuja's idea of God and Rahasyams of Vēdānta Dēśika.

The Pāncharātra āgamas are said to consist of 108 samhitās, some being of sātvika, some of rājasa and others of tāmasa character. Sātvika samhitā constitutes the part directly communicated by God. Those acquired by yōga practices are called Rājasa samhitās and what the Rishis wrote from their own thoughts not being inspired by yōga or otherwise go by the name of tāmasa samhitās. This system of worship is largely inculcated and adopted by the Sri Vaishnavas, and in fact the daily worship is more or less based on the Pāncharātra Śāstrās called Bhagavat Śāstrās by Śrī Vēdānta Dēśika. Out of these 108 samhitās only three samhitās seem to have been selected as the best by Vēdānta Dēśika and he calls them Ratnatrayam (the three gems). They are Sātvata samhitai, Paushkara samhitai and Jayākhya samhitai.

The Vaḍagalai Sri Vaishnavas call these three works Ratnatrayam. Some use the name Upabrāhmanams for Īśwara samhitai, Paramēśwara samhitai and Padma samhitai.

The temple Archakas that follow the Rahasyāmnāyam from a long period (a period at least prior to Āḷavandār's time) are said to fall into the four distinct classes, *viz.*— 1. Āgama Siddhāntis; 2. Mantra Siddhāntis; 3. Tantra Siddhāntis and 4. Tantrāntra Siddhāntis. The Āgama Siddhāntis are not now traceable. They have neither gōtra nor pravara nor gāyatrī. They are not expected to perform the Samskāras usually done by the Brahmans. They are to use for every ceremony the mantras "Om namō bhagavatē Vāsudēvāya". No other mantra is used by them for any kind of ceremony. Although the present day Archakas point out with pride these subdivisions, none of them are able to say to which of the sections they belong. So this appears to have only an academic interest.

Amongst the Archakas those who follow the Bōdhāyana, Vaikhānasa and Śaunakādi sūtrams are entitled to worship God in temples. This is so as rules pertaining to worship are given only in the Grihya sūtras of these three sūtras. The remaining sections belonging to the other fifteen sūtras are not authorized to do worship as no mention is made of the rituals of temple worship. It is believed that men belonging to these fifteen sūtras cannot do pūja without the Chakrābja maṇḍala dīkshai as stated in Pāncharātra sūtra. As already stated any person may adopt domestic worship and it is usually done according to the rituals laid down in the Pāncharātra Śāstras.

Although domestic worship may be carried out by any Brahman, temple worship can be carried out only by those who have been initiated into the system and specially made to undergo a ceremony called "Dīkshai" or "Chakrābja Maṇḍala Dīkshai". Though the Archakas following the sūtras of Bōdhāyana and Śaunaka may do the worship of God in temples without this initiation in practice they also undergo the Dīkshā ceremony now a days. The Archakas of the Bōdhāyana and Śaunaka Sūtras explain that they undergo the ceremony of Dīkshā instead of prapatti. As they consider prapatti to be an important ceremony, they go through the ceremony of dīkshai.

The Vaikhānasa system is of course entirely different and it has to be treated separately by itself.

The Archaka boy is made to go through the "Chakrābja Maṇḍala Dīkshai" only after the Upanayana ceremony. The ordinary Sri Vaishnava Brahman boy undergoes the Samāśrayaṇa ceremony after the Upanayanam. But the Archaka boy passes through the ceremony of "Chakrābja Maṇḍala Dīkshai" and does not pass through the Samāśrayaṇa ceremony as "Dīkshā" ceremony is considered equivalent to it.

THE CHAKRĀBJA MAṆḌALA DĪKSHAI CEREMONY.

This ceremony usually lasts for three days. It is usually commenced on a Śuklapaksha daśami day (10th day after New moon).

First Day.

On Śuklapaksha daśami or the 10th day after the New moon the Yāgamaṇḍapam (the sacrificial maṇḍapam) is laid out, decorated and worshipped; the Ankurārpaṇam ceremony is gone through towards the evening.

The Yāgamaṇḍapam is usually formed in a clean spot with good surroundings, such as a river side, temple compound or a good garden. The most important item in the Yāgamaṇḍapam is the fire pit.

The ceremony when elaborately performed, a large number of people knowing the rituals are engaged. When this is the case four fire pits are made and these are disposed round a dais. The pit to the east of the dais should have sides each measuring about twenty-four anguḷas (mānānguḷas which are a little smaller than the inches) and chaturasra of the pit is to be twelve anguḷas. This pit lying to the east is called "the depth kuṇḍam". To the west of the dais a fire pit of a circular type is made. The radius is to be about fifteen anguḷas and the depth of the pit about twelve anguḷas. This pit is to be round and goes by the name "Vritti kuṇḍam". On the southern side of the dais a semi-circular kuṇḍam called "Dhanush kuṇḍam" is made. The size of this kuṇḍam is to be sixty anguḷams round and about thirty-six anguḷams of diameter is to be provided. That is to say the straight line to be about thirty-six and curved line about sixty anguḷams. To the north of the dais a triangular pit is made, each side of the triangle being about twenty-four anguḷams. The depth is to be twelve anguḷams. This kuṇḍam is called the "Yōnikuṇḍam."

Round each of these pits three steps are to be made, called mēkhalas. These mēkhalas are to be six mānānguḷams high and four mānānguḷams broad, so that the lowest would be twelve anguḷams broad, the middle one eight anguḷams and the third or the uppermost would be four anguḷams. At the bottom of these pits, except the circular one, kamalams are drawn and in the front about the middle of the mēkhalai. *Ficus religiosa* leaf is drawn in the case of the three pits except the triangular "Yōnikuṇḍam." The ficus leaf is to be fifteen inches long, 10, 6, 4, 2, 1 and less inches gradually in breadth and with a long tip pointed downwards. When thus four fire pits are made four Archakas have to take part in doing the ceremony.

When sufficient number of Archakas are not available, it is usual to have only one sacrificial pit dug. The ceremony is usually conducted by two persons and in such cases only one pit is made for the fire. In this case the pit is to be a square about one yard each side and at least twelve anguḷams deep. Round this pit three mēkhalas are made, each of these six inches high and four inches broad. The lowest mēkhalai will be twelve inches, the middle one eight and the uppermost four inches broad. These mēkhalas are called sātvika, rājasa and tāmasa, respectively.

The space allotted for the maṇḍapa should be at least ten yards square. On each of the four directions, a doorway has to be set up and decorated. The frame work of the doorway for the east is to be made of the wood of the araśu tree (*Ficus religiosa*), for the south of the wood of the atti (*Ficus glomerata*), for the west of the wood of nyagrōdham (*F. bengalensis*) and for the north of the wood of juvvi tree (*F. tsiela*). As soon as the doorways are placed they are decorated with tōraṇams of mango leaves by tying them across the doorways. At each of the doors, two lights are placed. Kōlam (figures or designs of various things) is drawn and akshatai is sprinkled over the doorway.

On this day towards the evening the Ankurārpaṇam ceremony is gone through. For this ceremony usually, and when it is done on an elaborate scale three kinds of mud vessels are used. They are pāligais, ghaṭikais and sarāvams. The pāligai is the vessel in which seedlings are to be raised, the ghaṭikais are the four-faced vessels and sarāvams are dishes. Only the pāligai vessels may also be used. Each of the pāligai vessels is to be sixteen inches in circumference at the top, seven inches round at the constricted part. The ghaṭikaī is to be twenty-two inches high with four side holes and an open space in the top also. The top hole is to be six inches and the side holes four inches in circumference. The sarāvams should be twelve inches round and two inches deep.

The mud needed to fill the pāligais should be obtained from an ant-hill which is close to the place where the ceremony has to be gone through. The initiate proceeds towards the east or the north in procession accompanied by music until he reaches the place wherefrom mud is to be taken. A yāgabhēram or balibhēram of Vishvaksēnar, Garuḍa, Hanumān or Chakrat Āzhwār is also taken along in the procession. A digger or other weapon, intended for use to dig the mud, is cleaned and a new cloth is wrapped round it and it is taken along with the initiate in procession. On reaching the destination the space from which mud is to be taken is marked.

The initiate while going towards the east or north in procession for bringing the mud repeats the Śākuna sūtram.

Over the place selected for taking the mud, he sprinkles water repeating while doing so the astra mantram. At the same time Bhūsūktam also is repeated.

Varāhamūrti is next invoked and he is shown the usual upachārams of arghya, pādya and āchamanam, etc. Then with the implement taken in procession the mud is dug out with Varāha mantra and it is deposited in a metal or cane tray accompanied by the repetition of ashṭāksharam. When a sufficient quantity of mud is secured, it is covered over with a new cloth.

Sand also is brought in the same manner as the ant-hill mud is secured from the river bed from a clean place or from any clean spot if a river is not available anywhere nearby. Sand and mud are taken in procession round the village and then to the maṇḍapam where the seed-sowing ceremony is to be performed. Dry cowdung is also brought down in procession from a cow-shed. Along with the procession people who repeat Śrīsūktam, Bhūsūktam, sākanasūktam, also follow.

The initiate takes his seat in the maṇḍapam after dressing himself up properly for the occasion. He does sankalpam for the performance of the Ankurārpaṇam ceremony.

He then selects the Āchārya who is to initiate him and also the Ṛtviks who are to help the Āchārya in the various items of the ceremony.

After the usual worship to God the pāligais, ghaṭikās and sarāvams are got ready for the ceremony. All these vessels are well washed with the repetition of the mūla mantram and white cotton threads are wound round the pāligais. While washing the pāligais, etc., Vishnu gāyatrī may also be repeated.

The number of pāligais, sarāvams and ghaṭikais used for the Ankurārpaṇam ceremony varies. When the ceremony is done on an elaborate scale, these vessels number one hundred and eight—thirty-six vessels of each. When the full number is used they are arranged in a particular manner as detailed below. These vessels are arranged in three rows from east to west in separate groups of three,—sarāvams in one line, ghaṭikais in a second line and pāḷigais in the third line. Usually these vessels are placed in a square space marked off by lines as shown below :—

EAST.

SARĀVAMS. GHATIKAIS. PĀLIGAIS.

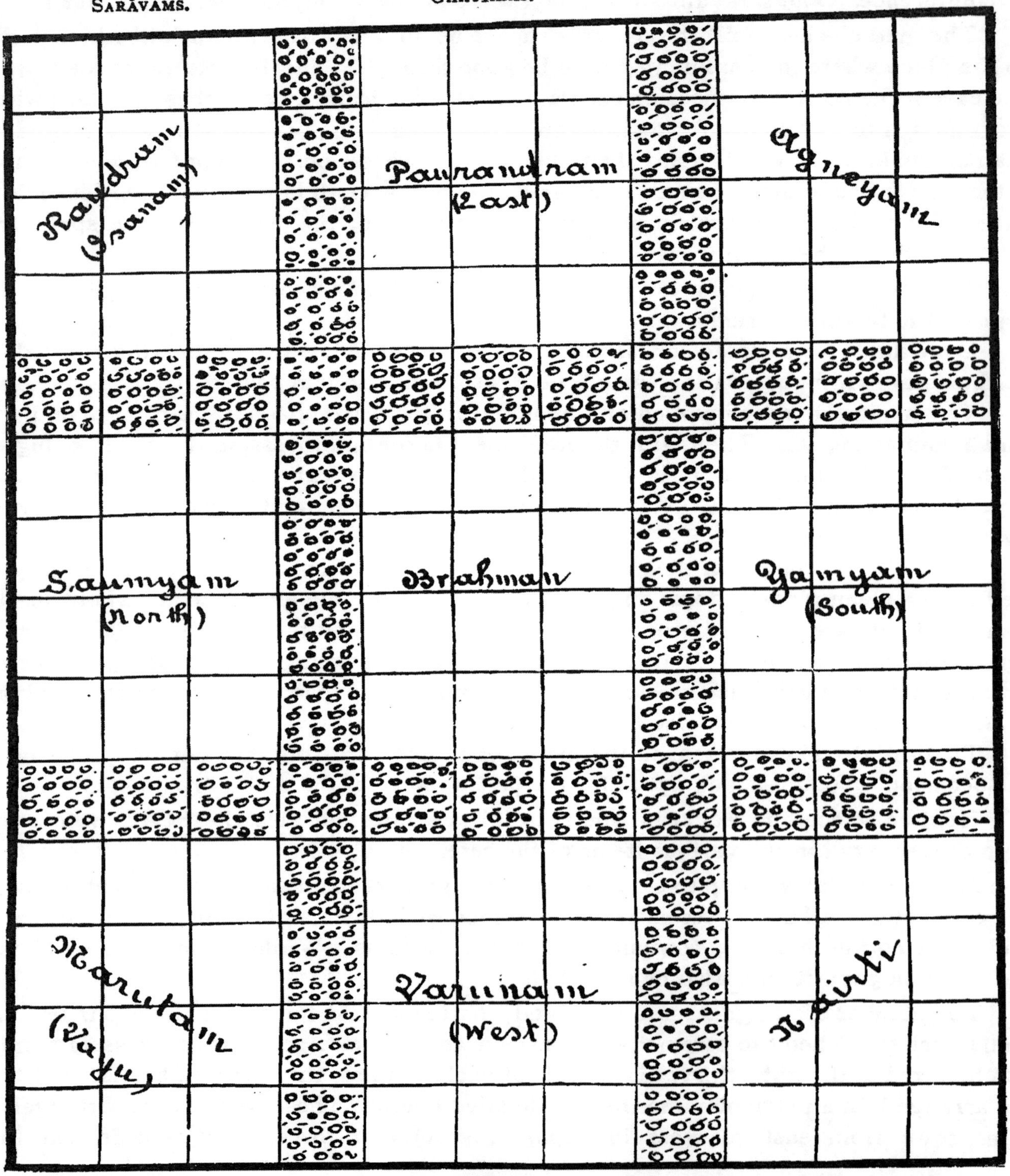

NORTH. SOUTH.

WEST.

When 108 vessels in all (36 of each) are not to be used less numbers may be used as shown below :—

48 in all (or 16 of each vessel) are used ;
36 in all (or 12 of each vessel) are used ;
24 in all (or 8 of each vessel) are used ;
12 in all (or 4 of each vessel) are used ;

When 48, 36, 24 in all are used it is considered to be madhyamapaksham and when 12 only are used it is considered to be adhamam. When pāligais alone are used sixteen, twelve or eight (16, 12 or 8) are used.

Round the necks of the pāligais (and if sarāvams and ghaṭikais are used to their necks also) blades of Cynodon grass and leaves of Pipal tree are tied. The lower openings of the pāligai are closed by means of some grass and Ficus leaves. The pāligais are then filled with mud, sand and then cowdung dry powder one over the other respectively. The pāligais are placed over a settle of paddy, rice or gingelly.

The initiate places the pāligais repeating the *purusha mantra*, ghaṭikās by repeating the *paramēshṭi mantra* and sarāvams by repeating the *vishṇu mantra*. Another vessel is cleaned in the usual way and after filling it with clean water and placing it to the north of the fire pit, some sandal paste is put into it and cotton thread is wrapped round it. This is called the sōma kumbham. When only pāligais are used the sōma kumbham is placed to their west. Nine kinds of seeds (those of Navadhānya) are obtained and milk and water are poured into the seeds. The whole thing is well mixed. Then puṇyāham is done and with the purified puṇyāham water the seeds are sprinkled and they are covered with a new cloth.

The initiate then proceeds to invoke the dēvatās and requests them to occupy the pāligais as detailed below :—

The twelve Kēśavādis are invoked and they are requested to occupy the pāligais. Brahmās are invoked and they are requested to be in the ghaṭikās. Sarāvams are to be occupied by the Rudras who are invoked. Upachārams are shown in the usual way to all these dēvatās thus invoked.

The initiate next proceeds to the doorways and begins to decorate them and invoke the dēvatās to occupy certain places in the doorways. The four doorways are decorated, and it is only after this decoration that the different dēvas are invoked and requested to occupy the doorways. The eastern doorway is to represent the Ṛg Vedas. The dēva that is invoked and requested to occupy this doorway is Suśōbhanar (சுசோபனர்). Another dēva who is also requested to be present is Indra. Two red flags are tied, one on each side of the doorway. While the right flag is being tied the word "Kumudāya namaḥ" is pronounced and the left flag is set up with the word "Kumudākshināya namaḥ." Two small pots are placed near the door after filling them with water. When the pot placed at the right side is being filled with water the word "Pūrṇāya namaḥ" is pronounced and the left pot is filled with water pronouncing the name "Pushkarāya namaḥ." These pots are then decorated with thread; some money is put in these pots and a kūrccham is also placed in each or across the mouths. The mouths of these pots are covered with mango or aśvattha leaves. The southern doorway represents the Yajur Veda. The dēva invoked is "Subhadraka." Another dēva invoked and requested to be present is "Yama." Two green coloured flags are tied one on each side. The right flag is put on invoking the dēvatā Puṇḍarīkar and left flag is inserted calling in Vāmanar. Two pots are placed filled with water on the right and left side and Ānandar is invoked when the pot on the right side is filled and Nandar when the left pot is filled with water. The western doorway is to represent Sāma Veda and the dēvas invoked are "Subandhu" and "Varuṇa." Two flags are hoisted on the doorway one on each side. The right flag is supposed to be occupied by "Śankukarṇar" and so he is invoked. Sarvanētrar is requested to occupy the flag to the left of the doorway. Two pots are filled with water and they are placed on the right and the left sides of the doorway towards the west. The dēva "Vīra Sēna" is requested to occupy the right pot and "Susēnar" is invoked and requested to be in the pot to the left. The northern doorway is made to represent Atharva Vēda and the dēvas called to occupy respectively the left and right sides are "Suhōtrakar" and "Kubērar." The top of the doorway is decorated with two flags white in colour. The right flag is believed to be occupied by "Sumukhar" and the left flag by "Supratishṭhitar." On the sides of the doorway pots are placed filled with water. While filling or after filling them with water, the right one is to be occupied by "Sambhavāya" and the left one by "Prabhavāya."

After thus arranging the various things and invoking the dēvas he next goes to the place where the pāligais are placed. There to the west of the pāligais a pot filled with water is placed, the moon is invoked and made to occupy the water in the pot. On account of this occupation by the moon, this pot is called "The sōmakaragam" or moon's pot. Pāyasam is offered to the moon.

The person presiding over the ceremony performs a hōmam and pours into the fire one hundred and eight oblations of ghee. Then he repeats the mūla mantra and while doing so he places in the fire as āhutis four samits or pieces of palāśa sticks (sticks of *Butea frondosa*). After offering these sticks offerings of cooked rice are made. Purushasūktam is repeated and offerings of cooked rice are made sixteen times into the fire. While the hōmam is being performed, ghee is secured from each of the 108 āhutis made, and this ghee is called sampātājyam (ghee secured). With this sampātājyam the five pāligais are smeared and the ghee that remains is poured into the seed-vessel. The Sōma mantra is repeated one hundred times.

Then getting permission from the assembled Brahmans the pāligais are filled with the nine kinds of grain already secured and kept. Though the Śāstras enjoin pāligai, ghaṭikai and sarāvams only pāligais are used. The ghaṭikais and śarāvams are used only when the ceremony is done very elaborately. At Lakshmipuram instead of sarāvams coconuts were used. In temples this is the case. But in regular marriages only pāligais are used and the other vessels are never brought in.

While filling the paligais with grains "Ōshadhi sūktam" is repeated and the actual ankurārpaṇam or the sowing of seeds is done with the repetition of dvādaśākshara mantra. After filling the pāligais with the nine kinds of grain bali (offering) is given to Kumudādis.

All the materials needed for use for the dīkshā ceremony next day are procured on this day only.

This fire pit is usually a single one and it is square. The four pits already described are usually used only when the ceremony is done on a very elaborate scale. The fire pit is usually made to the west of the vēdikai, at least three spans from it (27 inches).

The Second Day's Ceremony or the Śishyādhivāsam.

The ceremony is begun by worshipping the dēvas that are present in the various parts of the four doorways and upachārams are shown to them. The next item is the preparation of the Chakrābja Maṇḍalam on a dais. This maṇḍalam is to be drawn according to certain definite rules which are detailed below. As the result of carrying out the instructions a lotus is drawn with all its parts on the dais set apart for it.

Two directions are selected for the drawing and they are east to west and north to south. Seventeen lines are drawn in white colour from east to west, leaving a space of three inches between the lines. The same number of lines with the same interval of 3 inches are made on the lines from north to south. As a result of these lines crossing each other, there will be formed 256 squares, each square being about 3 inches. On each side there will be 16 squares. The threads that are used to make these squares are stained with chunam so that when they are placed on the ground the ground may have a line of chunam. This line is made by holding the thread hard at the ends and then raising it a little and striking on the ground twice or thrice. All the lines are marked off thus by this thread coated with chunam.

The 36 squares formed in the central portion of the square are rubbed off and in that space five concentric circles are made by drawing clearly the lines Of these circles the innermost one is called "The Karṇikakshētram." The second circle is subdivided into three circles and they are called (1) Kesarāvali, (2) Dalabhūmi, and (3) Nābhimaṇḍalam. The third and the fourth circles are called "Arakshētrams" and the fifth one is called the "Bahirnēmibhūḥ."

The single line of squares (28 in number) next to the circles formed out of the 36 squares in the centre, is called "Bahirāsanam." The two rows of squares numbering eighty lying outside the squares forming "Bahirāsanam" are called "Vidhikai." The remaining 112 squares are dealt with so as to form doorways in the centre of the four sides and other places by the sides. On each of the sides in the directions E, S, W and N the four central squares are rubbed off and are marked as doorways (dvārasthānams). At the four corners of the squares spaces are marked called "śankhasthānams." Now the spaces eight in number, existing between the " dvārasthānams " and " śankhasthānams " on each side are marked off into three kinds of spaces called " Ardha śōbhai," " Śōbhai," and " Upa śōbhai." Close to the dvārasthānams, one on each side of it, the " Artha śōbhais " are marked off. This space consists of three squares two adjoining the doorway and the one, the second of the outermost row from the doorway (see the figure). In all eight " Ardha śōbhais " are formed each consisting of two squares on one side of the doorway and one outer square, i.e., the second from the doorway. Next to this space called ardha śōbhais are marked off some spaces called " śōbhais." As they are marked off on both sides of the main doorway there will be eight śōbhais. Each of these eight śōbhais consist of four squares, three of the inner and one of the outer row. These four squares form a kind of T, the horizontal line of this letter being made of three squares and the vertical line of two squares (including the central one of the horizontal line). Between the śankham and the śōbhai there lie three squares and these are formed into a kind of ∠ space. This ∠ shaped space lying between the śankham and the śōbhai goes by the name of " upa śōbhai." As there are four sides and since two sets of upaśōbhais are formed on each side there will be eight upa śōbhais in all. Thus on each of the four sides E, S, W and N there will be the doorway in the centre and the sides of the doorway there will be ardha śōbhai, śōbhai, and upa śōbhais, one set on each side. So in all there will be eight sets of each. At the corners there will be śankhams, four in all, *i.e.*, one for each corner.

The set of squares is now divided into Padma, in the centre surrounded by a single row of squares called Bahirāsanam, which in its turn has two rows of squares enclosing it all round and called " Vēdikai." Outside the vēdikai lie the two rows of squares, now divided into 4 doorways, 4 śankha spaces at the four corners, 8 ardha śōbhais, 8 śōbhais and 8 upaśōbhais.

All round outside the squares two kamalams are drawn just near the dvārasthānams and one close to the Śankhasthānam. So in all there would be drawn twelve padmams or kamalams—2 at each doorway and 4 at the corners. All these should, if possible, be drawn to the same size as that of the central padmam.

The concentric circles, six around the central space and the central one are worked up into a lotus. In the central circle eight or twelve white dots are made to represent the seeds. When eight dots are made the presiding deity is believed to be Nārāyaṇa, and if twelve are made Vāsudēva is the presiding deity.

The whole of the inner circle is now filled with green powder (powdered green leaves); the seeds are represented over the green ground by white dots made by the white rice-flour. The boundary line or the limiting circumference is to be drawn with light red or black powder.

The space just outside limited by the circumference called " Kēsarāvali " is intended to draw the ninety-six kēsarams all round. Each line or kēsaram should be drawn in three colours, viz., white, green and red tips; the bounding line is drawn in dark green colour.

The space called dalabhūmi is intended to contain the twenty-four petals (or sixteen), the tips of the petals reaching the end of the arakshētram (the fourth main circle and the fifth in order). The space called dalabhūmi is occupied by 12 or 8 halams. The innermost row of petals (12 or 8) is to reach the limit of the circumference of the third main circle. Then alternating with these 12 or 8 petals are drawn again reaching the limit of the fourth circle *i.e.*, the main fourth. The bottom or lower part of the petals are made white, ends red and the line white.

The Nābhirēkhai, *i.e.*, the bounding line of the second main circle is to be of black, green, red lines between halams and upahalams. The tips of the upahalam are to be black and the line is red.

The line bounding the space called "Nēmibhūḥ" is marked with black powder and the space is to be white and for covering white powder is used.

The 28 squares forming the bahirāsanam or pīṭham are filled with green or yellow powder.

The space called vēdikai is sprinkled with white powder and is made to look white. On this back ground creepers and flowers of different colours are drawn.

The śōbhais are filled with red powder, upaśōbhais green and ardha śōbhais black. The eastern doorway is filled with white, south red, west green and north black. In the śanku corners both black and yellow powders are spread. (*See* Pl. XI-A.)

After the formation of the Chakrābja Maṇḍalam or simultaneously with it the Śishyādhi Vāsam ceremony is begun.

Puṇyāham or purificatory ceremony is done and the four doorways are then worshipped. The pots at the four doorways and the flags are worshipped, as on the Ankurārpaṇam day. A kumbham, called mahā kumbham, is cleaned in the usual manner and it is filled with perfumed water. Into this kumbham is next dropped a Nārāyaṇa idol if one is available or a piece of gold. It is then decorated by passing thread round it externally and placing near its neck flowers and sandal paste with akshata (rice). A new cloth is wrapped round this kumbham. Another small pot is prepared in the same manner and it is called the karagam. It is got ready and purified by the repetition of ashṭamantram. Both the kumbham and the karagam are taken round the Chakrābja Maṇḍalam in a pradakshiṇa manner or clockwise. They are placed to the north-east (Īsānyam) of the Chakrābja Maṇḍalam, the karagam (smaller pot) being placed to the left of the kumbham (larger pot). They are then covered with a new cloth.

Nārāyaṇa is then invoked and he is requested to occupy the kumbham and he is worshipped. The maṇḍalam is next occupied by several dēvatās, who are requested to come with their appropriate angams. They occupy their respective places in the maṇḍalam. The details of the āvāhanam and worship of these dēvātas are given below:—

In the centre of the maṇḍalam, which is now the centre of the lotus, Mantaradva is invoked and he is requested to occupy the place. Then bījam, piṇḍam, samugya, gāyatrī, mālā, mantram, are āvāhanamed in the same space and they are worshipped.

Then Para, Vyūha, Vibhava, Vibhavāntara, Archa, Antaryāmi, and Tatvam are āvāhanamed in the kēsarams and they are worshipped.

Kadhi Varṇams are invoked and are requested to occupy the petals and they are worshipped.

Jāgrat, Swapna, Sushupti, and Turīya mūrtis are invoked and are requested to occupy the "Nābhi maṇḍalam" and they are worshipped.

The Arakshētra is occupied by jñānam, Aiśwaryam, Śakti, Balam, Vīryam, Tējas after āvāhanam and they are worshipped.

The Nēmi bhūmi is occupied by Bhuvanādhvakramam (14 lokas) and they are worshipped.

In the centre the eight or twelve letters are supposed to be present and worship is done to them.

The following also are invoked and are requested to occupy the central space. Repetition of Vishṇu gāyatrī, Vishṇu shaḍāksharam, Vāsudēvādi mantras (4), Matsyādi mantras (10), Sudarśana and Hayagrīva mantrams, Śrī Bhūmi mantras, Ananta, Garuḍa, Vishvaksēna, Chanḍādi mantras and Pārashādi mantrams.

The twenty-four tatvas and thirty-three dēvatās are made to be present by request and they are worshipped. These occupy the kēsarams.

The daḷas (petals) are occupied by the letters ka to Kshakāra and they are worshipped.

The twelve Kēśavādis, the ten Matsyādis, Viśvādis, Kumudādis, Indrādis, Kumaryādis, Kinnaras, Kimpurushās, Vimaladis, Vyāptyādis, and Śrīvatsādis are invoked and are requested to occupy the Nābhi maṇḍalam.

The Akārādiswarams are repeated and they are believed to occupy the Arakshētram and then they are worshipped.

The fourteen lōkas or bhuvanās and lōkās of Vishnu are invoked and they are requested to occupy the Nēmi maṇḍala and they are worshipped.

Then fire is made or obtained for sacrifice. Strictly speaking for purposes of dīkshai "Balāgni" described below is considered to be the best. In very orthodox places and in most cases fire is obtained from "Vṛddhāgni" described below.

For sacrificial and religious purposes fire is usually obtained in one of the following three ways described below:—

(1) By means of the sticks of "Sami" or "Araṇi" fire is obtained. The end of one stick is inserted in a small hollow space made in another stick laid horizontally. Both these sticks are of the same kind. They are churned either by the hand or by means of ropes. The fire obtained by this method is termed "Balāgni" or young fire.

(2) It may be obtained from the sun by the use of a convex lens. This fire is called "Yauvanāgni" or adult fire.

(3) It may be obtained from the sacrificial fire kept burning by the very orthodox in their houses. This is called "Vṛddhāgni" or old fire.

As soon as fire is made or obtained from elsewhere it is put in the pit or kuṇḍam existing for the reception of sacrificial fire and some rice is cooked over this fire. The food thus cooked is divided into four parts and used as detailed below :—

(1) One part for using as oblations to the dēvatās that are present (āvāhanam) in the maṇḍalam.

(2) One part to be offered to the Nārāyaṇa kumbham.

(3) One part for putting into the fire as oblations during hōmam.

(4) One part to be offered to his own Āchārya.

The Āchārya makes 108 oblations of samit into the kuṇḍam or firepit repeating the mūlamantram. Oblations of cooked rice are made sixteen times repeating the purushasūktam.

Then the śishya or the candidate to be initiated into the dīkshai is to bathe and decorate himself with new cloths. He is seated on the right side close to his Āchārya with his eyes blindfolded facing east. By placing darbha grass between the two—Āchārya and the initiate—communication is made between the two individuals. The Āchārya makes twelve āhutis (pourings) of ghee repeating Puṇḍarīkāksha mantrams. After this twelve offerings of cooked rice are made, then twelve of samits, twelve of flowers and twelve of sesamum seeds. Then the Āchārya passes round the body of the initiate in a clockwise direction "Prasūti mudra" with his hands beginning with the head and passing to the foot, and also back to head. Taking a small quantity of ashes of the samit the Āchārya mixes it with the "Tirumaṇ" usually used for marking the forehead by the Vaishnavas. The initiate opens his eyes at this stage. With this mixture of ashes and nāmam the Āchārya makes a mark of ūrdhvapuṇḍram on the forehead of the śishya. After this the wrist thread is tied with the usual ceremonies that have to be gone through in this connexion. (This is "pratisara" or "Rakshābandhanam.")

Panchagavyam, prepared as usual, is next given to him to purify him. Then he is asked to take a little food offered as sacrifice.

The initiate is then made to clean his teeth with a stick brush. This brush is thrown on the ground after cleaning his teeth. The direction in which the apex of the stick falls is noted. The directions yāmyam, nairuti, and vāyavyam are considered bad and the other directions are considered to be good. If the apex or the unused part of the stick falls towards the bad directions already mentioned a sānti hōmam is performed. For this hōmam sesamum is offered in the fire 108 times repeating the Narasimha mantram.

The śishya then does āchamanam and afterwards is led to near God and is asked to prostrate. After prostrating to God the Āchārya on behalf of the śishya repeats a prayer which is somewhat as follows :—

"We who are bound by family ties completely like so many cows, can hope to be liberated from these bonds only by you ; we have no other means except you. For the removal of these bonds your grace is necessary and the only way to secure your grace is by worshipping you. So I pray to you to help this ignorant person depending only upon your mercy on his behalf to get him out of the bonds of Samsāra. To enable him to do so let him hereafter be permitted by you to worship you."

After this prayer the initiate is brought back to the dais and his eyes are tied over with a blindfolding cloth. The Āchārya ties round the body of the śishya the māyā thread. This thread must consist of red, black and white coloured threads twisted into one. Then three such tri-coloured threads are spun into a thicker thread. In other words, the māyā thread should consist of three black, three red and three white threads. The māyā thread is taken round the body so as to make twenty-five turns. While taking the thread round his body mūla mantra is repeated. After winding the māyā thread round the body, the disciple is seated next to the Āchārya and by placing the darbha grass between the Āchārya and the śishya communication between the two is established. Then the Āchārya does the hōmam. He takes the "Sruvam" and with it makes 108 oblations of ghee repeating the mūla mantra with each offering. After this offering of ghee cooked rice offerings are given. This is called "Pūrṇāhuti." Then taking another spoon called "Sruk" a small quantity of cooked rice is placed along with ghee and it is covered by another wooden ladle called "Sruvam" and the food is offered by pouring the food and ghee into the fire. Samit, darbha grass and flowers covered by sruvam are then offered in the fire. God is contemplated, svapnādi mantra is repeated and 108 ghee offerings are made by the Āchārya by repeating the mantram "Amṛtadhārām," etc.

To the dēvatās present in the doorways rice and black gram cooked is offered. The cloth tied across the eyes of the initiate to blindfold him and the māyā thread wound round his body are removed. The māyā thread is placed in a sarāvam which is placed near the kumbham. The sarāvam is covered over by another sarāvam after placing on it the māyā thread. The disciple sleeps for the night on the darbha grass spread on in a place with their tips to the east.

Third Day or the Diksha Day.

On this day the śishya comes to the maṇḍapam after snānam and sandhyā ceremony. If the śishya (initiate) had a bad dream during sleep, a śānti hōmam is usually done to remove the evil effects. The ceremonies of the day are first begun with upachāram and pūja to the dēvatās in the dvārams and maṇḍalam. It is only after this the śānti hōmam is proceeded with. For offerings to the dēvatas four kinds of rice are prepared—rice and sesamum mixed, milk and cooked rice, rice and green gram cooked together, and rice and jaggery cooked together.

The śishya (initiate) prostrates to God and then he is blindfolded as on the second day. He is then seated by the side of the Āchārya as usual. Then 108 samits are offered as sacrifice, one by one, repeating the mūla mantra for each. This is followed by offerings of ghee and food--ghee 108 times and food also 108 times. The māyā sūtram wound round the initiate as before, into 25 rounds around the śishya's body. The rounds of thread wound round the body of the initiate is then cut into twenty-five pieces repeating the tatva mantras. While cutting one piece a tatva mantra is repeated.

As each piece is cut, it is again cut into eight pieces and placed in the fire in the kuṇḍam. This is followed by oblation of ghee before the next thread is cut.

Soon after this the Āchārya must imagine that the initiate is burnt down and that his jīvan is placed at the feet of Vāsudēva, who is always present in the hrit-kamalam of the Āchārya. The śōshaṇa, dāhana and plāvanams are done respectively to the body of the disciple.

The jīva of the initiate existing at the feet of the God Vāsudēva in the hrit-kamala, is imagined to have passed into the body of the initiate now purified. When this is done, offerings of ghee are made in the kuṇḍam fire for twenty-five tatvams, repeating the tatvamantras in the order of creation (sṛshṭikrama). After the creation of the now pure body, water is sprinkled over it repeating the mūla mantram.

The cloth blindfolding the eye is now removed. A new cloth is worn by the initiate. He then lies down by the side of his Āchārya and his eyes are blindfolded again. The Āchārya who sits facing the east touches the body of the disciple in six places according to adhvakrama (Kāladhvam, Pādādhvam, Bhuvanādhvam, Mantrādhvam, Varṇādhvam and Tatvādhvam).

Oblations of ghee are offered repeating the Vyāhṛti mantram. Then with sampātajyam (ghee set apart) the feet and knee of the initiate are touched. Then oblations of sesamum seeds repeating the mūla mantra and with sampātajyam are done. After the āhuti, a part of the body of the initiate—knee to navel of the body—is touched. Next lotus petals are offered as oblations repeating the mūla mantram; the body is touched from nābhi to hṛdayam with ghee or lotus petal. Lastly, cooked rice oblations are offered. Hṛdayam to head is touched by charu (cooked rice).

Then taking hold of the right hand of the Śishya the Āchārya takes him round the maṇḍalam, kumbham and kuṇḍam once in a pradakshiṇa direction (clockwise). Then a flower, a pearl, a piece or coral and a coin are placed in his hands, with his eyes blindfolded and he throws all these on the Chakrābjamaṇḍalam. The place where the flower falls on the maṇḍalam is noted and the initiate is named after the name of the mūrti invoked and placed therein. (For example, the Buthugur Bhaṭṭar received the name of Tirunārāyaṇa Bhaṭṭar at the time of his dīkshai and his usual name given to him after birth was Srīnivāsa Bhaṭṭar). Usually the name that one is given during the dīkshā ceremony is the current one so far as temple matters are concerned.

Immediately after throwing the flower, etc., on the maṇḍalam the cloth tied across the eye is removed so that he may see the place where the flower falls and he adopts the name of the dēva presiding over the spot on which the flower falls.

Dīkshā may be gone through by men of all the four castes. The titles taken after passing through this ceremony are as follows:—

Brahmans ... ... call themselves *Bhaṭṭars* or *Bhaṭāraka* after this ceremony.
Kshatriya ... ... is called a *Dēvar* after this initiation.
Vaiśya ... ... is called *Bala* after this initiation.
Śūdra ... ... is called *Dāsa*.

But so far as is known these men are very rare. Only Brahman initiates are found now.

As soon as this ceremony is over God Nārāyaṇa is thought of. Into the right ear of the śishya, ashṭākshara and dvādaśākshara and mūrti mantrams are repeated in a very subdued voice so that these may not be heard by others than the initiate.

Then the kumbhams, the mandalams and the doorways are worshipped and saluted by the śishya.

The śishya after all this is taken to the presence of God and he is left there in the hands of God. This handing over is believed to be "self-surrender." So, for the person who passes through the ceremony of dīkshai, a separate bhārasamarpaṇam or prapatti ceremony need not be adopted by the Bhaṭṭars after having gone through the dīkshā ceremony. Some Archakas, in these days, do however adopt the prapatti also.

After the dīkshā ceremony a Bhaṭṭar is fit to undertake the ceremony of worshipping God in temples.

The idols in the temple are fit for worship only after the ceremony of Pratishṭhā. By this pratishṭhā ceremony the spirit of God is infused into the images or idols. So long as the worship is continued the idol is fit for worship. If the pūja is discontinued for more than three days a new pratishṭhā ceremony is necessary. But till one year the idol may be worshipped after "Snapanam" and after that period "Pratishṭhā" ceremony is necessary.

15. The Pratishṭhā Ceremony of Utsava Vigrahas in Temples.

In every temple we find one kind of image placed inside in the garbhagṛha and another just in front of it. The one in the garbhagṛha is one usually made of stone or mortar and its appearance is usually black and shining. In front of these stone or mortar vigrahas are placed metallic vigrahas. The mūla vigrahas are fixed to the spot and cannot be removed from the place. The metallic vigrahas placed in front of the mūla vigrahas are usually taken out whenever necessary in procession, and hence, they are called utsava vigrahas. Both these are prepared by smiths who are called Śilpis. They being to the Kammāḷa (Tamil) or Kamsali (Telugu) caste. The preparation of these images is done according to certain principles laid down in the Śilpa Śāstra. These rules or principles guiding them in the matter of making these images are either handed down from generation to generation by actual workers or learned from written works of Śilpa Śāstras.

Most of the Śilpis know astrology. So in preparing the images they select an auspicious time for beginning their work of making a vigraha in stone or metal. If they have to make a mūla vigraha they generally select a block of stone and at a selected auspicious hour begin their work of shaping this stone to the required image.

For making an utsava vigraha metals are mixed, boiled and after reducing them to a liquid state, it is used in casting the image. For this casting, at first they have to make the idol in mud, then shape it properly with wax and then pour the melted metal into the moulds containing the idols. For doing all this work proper time is chosen and then they do the various items of work at selected periods of time.

The metallic vigrahas required for the pūja in the temple are brought in the first instance to the temple by the Śilpis in an almost finished condition. Just before handing over the images to the archaka for the pratishṭhā ceremony the opening of the eyes or "Nētrōtghāṭanam" is usually done by the Śilpi. This is the last or the finishing touch of the Śilpi.

The pratishṭhā ceremony is performed usually by the bhaṭars or others interested in the pūja of the temple. For this purpose a very competent person is selected from amongst the bhaṭṭars. The person selected is one knowing the processes to be gone through during the pratishṭhā very well. In order to assist him in the ceremony two or three other Archakas are selected. The Archaka selected for performing the chief part of the ceremony is called the *Achārya* and the other assistants who help him in the ceremony are called *Rtviks.* The various articles that are needed for the pratishṭhā ceremony are secured and brought at the appropriate time by a person and he is termed a *Parichāraka.* The Parichāraka does not take part in the actual ceremonial. He is engaged only in getting ready the various things required during the performance of the pratishṭhā.

The pratishṭhā ceremony lasts five days, if on an elaborate scale and it lasts only three days under ordinary circumstances. The following account of the pratishṭha ceremony is mainly based on what was observed during the pratishṭhā ceremony performed at Lakshmipuram near Kuppam from the 11th to 13th of May—Wednesday to Friday—during the year 1927.

THE ANKURĀRPAṆAM CEREMONY.

This ceremony was carried out on the evening of the 10th of May 1927 (Tuesday). When the Ankurārpaṇa ceremony is performed on an elaborate scale it is usually done seven days prior to the main ceremony. But in most cases this ceremony is usually done on the evening of the day previous to the beginning of the pratishṭhā ceremony. This rule of doing the Ankurārpaṇam ceremony a week beforehand is adopted when the vigrahas are to be established in a temple newly built and when the ceremony has to be done on a grand scale.

The Brahmans connected with the temple or agents of the temple select the Āchārya and request him to carry on the ceremony of pratishṭhā. The Āchārya then requests certain people from amongst the Archakas to serve as Rtviks. The number of Rtviks may be any number up to 16 but the minimum number required is two.

At the appointed time or a little earlier Brahmans assemble and the Archaka requests them to permit him to begin the Ankurārpaṇa ceremony. On receiving their assent he performs a sankalpam which when freely translated is as follows:—"I am determined to do puṇyāham in order to purify the garbhagṛha, the inner portion leading to the garbhagṛha, the pillars, the central space, the big entrance, gōpura, the prākara, the kitchen, the several maṇḍapams, vessels used in the kitchen and the materials secured for the yāgam to be performed in connexion with the pratishṭhā ceremony." (*See* Pl. IX-A.)

The puṇyāham ceremony is gone through and the puṇyāha water contained in the vessel is sprinkled over the places and the things mentioned above in the sankalpam. After the sprinkling of the puṇyāham water the Āchārya, Ṛtviks and a few others start in procession carrying along with them cchattra, chāmaram, an idol of Vishvaksēna or Garuḍa. If these idols are not available Chakrattāḷvār alone is taken. The procession is formed and they all proceed either towards the east or north to a place where there is an ant hill to secure mud. As soon as the procession starts the Brahmans begin the chanting of the Vedas and this is continued during the procession. The people that have started in procession go to a river side or a tank side, or temple side or hill side. On reaching the spot selected for the removal of mud the Āchārya does sankalpam as follows:—"Pratishṭhā karma siddhyartham mṛt sangraham karishyē (karishyāmi)."

After performing this sankalpam the Āchārya purifies himself by going through the bhūtaśuddhi and doing mental worship of God as fully as possible. Here puṇyāham (Vāsudēva puṇyāham as it is called) is done. He then sprinkles water repeating the astra mantra "Sahasrōlkāya svāhā" over the spot from which mud is taken. Then the "Khanitram" or the implement intended for digging the mud is also purified by sprinkling some water over it and repeating the Vishṇu Gāyatrī. Then Varāhamūrti along with Bhūmidēvī is invoked by chanting mantrams praising them and a figure of Varāhamūrti is drawn on the ground and is supposed to occupy the space on which this figure is drawn. The figure drawn on this space will vary according to the time of the day it is drawn. After drawing the figure of Varāhamūrti bhūsūktam is chanted over it, as this is intended to purify the figure. Finally Varāhamūrti is invoked and he is requested to occupy a seat and then are repeated gāyatrī, cchandas, bījāksharams, kavacham and the mantram. All upachārams such as giving arghya, pādya and āchamanīyam are done in the usual manner.

Mud is dug out and taken from the belly portion of the figure drawn on the ground. For the removal of mud the head of the figure drawn is not to be selected. It may be taken from the region of the hands and the breast. But the portion of the belly is considered to be the best. The mud thus dug out of the ground is placed in a new plate of bamboo and it is covered with a new cloth. While placing the mud in the plate mūla mantra (ashṭāksharam) is repeated. The parichāraka who carries the bamboo plate of mud is shown some mark of distinction by tying round his head a silk cloth and it is called "parivaṭṭam". He retains this parivaṭṭam till he reaches the temple. During the return procession Bhūsūktam, Śrīsūktam, Sakhanasūktam, and Vedas are chanted. When the ceremony is elaborately done this mud, instead of being carried by a man, may be placed in a tray and carried on in a pallakku (palanquin) or on an elephant if one is available. Sand and cowdung also are brought with pomp.

On returning to the temple the mud brought is kept on the floor in a prepared place. Sankalpam for the ankurārpaṇam ceremony is done once again. The Āchārya and the Ṛtviks dress themselves in new clothes. In the Mysore Provinces and in some of the British territory adjoining it, it is a custom to dip the new cloths in turmeric. Round about Madras and in the southern districts of the Presidency, the new cloth is not dipped in turmeric.

Eight pāligais were used for placing the seeds. By the side of these pāligais were placed eight small pots, whose mouths were closed by placing coconuts. Ordinarily the mouths of these kumbhams (pots) should be closed by using earthenware lids. (*See* Pl. VI–A.)

When this ceremony is done on an elaborate scale four doorways are established and decorated as already described under dīkshā ceremony. But at Lakshmipuram this part of the ceremony was simplified. Instead of having doorways made of the woods mentioned, two kambhams or posts for each of the cardinal points were placed and they represented the doorways and the devatās present in each of them.

After fixing the doorways fire is brought and put in the kuṇḍam or pit made for fire. Then Lakshmī is thought of and she is āvāhanamed. She is requested to be present by means of a prayer. Then Nārāyaṇa is invoked and he is believed to be present. Both are believed to be on the ādhārapīṭha. After this āvāhanam of Vishṇu and Lakshmi fire is put in the kuṇḍam and it is generally believed to have been produced by them. The details of the hōmam are dealt with here.

In the fire-pit fire is put repeating the Vyāhṛtimantra. Into this pit containing fire some fuel is placed repeating the " Astra mantra." By using a fan the fire is made to blaze and while using the fan "Vāyu mantra" is repeated. A good quantity of fire must be in the pit, so that it may not go out.

Round the fire-pit water is sprinkled very sparingly. Then Vāsudēva mantra is repeated and darbha is spread with its tip towards the north and east. Towards the north of the kuṇḍam darbhas are spread with their tips to the east, and on these vessels are placed upside down. On these darbhas the following are arranged in two rows:—ājyapātram (ghee vessel), charupātram (vessel containing food), prōkshaṇapātram, samit (fuel in a bundle), darbha, praṇīti rice, water in a vessel for making charu, prīti (a bundle of 20 palāsa samits), sruk, srāvam, darvi, fan, firewood, bell, sandal materials, and rice (coloured with turmeric). A kūrcha made of two darbha grasses of about one "Ottai" (span) in length is put in the praṇīti vessel turning it over. Then water is poured into it and into it some rice, akshata, is put. The praṇīti pātra is placed just in front of the Āchārya and then he puts in some akshata and pours in some quantity of water. Then the prōkshaṇa pātra is turned up and it is taken out and kept in his front. Into this prōkshaṇa pātra he pours water from the praṇīti vessel and places the kūrcha also on this. Then with kūrcha placed on this vessel with its tip towards the north he mixes up the water by using it thrice. Taking water with this he sprinkles it on the vessels kept upside down. Then he places the up-turned vessels in the same place with their mouths upwards. When these vessels are touched by the darbha their names should be said. Then he does parishēchanam repeating the mantra "Satyam tvartēna pari shinchāmi" round the Praṇīti vessel taking water from the Prōkshaṇa vessel. Then he fills the praṇīti vessel with fresh water, requests Vāsudēva to occupy this space and then worships Him. This cup or vessel is placed to the Īsānya side on a spread of darbha grass. On this cup he places a kūrcha made of three darbha grass blades and to the south of the fire a kūrcha made of 12 darbhas on the ground, requests Brahma to occupy this and does archana to him. Then he takes the charu vessel and cleans it repeating the Vishṇu gāyatrī. He puts into this vessel some quantity of rice repeating the "Chakra" mantra. In the same vessel he pours water and cleans the rice and then pouring sufficient amount of water cooks the rice. While the rice is being cooked "Sudarśana" mantra is repeated. Sometimes when the ceremony is done elaborately four vessels are used and then four different kinds of food are prepared in these vessels. These preparations are ordinary food in a vessel, pongal in dhanushkuṇḍam, pāyasam in the vṛttakuṇḍam, and guḍānnam in śrīkōṇakuṇḍam (ordinary food, pulse and rice cooked in the vessel deposited on a figure of bow and arrow, sweet water containing dhal, coconut and jaggery in a vessel placed over a circle and food cooked with jaggery in a vessel deposited on a triangular figure made on the earth).

The charu pot containing cooked rice is placed in the north and some amount of ghee is poured into the rice within the pot by means of a darbha. The vessel, Prokshaṇa" pātra is placed to the south of the fire place and water is poured into it. He takes the "Ājya pātra" (vessel intended for ghee) and places it in front on a darbha grass. He puts into it a kūrcha made of two darbha grasses and pours into it a quantity of melted ghee. To the north of this ghee vessel he has some bit of redhot stick or vraṭṭi and places the vessel of ghee over it and then transfers this to the original place. He takes two bits of darbha grass, turns them round the ghee vessel in the pradakshiṇa way and puts the darbha grass in the fire. Then he takes the apical tips of two grass blades and cleans them in water and puts them in the ghee vessel. He takes a darbha grass and burning its tip takes it round the ghee vessel thrice and then puts the darbha grass into the fire. Then he lifts the ghee vessel and places it to the north of the fire, and puts the stick or vraṭṭi having fire back into the fire in the fire space or pit. After putting the fire into the pit he removes the ghee vessel to the front. Then with the kūrcha he mixes the ghee, undoes the knot of the pavitra, and touching water places the pavitra darbhas with its apex to the east into the fire pit. He shows the surabhi mudra to the ghee vessel and considers the ghee as amṛta that has been brought down from the maṇḍala of the Moon. Repeating the kavacha mantra and with agniprākāra mudra he takes his hands round the ghee vessel. Ārādhana is done to Indra and other dēvatās who are the ashṭadikpālakas who are around the fire. He takes one after the other the "sruk" and "sruvam" and touches them with a kūrcha made up of 5 darbhas, first with the lower part, then the middle part and lastly with their tips. While touching the "sruk" and "sruvam" he repeats the astra mantra. Then he heats a little in the fire these two—sruk and sruvam. Then he sprinkles some water over them and places them in their proper places on the ground. He unties the kūrcha, touches with the darbha water,. and places the darbhas in fire with their tips to the east. With the sruvam he takes some amount of ghee and touches all the materials that are to be put in fire (hōma articles) and places the sruvam in its place. The bundle of samits (twenty in number) are then taken and five are placed as detailed below and the remaining fifteen are put in the fire. One stick is placed in the west repeating the "Śrīdhara" mantra, one in the south repeating the "Narasimha" mantra, one in the north repeating the "Hayagrīva" mantra, one after touching the stick placed in the west is placed in the āgnēya corner and another after touching the same stick in the west is placed in the īśānya corner. While placing these mantras appropriate to the dēvatās occupying the corners are repeated. The remaining fifteen sticks are placed in the fire at the same time taking permission from Brahma, and repeating the karma for which these samits are to be put in fire. Then tying a darbha to the left hand he takes the vessel of ghee in his left hand, and does the āhuti of food (placing in fire some quantity of prepared food). Instead of having in his left hand the vessel of ghee it is usually kept on the ground and the left hand is placed on it Then ghee is taken in sruvam and it is dropped down taking the sruvam from the nirṛti side to īśānam first and then across from the vāyavyam corner to āgnēya corner. The ghee falling must form a continuous line. While taking ghee and dropping it from the nirṛti to īsānam corner he repeats the Brahma mantra and repeating the Indra mantra drops the ghee from vāyu corner to the āgnēya corner. Then repeating the dhyāna mantra of agni, he thinks of agni ("Dviśiraskam, saptahastam, tripādam, sapta jihvākam, etc." is the mantra that is usually repeated).

Then śānti hōmam is done. This consists of doing hōmam sacrificing sesamum 108 times in the agnikuṇḍam. After this the garbhādānādi hōmasamskāram is done. This consists in offering ghee 15 times into the sacrificial fire. After doing the 108 āhutis of sesamum and before doing the ghee hōmam, the dvādaśākshara mantra is repeated and āvāhanam done.

After each offering of ghee a small quantity of it is secured and is placed in a separate vessel. The ghee thus secured from the sacrificial offerings is called "Sampātājyam" (ghee secured).

As soon as oblations of ghee are over sticks of *Butea frondosa*, of bilva, of *Ficus glomerata* or *F. religiosa* (any one of these) are offered, the number of sticks varying from 108 to 28, 12 or even 8 of any one of the above-mentioned ones. The placing of each stick in the fire must be accompanied by the repetition of the mūla mantram.

The "Sampātājyam" or the ghee secured from the ghee which was used as oblations is smeared to the pāligais repeating the sparśa mantram. Some quantity of this ghee is also sprinkled and mixed with the grains to be used in the pāligais. The moon is invoked and requested to be present in the seed-grains.

With the permission of the Vaidiki Brahmans assembled there for the occasion the Āchārya gives the grain to the Ṛtviks and receiving the same back from them he puts the grain into the pāligais beginning with the central one and ending with the Īśāna corner, proceeding clockwise. He repeats the "Oshadhi sūtram" while putting the grain in the pāligais first and then the dvādaśākshara mantram is chanted. After the seeds have been put in the pāligais by the Āchārya, the Ṛtviks and some Brahmans may also do the same thing, if they choose to do so and if time permits.

The seeds put in the pāligais are covered with mud and whilst placing the mud over the seeds in the pāligais the "Mūrdhāna mantram" is chanted. After this the pāligais are watered by the water found in the kumbham, repeating the mantram. "Imam mē varuṇa, etc." The mud is covered either by cowdung powder or leaves.

The kumudādigaṇas who are occupying the doorways are shown respect and they should be fed every day until the close of the pratishṭhā ceremony. A light (akhaṇḍam) must be kept burning throughout the period of this ceremonial.

During the ceremonial Brahmans continue their reading of Vedas, Purāṇas, Gīta Prabandhas, Rahasyams, etc. This may continue for 3 or 5 days according to the duration of the ceremony.

First Day.

The ceremony is begun with the usual purifying ceremony for "Puṇyāham." All the materials obtained for the panchagavya ceremony are sprinkled over with this puṇyāham water.

For the panchagavya stāpanam paddy is spread over the ground and it is covered with a cloth or a leaf of *Butea frondosa*. Over this cloth or leaf rice is spread and after covering it with a leaf or cloth sesamum seeds are spread over it. On the sesamum (or rice if only two kinds of grain are used) the five kalaśams are placed as shown below :—

1. Cow urine
2. Cowdung
3. Cow milk
4. Curds prepared from cow's milk
5. Ghee prepared from cow's milk

	2	
5	1	3
	4	

All the materials used are the products from the cow.

If the panchagavya is intended to be taken in by men or women for purification these five products are arranged in a different manner and it is shown below :—

	2	
5	1	3
	4	

1. Milk ;
2. Curds ;
3. Ghee ;
4. Cowdung ;
5. Cow's urine.

The arrangement is evidently different in this.

After arranging these five products as shown above the panchōpanishadanmantrama repeated and āvāhanam is done as shown below :—

1st Om shaum namaḥ parāya		(1st pot).
2nd Om yām	do.	(2nd „).
3rd Om rām	do.	(3rd „).
4th Om lām	do.	(4th „).
5th Om vām	do.	(5th „).

Arghyam, pādyam and āchamaniyam are given as upachārams and they are worshipped :—

(1) At first he repeats the Vishnu gāyatrī and sprinkles over the idols to be established cow's urine.

(2) Repeating the mantram " Gandhadvārām " he sprinkles over the idols cowdung.

(3) Repeating the mantram "Āpyāyasvēti " he sprinkles over the idols milk.

(4) Chanting the mantram " Dadhikrāviṇṇō " he sprinkles over the idols curds.

(5) Chanting the mantram " Śukramasīti " he sprinkles over the idols ghee.

All the above purifications are carried out only after cleaning the vigrahas properly with water. During this cleaning process the usual mantra that is repeated is " Ashṭākshari."

The next item of the day is the performance of the śāntihōmam. This hōmam is done to purify and remove the evils of the idol prepared by the Śilpi. Repeating the sapta vyāhṛti mantram a mixture of rice and leaves of śami tree is offered as offerings in the fire. Each vyāhṛti has to be repeated 100 times and as many āhutis have to be made. So in all four hundred āhutis are made with the repetition of the vyāhṛti mantram. This hōmam is followed by another hōmam in which sixteen oblations of "Charu" or cooked rice are offered with the chanting of Purusha Sūkta. This hōmam is usually performed in close proximity to the idol.

After this hōmam " Panchōpanishad " mantram is repeated and 108 āhutis are made. Then pūrṇāhuti is put in this sacrificial fire and finally the fire is asked to leave the kuṇḍam (Udvāsanam). Then God is praised by repeating " Namastubhyam bhagavatē jātavēdasvarūpiṇē . . . pratimāyām hitāyāvaha." Then repeating the mūla mantram, darbha and a cloth are waved round. The cloth is placed over the idol and upachārams are done.

Now pratisarabandhana (wrist thread tying) is proceeded with. The tying of the wrist thread is done for the Vigrahas, Āchāryas and the Ṛtviks. On a spread of rice, threads, dyed yellow with turmeric paste, and as many coconuts as there are threads are placed. Close to them are also placed betel leaves, areca nuts, flowers and fruits. A new cloth also is deposited there. All these things are sprinkled over the puṇyāham water. Soon after depositing the threads and other things described above, " Ahṭa mantra " is repeated over the thread and then " The sudarśana " mantram is repeated one hundred times. After this a small quantity of sandal is taken and it is smeared to the threads with the thumb and the index finger. Next these threads are placed on the coconuts, one on each. Then Ananta is invoked and he is requested to occupy the threads. One of those threads is taken and it is tied to the wrist of the right hand of the vigraha of God. The thread is tied to the left hand in the case of the image of the Goddess. While tying the wrist thread to the right hand of God " The mūla mantram " is repeated and while doing the same to the left wrist of the Goddess " Śrī mantram " is repeated. Rakshai is done to these pratisaras tied to the hands of the two Vigrahas by repeating " Brihat sāmam." The Āchārya and Ṛtviks tie the threads to their right wrists repeating the Vishṇu gāyatrī.

To the utsava bimbam (new vigraha), pīṭha samyōjana hōmam was performed. On the ground paddy was spread and covering it with a cloth rice was spread over this. Over this a cloth was laid and sesamum was spread on it. A figure of padmam was drawn in the sesamum and a darbha was laid on it. Over this spread of sesamum a new cloth was thrown and the vigrahas were placed on this new cloth. Then agnipratishṭhai was done as already described. All the processes are repeated till the "Charu" hômam. Then puṇyāham is performed and this puṇyāham water is sprinkled over the new vigrahas. Then the vigrahas are placed on their pīṭhams and after making the pūrṇāhuti, agni (fire) is udvāsanamed (removed after the usual prayer).

Jalādhivāsam ceremony is next performed. For this ceremony of immersion the vigrahas are taken in procession to a river or tank when they are available. In the absence of good tanks, lakes, rivers, large vessels filled with water are used. In the pratisṭhā ceremony done at Lakshmipuram large vessels were used. (See pl. V-B.) For the same ceremony at Kangundi the vigrahas were taken in procession to an adjoining river.

For this ceremony close to the water in a river-bed or tank a pandal supported by 16 pillars is erected with four doorways towards the directions east, south, west and north. Within this maṇḍapam incense should be burnt constantly so that the smoke of the incense may be found everywhere in the pandal. The vigrahas are placed in a suitable place under the pandal and the Āchārya sits facing east or north and does the usual sankalpam for the usual jalādhivāsam ceremony.

In both the places Kangundi and Lakshmipuram there was no pandal erected over them. In the case of Kangundi the vigrahas were taken to the river for jalādhivāsam and in Lakshmipuram water was kept in big vessels in the temple compound itself for this purpose.

Close to the place where the vigrahas are immersed and to the south of them in a space ten kalaśams are placed. This is known as daśakalaśasthāpanam, as eight kalaśams are placed, one for each dik, one mahākumbham and one karagam. After cleaning and purifying the ten kalaśams in the usual manner, they are arranged as detailed below on a spread of paddy or rice.

In the place selected for kalaśasthāpana, in the centre, a pot is placed. This represents Brahma and to the south of this a karagam or small pot is placed to represent Sudarśana. Around these two pots are arranged the remaining eight pots and they represent the cardinal points. The pot placed in the eastern side represents Indra, the south-east pot Agni, the southern pot Yama, the south-west pot Nirṛti, the western one Varuṇa, the north-western Vāyu, the northern one Kubēra, and the north-eastern one Īśānam respectively. Rakshai is done to all these kalaśams or pots by repeating the "Rakshōghna mantra" and the "Agni prakaraṇa mudra" is presented to these pots.

The vigrahas in the best of circumstances ought to be under water for three days for the jalādhivāsam ceremony. At Kangundi for the jalādhivāsam a river was selected and the vigrahas were taken to the river side and the whole ceremony of jalādhivāsam was done there. At Lakshmipuram ordinary metallic vessels of large size were used. They were filled with water and the vigrahas were immersed in it and the ceremonial was gone through.

Before actually placing the vigrahas in water, puṇyāham is done in the beginning. The water ot puṇyāham is sprinkled over the idols and the water, tank or vessel is also subjected to the same sprinkling of this water. For the water in the vessel or tank or river, śōshana, dāhana and plāvanam are done. Then the holy waters Ganges, Yamunā, Sarasvatī, and Kāv rī are invoked and are requested to be present in the water to be used for jalādhivāsam. Then the Āchārya has to imagine a pīṭham to lie in the water. He then invokes the 32 dēvatās of the ādhāra pīṭhams and requests them to be present in the pīṭham. Then archana is done to the dēvatās, of course only mentally. The gaṇas in the door way are also worshipped. Afterwards the Āchārya with the assistance of the Brahmans present lifts the Vigrahas and immerses them in the water repeating the "Śākuna Sūtram". The face of the vigraha is turned towards the north and its head towards the east. After placing the idols in water Chakra Mudra is shown.

The Vigrahas are allowed to remain under water for three days only when the pratishṭha ceremony is celebrated on an elaborate scale. In cases where this ceremonial period is shortened the jalādhivāsam ceremony has to be done on a less expensive scale, in one night, one muhūrtam or even in half of a muhūrtam. At Kangundi and Lakshmipuram the immersion of the vigraha was only for a muhūrtam.

The water in which the vigrahas are steeped is considered sacred and no one may touch the water as long as the images lie in the water. The vigrahas are lifted from the water and then abhishēkam is done with milk, curds, and water. After abhishēkam the usual upachārams are shown to the vigrahas.

Second Day.

This day panchāmṛta sthāpanam is begun and tatva hōmam is the last item of this day.

The ceremonies are begun with the panchāmṛta abhishēkam. Then Vāstu hōmam is done, as detailed below. A figure of Vāstu purusha is drawn by kōlam in the īśāna side of the maṇḍapam. The figure is drawn head east-ward, right hand āgnēyam, left hand īśānyam, right leg nirṛti, and left leg vāyavyam. This figure, whose face is downward, is worshipped. On the back of this figure a kūrcham of seven darbhas was placed, puṇyāham was done and the puṇyāham water was sprinkled over the figure. Then prāṇapratishṭhai is done for the figure drawn and he is worshipped as "Kshētranāthan." On the head of the figure Amśumālī is believed to be present and he is worshipped after calling him and requesting him to occupy the space. Jashadhvajans are invoked and they are requested to occupy the two shoulders; Kumāran is invoked and he is to occupy the joints and front part of the arms; Vināyaka is invoked and he is to occupy the arms of the hand; Aśvini dēvas are invoked and they occupy the feet; the Moon is invoked and he occupies the waist; Durgā is invoked and she occupies the palms; the Seven mothers are invoked and they occupy the sides of the body; the chest is occupied by Rudra who is invoked; Vishṇu is invoked and he occupies the heart;

Brahma is invoked and he remains in the nābhi; Indra, Agni, Yama, Nirṛti, Varuṇa, Vāyu, Kubēra and Īśānan are invoked and are requested to occupy the eight corners of the compass.

Kshētranāthan is āvāhanamed to the north of the above dēvatās. (Kalaśams may be used for these digdēvatās and Kshētranāthan.)

To the west of the Vāstu purusha figure drawn on the floor Vāstu hōmam is done. Agni is made as usual and repeating the "Panchōpanishada mantram" 1,000 or 100 āhutis of ghee (pourings of ghee) are made. Then eight sticks each, of śami, apamarga (*i.e.*, Nāyurivi) and Kadira are put in fire as āhutis. After this "Charu" (cooked rice) hōmam of 16 offerings are made repeating the purusha sūkta. Finally āhutis for all the dēvatās (one āhuti for each dēvatā) named above are made in the fire. Then food is given to kshētranāthan and he is worshipped. The fire is then (udvāsanamed) requested to leave the place and it is disturbed a little.

Nayanōnmilanam or the ceremony of opening the eyes of the vigrahas is performed. For this ceremony a beginning is made by the spread of paddy, rice and sesamum one over the other, separating them either with new cloths or Butea leaf-platters. Sesamum is on the top and on it two cups, preferably one of gold and another of silver are placed. But generally they use only silver cups and so both are of silver. If money is not available for silver cups leaf cups are used instead. In case leaf cups are used, they are generally of the leaves of *Butea frondosa*. Both at Kangundi and Lakshmipuram Butea leaf cups were used. One of the cups is filled with honey and the other with ghee. In both small sticks of silver were placed, one in each. The two cups were covered with a new cloth after sprinkling them with puṇyāham water. After covering these cups with cloth, it was also sprinkled with this water. Sun and Moon are then invoked and they are requested to occupy the two cups containing honey and ghee, respectively. Afterwards the usual sixteen upachārams beginning with "Arghya" are gone through.

The honey in the cup is sanctified by repeating the mantram "Madhuvāteti" and the ghee by the mantram "Śukramasi". Then taking the stick from the cup containing honey, it is again dipped in the cup so as to immerse it in the honey. When the stick is lifted some quantity of honey sticks on to it. With this honey on the stick the right eye is smeared repeating the mantram "Chitram dēvānām". Then the left eye is smeared with ghee with the silver stick repeating the mantram "Tacchakshuriti". During this process of opening the eyes a screen is put across so that people assembled in front may not see the process when it is done. As soon as the screen is removed a cow, a kanyakā and nine kinds of grains are to be seen by the vigrahas. At Kangundi, the cow and the grains were shown and the cow was given away to the Āchārya. At Lakshmipuram the cow was not given, but some money was given in its stead.

After the ceremony of Nayanōnmīlanam mṛttikā snānam was gone through. At first mud brought from an ant-hill was smeared and washed. Then mud taken from the place where the tulasi plant is growing was used. The mṛttikā snānam was followed by the ordinary abhishēkam using ordinary water. Then the upachārams followed Close to the vigrahas to the east kalaśams (9 or 17) are usually placed and worshipped.

Saptadaś kalaśa sthāpanam.—Seventeen kalaśams (pots) were arranged as detailed below. As usual paddy, rice and sesamum are spread one above the other separating them by cloths or leaf-platters. The seventeen kalaśams that are to be established over the spread of grains are cleaned with pure water repeating the Vishṇu gāyatrī and the threads are then passed round the pots repeating the mantram "Indram natēti". The space between the threads should be either ½ inch or 1 inch and not more. Close to the settle of grains darbhas with their tips towards the east are spread and the kalaśams are placed on them inverted, *i.e.*, upside down. Over this praṇava mantra is repeated. Then repeating the Panchōpanishad mantram the pots are placed properly, *i.e.*, turning them up. Rice is then thrown over these pots.

The usual sacrificial fire is made in the pit or kuṇḍam and 108 āhutis of ghee are made in this fire repeating the "Vishṇu gāyatrī". While doing these āhutis ghee must be secured from the āhutis. The ghee thus secured is called "sampatājyam". The seventeen pots are arranged as shown below in the diagram after filling them with the appropriate liquid as detailed below :—

17 Kashāya.		10 Pādyam water.		14 Curds.
	9 Wheat and water.	2 Hot-water.	6 Ratnam and water.	
13 Panchagavya.	5 Rice and water.	1 Ghṛta kalasam (ghee pot).	3 Fruits and water.	11 Arghyam water.
	8 Sandal and water.	4 Roots and water (Mārjanōdakam).	7 Metal and water.	
16 Honey.		12 Āchamanam water.		15 Milk.

The numbers indicate the places where the pots are to be deposited and filled in. The materials for filling the pots are given below :—

(1) In the centre is placed the pot filled with ghee with a kūrcham made up of 27 darbha grass blades. *Vāsudēva* is invoked and he is requested to occupy the kalaśam.

(2) A pot is filled with hot water and it is placed towards the east of No. 1. A kūrcham of 3 or 5 darbha grass blades is put in. *Purusha* is invoked and he is requested to occupy the pot.

(3) A pot is filled with water and fruits and it is placed towards the south of No. 1. A kūrcham of 3 or 5 darbhas is put in. *Satyar* is invoked and he is requested to occupy the pot.

(4) A pot is filled with water and roots and it is placed to the west of No. 1. A kūrcham of 3 or 5 darbhas is also placed in it. *Achyutar* is invoked and he is requested to occupy the pot.

(5) A pot is filled with rice and water and it is placed to the north of No. 1. A kūrcham of 3 to 5 darbhas is placed in it. *Anantar* is invoked and he is requested to occupy the place.

(6) A pot is placed in the āgnēyam corner (south-east corner) filling it with water and some precious stone, preferably a ratna is put in. *Kēśava* is invoked and he is requested to occupy the place.

(7) A pot is placed in the nirṛti corner (south-west) and it is usually filled with water and some gold is put in. A kūrcha of 3 to 5 darbhas is also put in. *Nārāyaṇa* is invoked and he is requested to occupy the place.

(8) A pot is placed in the Vāyu corner (north-west) and it is usually filled with sandal and water. A kūrcha of 3 to 5 darbhas is also put in it. *Mādhava* is invoked and is requested to occupy the place.

(9) A pot filled with water in which a small quantity of wheat is put is placed in the Iśānya or north-east corner. A kūrcha of 3 to 5 darbhas is placed in it. *Gōvinda* is invoked and he is requested to occupy the place.

(10) A pot is filled with water and tulasi, bilvam, rice and lotus petals are dropped into it. A kūrcha of 3 to 5 darbhas is put in it. *Vishṇu* is invoked and he is requested to occupy the place.

(11) A pot is filled with water and after putting in it tips of darbha grass, flowers, gingelly and sandal water it is deposited towards the south. After putting in the kūrcham of darbha, *Madhusūdana* is invoked and he occupies the place.

(12) A pot is filled with water and takkolam, champaka and vakuḷa flowers, camphor, sandal and jajipal are dropped into the water. The usual kūrcha of 3 or 5 darbhas is also put in. It is placed in the west. God *Trivikrama* is invoked and he is requested to occupy the place.

(13) A pot is filled with water and in it are poured curds and a small quantity of panchagavyam. The usual kūrcham is put in. It is placed in the north. *Vāmana* is invoked and he is requested to occupy the place.

(14) A pot is filled with water and in it are poured curds and the usual darbha kūrcha is put in. The pot is placed in the south-east corner (Āgnēya) Then *Śrīdhara* is invoked and he is requested to be present in the place.

(15) A pot is filled with milk and water and the usual kūrcham is dropped in and it is placed in the south-west corner, *i.e.*, nirṛti. *Hṛshikēśa* is invoked and requested to occupy the place.

(16) A pot is filled with water and honey is poured into the pot and the usual kūrcha is put in. It is deposited in the north-west corner or Vāyu corner. *Padmanābha* is invoked and he is requested to occupy the place.

(17) A pot is filled with water and a kāshayam is poured into it. Then sami, nyagrodham, and aśvatham juices are poured into the water. Darbha kūrcha is also put in. This is placed in the north-east corner. *Dāmōdara* is invoked and he is requested to occupy the place.

Sometimes this ceremony is simplified by the use of only nine kalaśams, as was done at Lakshmipuram and Kangundi. The pots are placed as shown below and the filling is also shown :—(See Pl. VI-B).

9	2	6
5	1	3
8	4	7

(1) Madhyakalaśam with jaggery water—Vāsudēva.
(2) East—milk—Vāsudēva.
(3) South—curds—Sankarshana.
(4) West—ghee—Pradyumna.
(5) North—honey— Aniruddha.
(6) Āgnēya—arghya water—Śriyai namaḥ.
(7) Nairṛti—pādyam water—Pitur.
(8) Vāyavyam—Āchamanam—Vāgīśar.
(9) Īśānam—Snānīyam—Varuṇa.

The contents are dealt with as in the case of 17 kalaśams.

All are used for abhishēkam after taking out from the Jalādhivāsam, one after the other.

Round the central kalaśam a new cloth is wrapped and upachārams are done to it. Ghee oblations are made seventeen times, repeating the mūla mantra with every āhuti. Cooked food is offered sixteen times repeating the purusha sūktam. All the kalaśams are touched with Sampātājyam. The sacrificial offerings are closed by giving the Pūrṇāhuti of cooked rice and then udvāsanam to agni is done.

Then coming near the vigrahas and repeating the mantra "Uttishṭhēti" they are removed to the Snāna pīṭha. With the mud secured from the bed of a holy river and sprinkled over with puṇyāham water the Vigraha is smeared 21 times. While smearing the mud over the body of the vigrahas the mantra "Mūrdhāna vidhi" is repeated. The vigrahas are to be smeared with the mud from head to feet. After smearing 21 times with this mud they are bathed in clean water repeating the mantra "Imammē Varuṇa." Then the usual upachārams are shown Afterwards upachārams are shown to the kalaśams and one by one the pots are taken and the contents are used for abhishēkam. At first the pādyam water (when 17 pots are used) is poured repeating the mantra "Idam Vishṇu." Then arghyam water is poured repeating the mantra "Āpōhishṭhāma yōbhuvaḥ." Next āchamanam water is used repeating the mantra "Imammē

Varuṇa." This is followed by the panchagavya water and the mantra repeated is "Pavitramiti." Afterwards the pot with curds is used and the mantra chanted is "Dadhikrāviṇṇō." Subsequent to this the pot containing milk is utilised and the mantra repeated is "Payōvrithow." Next honey is utilised and the mantra repeated is "Madhuvātāritā." Then the kāshāyam vessel is used and the mantra repeated is "Yajña Yajñēti." The hot water is then used and the mantra repeated is "Mānastōkēti." The next vessel to be used is the one containing ratnam and water and the mantra to be used is "Vashaṭ tē Vishṇō." After this the pot containing fruits and water is used and then is repeated the mantra "Palinīti" The next vessel containing metal and water is taken and used. The mantra repeated is "Hiraṇyagarbha." The vessel containing mārjanōdakam is taken and its contents are used. The mantra to be repeated is "Śannōdēvī" After this the pot containing sandal and water is used and then the mantra chanted is "Gandhadvārēti." The vessel containing water and rice is next used and the mantra to be repeated is "Tratara." The pot containing water and wheat is next taken and used. The mantra repeated then is "Idam Vishṇu." Lastly the central pot containing ghee and water is used and the mantra used is "Ghṛtam snānēti."

When only nine pots are used the arrangement is to use arghya, pādya, āchamanīyam first and then milk, curds, ghee and honey and lastly the central one. The mantras repeated after each operation is the same as above corresponding to the material used.

The next item is *Śayyādhivāsam* or *Bimbādhivāsam*. On the vēdikai a suitable place is selected for placing a cot and this space is sprinkled with water repeating the dvādaśākshara mantram. On the space selected darbha grass with their apices to the east or north is placed. On this paddy is spread. Over the paddy rice and sesamum are spread in the usual way separating them from one another by means of cloths. When the ceremony is done on a large scale at least one khaṇḍagam of paddy should be spread. Over this rice about ½ a khaṇḍagam is to be spread and ¼ of a khaṇḍagam of sesamum over this. If available a tiger skin is used to cover the sesamum. If this is not available a good ratnakambali or a good silk cloth or cotton cloth is spread over it. Over this cloth covering the sesamum, other cloths variously decorated are put on. On the cloths a mattress, if available, is put on and it is covered with a cloth. The coverings over the sesamum is regulated according to the money available. Over this sesamum covered variously, according to the money available, a cot made of good wood and measuring at least 4 feet is placed. On this cot mattress, cloths and pillows are placed in the usual manner. At Lakshmipuram the cot was placed over a settle of paddy covered with a cloth. No mattress was used over the paddy. When the ceremony is performed on a smaller scale, the covering of the grains with mattress, cloths, blankets and silk is dispensed with (See Pl. V-A, VIII-A.)

Then ārādhana is done to God (this is called yōga pīṭha ārādhanam). Then the vigrahas are taken round the cot once and then they are placed on the cot in a lying posture.. At this time Purusha sūkta and other Vedic ṛks are chanted and mangaḷa vādyams are played. While taking the vigrahas round the cot the mantra "Uttishṭhēti" is repeated. The vigrahas are usually placed in a lying posture. The head of the vigraha is to be turned to the east or towards the sannadhi side repeating the mantra "Idam Vishṇu" and "Viśvataśchakshuḥ" mantras. The vigrahas are covered with a silk cloth and then the mantra "Yuvāsu vāsa" is repeated.

After doing these to the Vigrahas, the four doorways are attended to. The Gods, etc., believed to occupy the places are worshipped. At Lakshmipuram the ceremony was very much simplified, by representing the doorways, etc., by Kalaśams, two for each direction. The wooden posts were merely imagined to have been set up.

(1) The eastern doorway is made of the wood of *Ficus religiosa* or pipal tree (Aśvatham tree).

Pūrvadvārē, Ṛgrūpam, suśōbhanam āvāhayāmi. (The eastern door represents the Ṛg Veda and Suśōbhanar is requested to be present.) "Aśvattha tōraṇē Indrāya namaḥ" is repeated and āvāhanam is done.

(2) The southern doorway is made of the wood of *Ficus glomerata.*

Dakshiṇadvārē Yajur rūpinam Subhadrakam āvāhayāmi. (The southern doorway represents the Yajur Veda and Subhadraka is requested to be present and worshipped.)

"Audumbara tōraṇē Yamāya namaḥ" is repeated and āvāhanam is done.

(3) The western doorway is made of the wood of *Ficus bengalensis.*

"Paśchimadvārē, sāmarūpiṇē, sambandhavē namaḥ." (The western doorway represents the Sāma Veda and Sambandha is requested to be present.)

"Nyagrōdha toraṇē Varuṇāya namaḥ" is repeated and āvāhanam is done.

(4) The northern doorway is made of the wood of *Ficus tsiela.*

"Uttaradvārē atharvaṇa rūpinam suhōtrakam āvāhayāmi. (The northern doorway represents the Atharva veda and Suhōtraka is requested to be present.)

"Plakshaja tōraṇē Kubērāya namaḥ" is repeated.

The flags and pots on these doorways are also worshipped as already described under ankurārpaṇam ceremony under Dīkshai. Eight flags are used in regular doorways as shown below:—

(1) East—Two red flags are tied to the eastern doorway and they are called *Kumuda* and *Kumudāksha.* The pots are occupied by *Pūrṇa* and *Pushkara.*

(2) South—Two green flags are tied to the southern doorway and they are called *Puṇḍarika* and *Vāmana.* The pots are occupied by *Ananda* and *Nandana.*

(3) West—Two blue flags tied to the western doorway and they are called *Sankukarṇa* and *Sarpanētra.* The pots are occupied by *Vīrasēna* and *Susēna.*

(4) North—Two white flags are tied to the northern doorway and they are styled *Sumukha* and *Supratishṭhita.* The pots are occupied by *Sambhava* and *Prabhava.*

After doing the ārādhana to these things Chakrābaja Maṇḍala is worshipped as detailed below. The Chakrābja Maṇḍala Vēdikai should be to the north of the chief vēdikai on which the cot and the nine pots are placed.

The central part of the floor is called the Yōgapīṭham. The worshipping of this part is called the yogapīṭha ārādhanam. God Nārāyaṇa is requested to occupy the place.

He is believed to be in the forms Para, Vyuha, Vibhava, Antaryāmi and Maṇḍala (Vāsudēva). He is worshipped, by giving him arghya, pādya and āchamanīyam and he is prayed to.

In the staminal part of the floral diagram Lakshmī, Earth, Sarasvatī, Rati, Prīti Kīrti, Śānti, Tushṭi, and Pushṭi are āvāhanamed and worshipped.

In the petals of the row near the stamens the Śaktis named below are invoked and are worshipped. The Śaktis invoked are Śrīvatsam, Pūrṇakumbham, Bhēri, Darpaṇamaṇḍalam, Matsya yugmam, Pānchajanyam, Chakram and Garuḍa.

In the dalānta valayam Vyāpti, Śānti, are āvāhanamed and worshipped.

In the Nābhi part Vishṇu is āvāhanamed and worshipped.

In the Arakshētra the dēvadāsādi mūrtis (*viz.*, Vishṇu, Madhusūdana, Trivikrama, Vāmana, Śrīdhara, Hṛshīkēśa, Padmanābha, Dāmōdara, Kēśava, Nārāyaṇa, Mādhava and Gōvinda) are requested to be presented and they are worshipped.

In the Anantavalayam the twelve Matsyādi Mūrtis (*viz.*, Matsya, Kūrma, Varāha, Nārasimha, Vāmana, Paraśurāma, Śrī Rāma, Bala Rāma, Kṛshṇa and Kalki) and the eight arms—Chakra, Śankha, Gada, Padma, Musala, Khaḍga, Sāṛngam, and Chāpam—are āvāhanamed and worshipped.

In the first square on the Āgnēya corner Varāgar is invoked to be present, in the nirṛti corner Narasimha, in the vāyavyam Anantar and in the Īśānyam Hayagrīva are invoked. They are worshipped.

In the Vēdikai the eight Indrādi lōkapālakas are invoked to be present. They are Indra, Agni, Yama, Nirṛti, Varuṇa, Vāyu, Kubēra and Īśāna in their places and they are worshipped.

In the four doorways, towards the east Chanḍan and Prachanḍan, towards the south Dhāta and Vidhāta, west Jaya and Vijaya and north Bhadra and Subhadrakan are invoked and they are worshipped.

In the Vēdikai in the Īśāna side Vishvaksēnar is invoked and is requested to occupy the place.

Lastly just in front of the eastern doorway Garuḍa is requested to be present, in the southern side in front of the door Sudarśana is requested to be present, in the west Gada is requested to be present and in the north Śankham is requested.

The *Mūrtikumbhasthāpanam* or the *Mahākumbhasthāpanam* is then done. For this a small quantity of paddy is spread and on it nine kalaśams, one being a large one, are placed after cleaning them in the usual manner. All these vessels are wound round externally with cotton thread and decorated with sandal and turmeric paste, flowers akshata, ūrdhvapuṇḍram. All the vessels are filled with pure water and into each vessel are dropped precious stones or coins if precious stones are not available.

The larger vessel is placed in the centre and it is the most important kumbham. It is called the maha or mūrtikumbham. Into this kumbham is poured water scented with sandal paste, and into it is dropped a small silver pratimā of the mūrti. By the side of this mahākumbham a small pot or karagam is placed. By the side of this mahākumbham, if available, a small wooden tablet in which are engraved the āyudhas of Vishṇu is placed.

The water in the central pot is subjected to the processes of śōshaṇa, dahana and plāvana processes, and then God who is present in the hṛtkamalam is requested to occupy this mahākumbham. While invoking God the mūla mantra is repeated. Then the mudras of āvāhana, sammukhīkaraṇa and prārthanā are shown to the kumbham or pot. This central pot is generally covered with two new cloths. Then the usual upachārams of arghya, etc., are gone through. The karagam or smaller pot is usually kept to the south of the bigger pot or kumbham. Into this karagam or smaller pot Sudarśana is āvāhanamed (that is to say Sudarśana is requested to occupy this karagam). After doing the usual upachārams the chakra mudra is presented to the karagam.

In the remaining 8 kalaśams several mūrtis are āvāhanamed (that is they are invoked and requested to occupy the place). Beginning with the east the kalaśams are placed and the mūrtis āvāhanamed and they are placed on the paddy spread on the ground one by one. The mūrtis āvāhanamed in the pots are respectively Vishṇu, Madhusūdana, Trivikrama, Vāmana, Śrīdhara, Hṛshīkēśa, Padmanābha and Dāmōdara. After requesting the abovementioned mūrtis one by one in each of the pots, they are arranged respectively beginning with the east, then south-east, south and south-west, etc., to the north-east. There are eight mūrtis occupying each a direction of the compass.

Before the establishment of these pots on the spread of paddy, fire is kindled in the pit and hōmam with ghee is made in the usual way. Then the usual hōmams with samit, charu and sesamum are performed. This agni (fire) is considered to be *divāgni.*

Then the pots are placed properly in their places as are already described. The Āchārya after placing the pots, sits near the Vigrahas and goes through the śṛshṭi, samhāra, and śṛshṭi nyāsas on his own body and then begins to perform the tatva hōmam.

The tatva hōmam being an important one it is never shortened or left out. There are 25 tatvams represented by the consonants of the Sanskrit alphabet. For each tatva eight āhutis of ghee are made. (18, 28 āhutis also can be made if a large quantity of ghee is available.) After each oblation of ghee sampātājyam is secured and this is used in smearing it over the appropriate places of the Vigraha, when the āhutis of ghee are over for the particular tatva. While touching the part the name of the dēva is pronounced adding to it the word "Namaḥ." The mantras of tatva hōmam are given below in the order in which the hōmam has to be done with the proper ceremonial actions:—

(1) 8 (Ma)—Makāraya spaṭikā bhāsāya jīvatatvāya svāhā (saying the above mantra pour the ghee into the fire.) Jīva tatvātmane namaḥ. Touch the heart with sampātājyam after pouring the ghee oblations eight times (or 28 times or 108 times) according to the availability of ghee and time.

(2) ഭ—Bhakārāya sitavarṇāya prakṛti tatvāya svāhā (pour the ghee) prakṛuti tatvāya namaḥ. Touch the heart with the sampātājyam (ghee).

(3) ബ—Bakārāya spaṭikābāsāya buddhi tatvāvasvāhā (pour ghee) buddhi tatvātmanē namaḥ—touch the heart.

(4) ഫ—Phakārāya ahaṁkārāya pāṭalabhāya svāhā (pour ghee) ahaṁkāra tatvāya namaḥ—touch the heart.

(5) പ—Pakārāya sitavarṇāya manasē svāhā (pour ghee) manasē namaḥ—touch the heart.

(6) ന—Nakārāya śukla varṇāya saptatanmātrātmanē svāhā (pour the ghee) saptatanmātrē tanmatrātmanē namaḥ—touch the ears.

(7) ധ—Dhakārāya lōhita varṇāya sparśatanmātrātmanē svāhā (pour ghee)—sparśa tanmātrātmanē namaḥ—touch the skin.

(8) ദ—Dakārāya jyōtirmayāya rūpatanmātratmanē svāhā (pour ghee)—rūpatanmātrātmanē namaḥ—touch the eyes.

(9) ഥ—Thakārāya pāṇḍarābhāya rasatanmātrātmanē svāhā (pour ghee)—rasatanmātrātmanē namaḥ—touch the cheeks.

(10) ത—Takārāya asitavarṇāya gandhatanmātrātmanē svāhā (pour ghee)—gandhatanmātrē namaḥ—touch the nose.

(11) ണ—Ṇakārāya pāṭalavarṇāya śrōtrātmanē svāhā (pour ghee) śrotrātmanē namaḥ—touch the ears.

(12) ഢ—Ḍhakārāya hēmavarṇāya tvagātmanē svāhā (pour ghee) tvagātmanē namaḥ—touch the skin.

(13) ഡ—Ḍakārāya kṛshṇavarṇāya dṛgātmanē svāhā (pour ghee) dṛgātmanē namaḥ—touch the eyes.

(14) ഠ—Ṭhakārāya gauravarṇāya jīvātmanē svāhā (pour ghee)—jīvātmane namaḥ—touch the tongue.

(15) ട—Ṭakārāya asitavarṇāya ghrāṇēndriyātmanē svāhā (pour ghee)—ghrāṇēndriyātmanē namaḥ—touch the nose.

(16) ഞ—Ñakārāya sitavarṇāya vāgātmanē svāhā (pour ghee)—vāgātmanē namaḥ—touch the mouth.

(17) ഝ—Jhakārāya raktavarṇāya pāṇyātmanē svāhā (pour ghee)—pāṇyātmanē namaḥ—touch the hands.

(18) ജ—Jakārāya raktavarṇāya pādātmanē svāhā (pour ghee) pādātmanē namaḥ—touch the feet.

(19) ഛ—Cchakārāya raktavarṇāya pāyuvātmanē svāhā (pour ghee)—pāyuvātmanē namāḥ—touch the thighs.

(20) ച—Chakārāya hêmavarnāya mēhanātmanē svāhā (pour ghee) mēhanātmanē namaḥ—touch the secret parts.

(21) ങ—Ṅakārāya chaturaśrāya pītābhāya prithvītatvātmanē svāhā (pour ghee tatvātmanē namaḥ—touch from knee to feet.

(22) ఘ—Ghakārāya śvētābhāya ardhachandrākārāya aptatvātmanē svāhā (pour ghee)—aptatvātmanē namaḥ—touch knee to navel.

(23) గ—Gakārāya lōhitavarṇāya trikōṇakāṇāya tējastatvātmanē svāha (pour ghee)—tējastatvātmanē namaḥ—touch navel to heart.

(24) ఖ—Khakārāya dhūmravarṇāya vēdikākārāya vāyvātmanē svāhā (pour ghee)—vāyvātmanē namāḥ—touch heart to septum of nose (between the holes of the nose).

(25) క—Kakārāya anjananābhāya nirākārāya ākāśatatvātmanē svāhā (pour ghee)—ākāśatatvātmanē namaḥ—touch from nose to the head.

Third Day.

This ceremonial is followed by the Prāṇadi daśa vāyu nyāsa. The various parts of the Vigraha are touched pronouncing the appropriate mantrams as shown below:—

(1) Ōm namaḥ parāya prāṇāya svāhā—nose to head is touched.
(2) Ōm namaḥ parāya apānāya svāhā—nose to head is touched.
(3) Ōm namaḥ parāya vyānāya svāhā—head to tongue is touched.
(4) Ōm namaḥ parāya udānāya svāhā—head to left eye is touched.
(5) Ōm namaḥ parāya samānāya svāhā—head to right eye is touched.
(6) Ōm namaḥ parāya nāgāya svāhā—left head to left ear is touched.
(7) Ōm namaḥ parāya kūrmāya svāhā—right head to right ear is touched.
(8) Ōm namaḥ parāya krikarāya svaha—knee to thigh is touched.
(9) Ōm namaḥ parāya dēvadattāya svāhā—thigh to secret parts are touched.
(10) Ōm namaḥ parāya dhanañjayāya svāhā—foot to knee is touched.

After this nyāsá the Āchārya does the nyāsa on himself as detailed below. This is only a preliminary stage to prāṇa pratishṭhā hōmam.

1. Aum bījam	...	Hrām Hrim Krōm	ka, kha, ga, gha, ṅa—prithvi, ap, tējas, vāyu, and ākāśam—touch with the thumb the heart.
2. Aiym bījam	...	Hrām Hrim Krōm	cha, ccha, ja, jha, ña,—śabda, sparśa, rūpa, rasa, and gandha—touch with the thumb the head (śiras).
3. Eem bījam	...	Hrām Hrim Krōm	ta, tha, da, dha, na—tvak, chakshuḥ, śrōtram, jihvā, āghrāṇa śikhā madhyam—touch the centre of the head.
4. Um-bījam	...	Hrām Hrim Krōm	ṭa, ṭha, ḍa ḍha, ṇa—vāk, pāṇi, pāda, pāyu, upasthātmanē kavachāyahūm—with anāmika finger touch the heart.
5. Ūm-bījam	...	Hrām Hrim Krōm	pa, pha, ba, bha, ma.—vachana, dāna, gamana, visarga nandātmanē, nētrāyai vaūshaṭ—last finger is touched.
6. Aym-bījam	...	Hrām Hrim Krōm	ya, ra, la, va, śa, sha, sa, ha—manō buddhi, ahankāra, chitta, vritti, ātmanē sahasrōlkāya svāhā—karatalakarapṛshṭābhyām-namaḥ—Smear hand over hand.

After doing the nyāsa on himself as described above the Āchārya does dig-bandhanam by repeating the mantram "Sahasrōlkāya svāhā".

Then the prāṇapratishṭhā hōmam is proceeded with, as described above (six items only).

This is followed by Āyudha hōmam as described below:—

The Āchārya offers ghee and touches with sampātājyam, the chakram in the right hand, śankham in the left hand, padmam, śārngam and vajram in the right lower hand gada, musalam and khaḍgam in the left lower hand. The kirīṭa is also touched after the hōma with sampātājyam. So also the Śrī Vatsa, vanamālā and Garuḍa are touched.

The utsava Vigrahas are then placed in front of the mūla Vigraha for prōkshaṇam, etc.

In the case of mūla Vigraha sthāpanam more hōmams (16 more) are done. They are praṇava nyāsam, vyahṛtinyāsam, akshara nyāsam, nakshatra nyāsam, navagraha nyāsam, kāla nyāsam, jāti nyāsam, tōya nyāsam, nigama nyāsam, dēvatā nyāsam, vairaja nyāsam, kratu nyāsam, guṇa nyāsam, mūrti nyāsam, śakti nyāsam and lōka nyāsam. The Āhutis of ghee are to be poured into the fire and then the bimbam has to be touched (16 times) with sampātājyam. Āhutis of 8, 28 or 108 have to be made.

16. The Daily Worship in Temples according to the Pāncharātra System.

The Archakas concerned should finish their daily observances (nitya karmas) before beginning the worship of God in the temple. They should wash their legs up to the knees and clean their hands up to the wrist with clean water, before entering the temple. After cleaning their legs and feet they come to the front of the temple and standing in front of the outer doorway which is closed they repeat the suprabhātam to awaken God and then salute him in the temple. The musicians, if available, play on their nāga-sarams. The front doors of the temple are opened after the recital of the suprabhātam as the Archakas think that God is awakened. As soon as they enter the temple precincts they show respect to God by obeisance and then, with the permission of the dvārapāla-kas, they enter the temple after going round the prākāram once. (See Pl. IX-B.)

Then the Archaka stands to the south of the closed door of the garbhagṛha and performs on himself the "*Shaḍanganyāsam*" and then slaps his hand three times and pronouncing the words "Om Yem Vāyavē namaḥ" opens the door. Just before pronouncing these words and after slapping his hands thrice, he sounds the bell by shaking it.

The shaḍanganyāsam is done as follows:—The Archaka touches his body in six places with appropriate mantrams. (1) He touches his heart (hṛdayam) saying "Jñānāya hṛdayāya namaḥ." (2) He touches his head repeating "Aiśvaryāya śirasē svāhā": (3) He touches his tuft of hair saying "Śaktyai śikhāyai Vaushaṭ." (4) He touches his shoulders saying "Halāya kavachāya hūm." (5) He takes round his head his right hand and slaps both the palms twice saying "Vīryāya astrāya phaṭ" and

(6) lastly he touches his eyes with his right hand repeating "Tējasē nētrābhyām voushaṭ."

The Archaka after opening the door enters by placing his right leg inside. While entering he chants the mūla mantra and dēva vrata sāmam also if he knows it. On entering the temple he prostrates on the ground before God and repeats the mantra "Jitantē Puṇḍarīkāksha namastē viśvabhāvana | namastēstu hṛshīkēśa mahāpurusha pūrvaja". Getting up from the prostrating position he goes inside and puts the burning light near God into order and lights it. While it is burning properly he repeats the mantra "Tējasām adhipatayē agnayē namaḥ." He may also repeat "Jagajjyōtirūpāya namaḥ" and salute the light.

The Archaka then removes the faded garlands and flowers worn by the mūla and utsava vigrahas. These garlands and flowers are put on Vishvaksēna. Then the temple precincts are cleaned by the proper persons. The vessels used in worship are then given to the parichāraka to be cleaned. The dirt, etc., found on the body of God are cleaned by the Archaka by means of a kūrcha of darbha grass.

The dvārapālakas and others found around the temple in the prākāra and vimānā dēvatās are shown respect by a pūja which is done by the parichāraka or others if a parichāraka is not available.

ENTRANCE INTO THE TEMPLE.

The Archaka staying on the right side of the mūla vigraha repeats the "Mūla mantra" and sprinkles water on the floor. Then he repeats the astramantra and sprinkles water over the same space. The astramantra which he repeats is "Om sahasrōlkāyasvāhā vīryāya astrāyaphaṭ". On the purified space the Archaka places a "Kūrmāsanam" (a wooden seat), or uses "Darbha" when the wooden plank is not available and sits on the plank or darbhāsana. He assumes while sitting "Padmāsanam" or "Svastikāsanam" according to circumstances. For Padmāsanam he has to sit squatting his legs at the knee and place his hands under the knees. For "Svastikāsanam" he sits merely squatting with both the feet above. Both these are described in "Vishṇutilakam" in the second chapter.

The Archaka draws the curtain just at the time of sitting on the space and after sitting he sounds the bell and does sankalpam saying "By the strength of God, by His śakti, by His tējas, by His karma and by His influence I am about to begin his worship."

THE ARCHAKA PURIFYING HIMSELF TO BE FIT FOR THE WORSHIP OF GOD.

He then repeats the qualifications of God as follows :—God is the master of every thing and so He has created everything. He influences us to do pūja to him with things created by Him. He influences us to present to Him things created by Him and thus satisfy Him during the Ārādhana. (This is called sātvikatyāgam.)

After this sātvikatyāgam the Archaka repeats the astra mantra "Om sahasrōlkāyasvāhā vīryāya astraya phaṭ" and does digbandhanam on the eight sides and sky and earth (10 directions in all). For each direction he has to repeat the abovesaid astra mantra, so he has to repeat ten times this mantra in all.

The Archaka repeats next the mantra "Ghīm namaḥ parāya tējа ātmanē namaḥ" and imagines that he is surrounded on all sides by fire. In his right hand the last three fingers are folded and the remaining two fingers, the index finger and the thumb, are kept straight and the palm is taken round the head. Instead of the above mantra some repeat " Ram namaḥ parāya kalanalātmanē namaḥ ".

Repeating the mantra " Om Namassudarśanāya " or " Sahasrāra Hum phaṭ " Chakra mudra is shown on the head. The chakra mudra is made as follows :—" Maṇibandhana samau hastaū tiryak sambhrāmya cha kramāt paryāyēṇa prayōktavyā chakra mudrā mahōdaya. " He then imagines himself to be covered by it.

Then he does prāṇāyāmam and then sankalpam for bhūta śuddhi. He then does three prāṇāyāmams. The proper way of doing prāṇāyāmam is as follows :—

The left nostril is closed by pressing outside the nose and closing it by the last two fingers (*i.e.*, the 4th and 5th fingers); then through the right nostril breath is left out (*i.e.*, air is breathed out) for about 32 mātras (leaving out by the piṅgaḷa nāḍi) and then with the right hand thumb the right nostril is closed and by the left nostril air is taken in for sixteen mātras. These processes of breathing out and breathing in are being called " Rēchakam " and " Pūrakam," respectively. Then closing both the nostrils for 64 mātras as " Kumbhakam " (or holding in the breath) is done. This is the proper prāṇāyāma-nyāyam.

After prāṇāyāmam he does the yōga mudra and places it near the navel. The yōga mudra is shown as described below :—Below the navel (nābhi) place the left palm with the hollow above and put the outer part of the right palm over the inside of the left palm. Then "saying Yam" (bījaksharam) think of Vāyubījam (The Vāyubījam will be of " Vēdyākāram "). By this Vāyubīja all the dōshams in his body are believed to be destroyed and so he thinks that all his dōshams have also disappeared. He should think of " Rakta varṇam " (red colour) and the syllable " Ram " which is the agni bījāksharam, in his heart. He should also think that the syllable " Ram ", the agni bījākshara lies in a triangular space. He has to imagine that his whole body has been consumed by fire.

In his neck he should think of a chaturasra kuṇḍam of green colour with the bījāksharam of Indra " Lam " (லம்) being present. By this he has to think that the agni jvālā that has been connected with Vāyu has been extinguished by the Vāyu. He should then think of the Varuṇa bījāksharam " Vam " (வம்) as existing in his head in a round form of spaṭika colour and think that his whole body from head downwards was wetted by amṛtadhāra.

Then he shows the yōga mudra, yōgasampuṭa mudra below his navel and the samhāra mudra at the navel. The yōga mudra has already been described above. Yōgasampuṭa " mudra is one in which the left palm is placed below the navel close to it and the right palm is placed over the left in such a way that the palms of both hands are together; the samhāra mudra is leaving the middle finger straight up and folding the other fingers. In the nabhi proper tatva mudra is shown. Tatva mudra is joining the thumb and the first finger at the tips the other fingers being free and straight.

Then God, who is always in his heart, is thought to have come out through the right nostril and staying in a kamalam of one thousand petals above his head. He next pronounces

"Om Ṅīm (ஙி) namaḥ parāya"—prithvi bījam.
"Om tīm namaḥ parāya"—ghrāṇam.
"Om chīm namaḥ parāya"—upastham.

Repeating these three mantras he has to imagine that he has destroyed by burning the Prithvi tatva with its attributes of śabda, sparśa, rūpa, rasa and gandha (the five qualities of sound, touch, form, taste and smell) and greenness in colour along with "Ghrāṇam" and "Upastham."

Samhāram is done in gandha tanmātra.
"Om tīm namaḥ gandha tanmatram".

Gandha tanmatra is destroyed by aptatvam.
"Om ghīm namaḥ parāya"—aptatvam (water).
"Om tīm namaḥ parāya"—jihvātatvam (tongue).
"Om chīm namaḥ parāya"—pāyutatvam (hips).

Saying the above words he has to imagine that the Aptatva (water) which is white and having the qualities of śabda, sparśa, rūpa and rasa (the four qualities—sound, touch, form and taste) having the form of ardhachandra along with the tongue and hips has been destroyed by rasatanmātra.

"Om thīm namaḥ parāya"—rasatanmātra is destroyed in fire (tējas).
"Om ghīm namaḥ parāya or namaḥ"—fire (or tējas).
"Om tīm namaḥ parāya or namaḥ"—eyes.
"Om jīm namaḥ parāya"—legs.

Repeating the above he has to imagine that agni or tējas tatva which is triangular and a mixture of red and white in colour and which has the senses śabda, sparśa and rūpa (three qualities—sound, touch, and form) has been destroyed along with eyes and legs by rūpa tanmātra.

"Om thīm namaḥ parāya"—rūpatanmātra is destroyed by Vāyu.
"Om ḳhīm namaḥ parāya or namaḥ"—marut (wind or Vāyu).
"Om ṭīm namaḥ parāya or--namaḥ"—tvak (skin).
"Om jhīm namaḥ parāya or namaḥ"—pāṇi (hands).

Saying these words he has to imagine that Vāyu (marut) tatva which is round, smoke coloured and having the qualities of the senses śabda and sparśa (two qualities—sound and touch) has been destroyed along with tvak or skin and pāni or hands by sparśa tanmātra.

"Om ḍhīm namaḥ parāya"—sky (vyōman).

Sparśatanmātra is destroyed by Ākāśam.

"Om kīm namaḥ parāya or namaḥ"—sky (vyōman or Ākāśam).

"Om ṇīm namaḥ parāya or namaḥ"—śrōtram (hearing).

"Om jīm namaḥ parāya or namaḥ"—vāk (tongue).

Saying these he has to imagine that the sky which has no form, blue in colour and which has the quality of the sense of śabda only has been destroyed along with hearing (śrōtram) and speech (vāk) or śabda.

"Om nīm namaḥ parāya"—śabda is destroyed by manas.

"Om pīn namaḥ parāya"—manas is destroyed by ahankāram.

"Om phīm namaḥ parāya"—ahankāram is destroyed by mahat (or buddhi).

"Om bhīm namaḥ parāya"—mahat (or buddhi) is destroyed by prakṛti.

"Om bhīm namaḥ parāya"—prakṛti is destroyed by jīva.

The Jīva which is now devoid of smell is now thought of and by "Kumbhaka" the Jīva is believed to make its way out by piercing the brahmarandhra in the head and passing out through a delicate lotus thread like sushumnā nāḍi. After passing out of the body it is believed to enter the sun and from there it reaches the feet of Para Brahma. The worshipper has to imagine that his Jīva joins the feet of God. When the Jīva joins the feet of God he has to repeat "Om mīm parāya." The body born out of the yōni, he must imagine to have been burnt by the agnibīja in his angushṭham. (രം Ṛam-agnibīja mantra). He must imagine that the body, from head to feet, has been burnt.

The Archaka next makes and shows on himself the yōga mudra, yōga sampuṭa mudra, śṛshṭi mudra and tatva mudra. (Śṛshṭi mudra is the one in which the fingers of the right hand except the tarjani are closed—"Samhata viśēsha tisṛbhiranguḷi viśēshasangatiḥ / vimukta tarjanī bhūyas sṛshṭi mudrēti kīrtyatē"). He must then think that the nivarti bīja "Vam" is equivalent to a thousand moons in the heavens over the head.

From the nivarti bīja "Vam" an amṛta samudra has sprung and on it a white padma (lotus) has grown. And from the Brahma sitting on this padma the Jīva is believed to have come.

Saying "Om mīm namaḥ parāya" Jīva is āvāhanamed in the lotus. (Jīva is believed to be present in the śvēta pankajam or white lotus.)

Then the body is believed to have come into existence by the influence of Jīva and so he says "Om Bhīm namaḥ parāya." From the body buddhi is believed to have sprung and he repeats "Om Bhīm namaḥ parāya." From buddhi he imagines that ahankāra has sprung and so he is enjoined to say "Om phīm namaḥ parāya"; and manas is believed to spring from ahankāra and he says "Om phīm namaḥ paraya" (manas ப pa : ahankāra ഫ pha ; buddhi ബ ba ; deha ഭ bha ; and Jīva മ ma.)

Then he repeats "Om Nīm parāya" and believes *śabda tanmātra* to arise from ***manas.***

"Om khīm namaḥ parāya"—ākāśam (sky).

"Om Nīm ... ... "—śrōtram (ears).

"Om Jīm ... ... "—vāk (speech).

He is to think that the sky which is blue in colour and without any form and having the guṇa of śabda to have come into existence with śruti and vāk.

Then he repeats "Om dhīm namaḥ parāya" and imagines *sparśatanmātṛa* to have arisen out of *ākāśam.*

"Om—khīm namaḥ parāya"—Vāyu (wind).
"Om—ṭīm ... ..."—tvak (skin).
"Om—jīm ... ..."—pāṇi (hands).

He must imagine that from the round smoke-coloured Vāyu with the characteristics of śabda and sparśa and the organs of skin and hands to have sprung from sparśatanmātra.

Then he says "Dhīm namaḥ parāya" and imagines *rūpa* (agni) tanmātra to have sprung from *Vāyu.*

"Om—ghīm namaḥ parāya"—Agni (fire).
"Om—tīm ... ..."—nētram (eyes).
"Om—jīm ... ..."—pādam (feet).

He must imagine that the triangular white and red-coloured fire possessing the characteristics of śabda (sound), sparśa (touch) and rūpa (form) and the organs of eyes and feet have sprung from *rūpa tanmātra.*

Then he says Om ḍhīm namaḥ parāya and imagines *rasa* to have *sprung* from fire (Agni).

"Om—ghīm namaḥ parāya"—jala (water).
"Om—tīm ... ..."—jihvā (tongue).
"Om—chīm ... ..."—pāyu (hips).

He must imagine that the crescent-shaped white-coloured water with the characteristics of śabda, sparśa, rūpa and rasa (sound, touch, form and taste) with the organs of tongue and pāyu (hips and private parts) has sprung from *rasa tanmātra.*

Then he says "Om—thīm namaḥ parāya and imagines gandha tanmātra to have sprung from Ap or Jala (water).

"Om—ngīm namaḥ parāya"—prithivi (earth).
"Om—tīm ... ..."—ghrāṇam (nose).
"Om—chīm ... ..."—upastham (private parts).

He must imagine that the square green-coloured prithvi tatvam with the characteristics of the guṇas, śabda, sparśa, rūpa, rasa and gandha (sound, touch, form, taste and smell) has arisen from gandhatanmātra along with the organs of ghrāṇam and upastham.

He has to imagine in this manner that his body is composed of earth and other bhūtas (elements). He has to imagine that the lotus bud has opened and the petals are spreading out. From the petals of the flower, he has to imagine, that water has issued and wetted his body. Then he should think that his body, which is now purified is fit for worshipping God and contemplate God in the mind saying "Om sahasrōlkāya svāhā vīryāya astraya bhaṭ" and after repeating this mantra wash or clean the back and front of the hands with water.

He performs afterwards the following nyāsa or touching the parts of the body :—

With the right thumb he smears the corresponding fingers repeating the mantras in the manner given below :—

"Om, Om, Om, śuklam"—touch the right first finger (or the index finger).

"Om—nam—Om svarṇa varṇam"—touch the right middle finger.

"Om—mom—Om kṛshṇam"—touch the right third finger (anāmikam)

"Om—nam—Om raktam"—touch the right last finger.

"Om—ram—Om kunkumasannibham"—touch the left tarjanī (first or the index finger of the left palm).

"Om—yam—Om padmakinjalkasadṛśam"—touch the left middle finger.

"Om—nam—Om nīla varṇam"—touch the left anāmika finger.

"Om—yam—Om sarva varṇam"—touch the left last small finger.

Then with the first finger he smears the right thumb and says the mantra "Om jñānāya hṛdayāya namaḥ"; then with the thumb he smears the first finger and says the mantra "Om balāya svāhā"; then with the thumb he smears the second or the middle right finger and repeats the mantra "Om vīryāya vashaṭ"; then with the thumb he smears the anāmikā (or the third right finger) and says the mantra "Om aiśvaryāya hum"; then with the thumb he smears the last finger and says "Om śaktyai vaushaṭ"; then he touches with the tip of the thumb the tips of all the other fingers and says "Om tējasēphaṭ."

In the left hand he must imagine that the gadā is held and think of it by repeating "Om namō bhagavaṭyai" and also think that in the same hand kaumōdakam is held and repeat "Hum paṭsvāhā."

In the left hand he must imagine that the śankham is held and repeat "Om namō-bhagavatē puṇḍarīkākshāya vāyumukhāya dīptarūpāya śankhapālāya svāhā."

He imagines that in the right hand he is holding the chakra and repeats the mantra "Om āditya pratimāya māyarūpiṇē hum phaṭsvāhā."

Then he does dēhanyāsa as follows :—Make the nyāsa mudra. (Nyāsa mudra is done by touching the hollow of the left palm by the right middle finger and then taking the left hand to the hṛdaya.) Imagine that the mantra is shining in the hollow of the left hand. Then think that the whole body from head to feet is covered by the asṭākshara mantra. Say or repeat this asṭākshara as shown below :—

(1) Om—*om*—Om śuklam—Say this and touch the nābhi with the thumb and the last finger.

(2) Om—*nam*—Om svarṇa varṇam—Repeat this and touch the nābhi with all the fingers except the thumb.

(3) Om—*mom*—Om kṛshṇam—Repeat this and touch with the four fingers the knees.

(4) Om—*nam*—Om raktam—Repeat this and touch the back of the legs with all the fingers.

(5) Om—*ram*—Om kunkumavarṇam—Repeat this and touch the middle of the head with the middle finger.

(6) Om—*yam*—Om padmakinjalkasadṛśam—Repeat this and touch with the first (index) finger and the middle finger the two eyes.

(7) Om—*nam*—Om nīla varṇam—Repeat this and touch with the thumb and anāmikā (*i.e.*, third finger) the nose at the top.

(8) Om—*yam*—Om sarva varṇam—Repeat this and touch with the thumb and the first finger (tarjanī) the heart.

Then he does shaḍanganyāsam as detailed below:—

(1) The heart is touched repeating the mantra "Kuruththolkāyasvāhā jñānāya hṛdayāya namaḥ", the mantra having the white colour of the lotus.

(2) The head is touched repeating the mantra "Mahōlkāyasvāhā aiśvaryāya śirasē-svāhā" the mantra having the colour of "karuṇaital" (blue-lily) flower.

(3) The knot of hair on the head is touched repeating the mantra, "Vīrōlkāyasvāhā śaktyai śikhāyai vaushaṭ" the mantra having black colour.

(4) The flanks of the body are touched repeating the mantra "Dvelkāyasvāhā balāya kavachāya hum," the mantra possessing the colour of the stamens of the lotus flower.

(5) The eyes are touched repeating the mantra "Sahasrōlkāyasvāhā vīryāya astrāya phaṭ," the mantra having the colour of rose or kamalam.

(6) All the eight cardinal points are touched repeating the mantra "Ambhōjāsamam sahasrōlkāyasvāhā vīryāya astrāya phaṭ," mantra having the colour of the lotus (rose colour).

After the above he makes the mudras mentioned below and touches the parts of the body as detailed:—

(1) The mudra of the heart:—Fold the thumb and over it the middle and the next finger should be folded over and with these three fingers bent touch the heart.

(2) The mudra of the head:—Fold all the fingers, except the tarjani finger, with the thumb above and touch the head.

(3) The mudra of the tuft of hair:—Fold all the fingers except the thumb which ought to be kept extended and touch the tuft of hair.

(4) The mudra of the kavacha (dress):—Fold all the fingers over the thumb and touch the sides.

(5) The mudra of the eyes:—Touch the base of the first finger with the thumb and close the other fingers over it and then turn them before the eyes.

(6) The mudra of the hastam (hands).—Close all the fingers having the thumb outside and show it towards the cardinal points (eight or four).

The Worship of God.

The Archaka who is carrying on the worship ought to think that he is now the Nārāyaṇamūrti who is having gadā, śankha, padma, sudarśana, who is dressed up in pītāmbarā, whose body is smeared with sweet scented gandha and who is wearing the Vanamāla and Kaustubha.

Then he thinks of the mantra bīja "Om Namō Nārāyaṇāya" and imagines that it is being worshipped by offering sandal, flowers and light.

Then he places the hands fully extended in the navel and keeps his mind clear of all things; then adds the mind to buddhi and makes the buddhi think of only God and nothing else. Then he thinks in his heart of the " Ādhārādi svarūpa paryantam " and of the pīṭha of God.

He should imagine that God exists in his heart as small as his angushṭha and bearing śankha and chakra, having the colour of śuddha spaṭika, carrying gadā and padma and existing amidst the effulgence of light.

Now he thinks of mūlamantra in the mind and imagines that he has done sammukhī karaṇam and maṇtranyāsam.

He imagines that from sushumnā nāḍi to hṛdayakamala Ganges water has flowed; from this water he thinks that he has filled the vessels for doing arghya, pādya and āchamanam; then he thinks that he has done arghya, pādya and āchamanam and offered madhuparka, etc., to God.

Then he thinks that he has requested God to occupy the Snānāsanam and that He has done so.

Then he imagines to have offered and done the following things to God:—Arghya, pādya, and āchamanam; dantadhāvanam, cleaning of the tongue, cleaning of the mouth by water by taking it into the mouth and throwing it out and doing āchamanam; taking into the mouth and biting the tāmbūlam; then bathing, cleaning the body by rubbing; smearing the body with "Nellipparuppu" (the kernel of *Phyllanthus emblica* fruits); the establishing of nine kalaśams; smearing turmeric powder and washing it; smearing kunkumam and washing it; doing parishēchanam; bathing in one thousand dhāras of water; drying up the body by using a cloth and removing the water over the body with it; wearing the cloths, and wearing the sacred thread and doing āchamanam.

It should also be thought that arghyam, pādyam, āchamanam, drying up of the hair, putting on the tilakam on the face, wearing chandanam and jewels, putting on flowers akshata, collyrium and then looking up in the glass have been attended to by competent persons. Seeing dīpam, dhūpam and rice and sesamum and cloth in a plate must also be done by competent persons. He thinks that vedas, vedāngas, stōtras, vādya and nartanam and singing are performed by competent persons.

Then he imagines God to occupy the seat bhōjyāsanam on request.

Then he thinks that the following were offered and accepted by God:—Arghyam, pādyam and āchamanam; madhuparkam, tāmbūlam, āchamanam and arhajalam; sweets and other preparations; lēhiyams and things made up of greens (kīrai); four things (generally offered to God), *viz.*, pānakam, pānīyam, hastaprakshāḷaṇa and tāmbūlam. Then God is respected by dhyāna.

He thinks that in the nābhi there exists a trikōṇakuṇḍam and also imagines fire to have sprung from the dhyāna araṇi wood and to the Vaishnavāgni, which is purified and so pure now, oblations are made and thinks of the fire as Vāsudēva agni.

Idhmapprākshēpaṇam.—Out of twenty samits he imagines fifteen to have been put in this fire as āhāra āhuti and that oblations of ghee were given four times by reciting the vyāhṛti mantras.

By dvādaśākshara mantra, it should be imagined, that 108 sesamum āhutis were done; and that pūrṇāhuti was done by repeating agni mantra.

Also he thinks that sandal, flowers, and akshata were used while worshipping and that parishēchanam was done after pūja.

He thinks also that Ādhāraśaktyādi hōmam was done and imagines God to be present in the middle of the agni; that āhuti was done in fire by eight samits; that sixteen āhutis were done by offering sixteen charus; that ghee offerings were done by the repetition of purusha sūkta; and that the prāyaśchitta āhuti and pūrṇāhuti were also done.

Then he thinks of God as having entered the mind and then performs the following by repeating the appropriate mantrams:—

(1) The ōmkārādi ashṭākshara is dried up by the repetition of the mantra "Yam."

(2) The ōmkārādi ashṭākshara is burnt up by the repetition of the mantra "Ram."

(3) The ōmkārādi ashṭākshara is 'stambanamed' by the repetition of the mantra "Lam."

(4) The ōmkārādi ashṭākshara is washed up by the repetition of the mantra "Vam."

(5) The ōmkārādi ashṭākshara is made to be present by repeating "Hum."

(6) The ōmkārādi ashṭākshara is made to be present before by repeating "Phaṭ."

Then in the end cleaning is done repeating "Om chōdayāmi."

Then he does nyāsam repeating the mantra "Srimad ashṭākshara mahā mantrasya antaryāmi nārāyaṇarshiḥ dēvīgāyatrīśchandaḥ śrīmān nārāyaṇō dēvatā. Am bījam, āya śakthḥ, śuklādi varṇaḥ, buddhistatvam, paramavyōma kshētram, bhagavadārādhanārthē japē vinyōgaḥ."

Then God is praised by repeating as follows:—He is one having four bhujas; One possessing bright angas; One having the āyudhas, śankham and the chakram; One possessing a body of the colour of clouds full of water vapour; One having eyes like the petals of a lotus flower; One wearing a pītāmbara; One easily accessible; One having a face like that of a brilliant full-moon; One having a very pleasing and smiling attitude; One having red lips; One having ears with kuṇḍalas set with brilliant stones; One having a superior eye-browed face, a good kirīṭa on his head and wearing all ornaments; One having a charming tilaka on his forehead; One having a face with streaks made of tirumaṇ and so bright like light; One wearing bright ornaments on the hands and legs, such as, arm-bracelets, garlands and kaustubha; One having the brightness of one thousand sūryas; One appearing bright with vanamālā; One ornamented by a host of ornaments; One wearing excellent sandalpaste; One wearing a superb "mālā" (garland of flowers); One sitting comfortably and snug with Śrī and Bhūmi dēvis; One sitting on a simhāsana made of gold.

He should repeat the ashṭākshara, 8 or 28 or 108 times, count either by using lotus seeds or the streaks in the hand and show the japa mudra and get up.

Then he cleans the pūjā dravyas by sprinkling water over them and by repeating the gāyatrī of Vishnu; thinks that a kamalam is existing in the right hand; that in the midst of this flower fire exists in the form of a triangular tējas; then shows this imaginary fire in the hand over the pūjā dravyas; thinks that all the pūjá dravyas are burnt and reduced to ashes; thinks that a lotus of sixteen petals, white in colour, exists in his left hand; thinks that the moon with "Shoḍasakaḷās" is existing in it; with the amṛtadhāra arising from this moon, the ashes above referred to are considered to have been wetted and again created.

Then he shows the surabhi mudra over the pūjā articles and keeps to his south a big vessel of water; then he transfers it to his left.

He then repeats Vishnu gāyatri, cleans the vessels to be used for arghya, etc. and places the vessels in front of God as stated below:—He keeps the pādya vessel in the centre, arghya vessel to the south, and to the left the āchamanam vessel, fills these arghya, pādya and āchamana vessels with clean water; touches these vessels repeating the praṇava; places in the arghya vessel darbha tips, akshata, flowers, fruits, sandal paste, white mustard and wheat grains; in the pādya vessel he places the six things sesamum, *Cynodon dactylon* grass, Vishnu leaf, Śyāmākam, lotus flowers and rice nutmeg grains (akshata) and places in the āchamana patra cardamoms, cloves, camphor, fruit, takkōlam and sandalwood paste.

He imagines in his right hand a lotus with twelve petals to be present and the sun in the centre, and thinks that it is reduced to ashes by the rays of the sun; imagines that a lotus with sixteen petals is in the left hand and thinks that the moon is present in it and that the moon wets it with his amṛta rays. He thinks that everything has been created again and that they are fit for God's worship now; *i.e.*, after burning and creating them and washing them with amṛta.

Then he thinks of Nārāyaṇa and imagines Him to be present in both his hands; then with the hands he touches the arghyādi vessels; then repeating the Vishnu gāyatrī he cleans these vessels; then repeating the surabhi mudra mantra "Ōm sūm surabhyai namaḥ" shows over the vessels the surabhi mudra; imagines that he has filled these vessels with milk; touches the arghyādi vessels with the right palm repeating "Arghyam parikalpayāmi pādyam parikalpayāmi, āchamanīyam parikalpayāmi."

He pours from the arghya vessel water into another vessel and places it in the left hand; then repeats mūla mantra seven times and with the water in this vessel taken with a kūrcha sprinkles over the pūjādravyas and over himself repeating the mantram "Vīryāya astrāyāphaṭ."

Saying "Ōm Śrîyai arghyarūpiṇyai namaḥ" pūjā is done to arghya vessel; saying "Ōm gangāyai pitṛpriyāyai pādyarūpiṇyai namaḥ" pūjá is done to pādya pātra; saying "Ōm sarasvatyai amṛta rūpiṇyai āchamanarūpayai namaḥ" pūjā is done to āchamana pātra. He does pūjā with sandal paste and flowers.

Then saying "Ōm dhūmrōdkarāya nama iti" pūja is done to dhūpapātram. Then saying "Ōm trūm ghanṭāyai namaḥ ōm jāgratjyōtirūpāyanamaḥ" pūjā is done to the bell and light vessel.

He divides mūlavars pīṭha into twelve parts and in the first part says the mantra describing the form of ādhāra śakti and then does pūjā with flowers and contemplates on it. While doing pūjā he says "Om brūm trum ādhāra śaktyai namaḥ." He thinks of "Ēkavakram" and saying "Om krūm kūrma kālāgnayē namaḥ" thinks of kūrma kālāgni. He thinks of "Spaṭikādri" repeating "Ōm ham anantāya namaḥ" and does pūjā with flowers. He thinks of "Sarva lōkaika" and repeating "Ōm ḍham ḍharaṇyai namaḥ" does pūja to dharaṇi with flowers. Then he repeats one after the other "Om 'dham' dharmāya namāḥ; ōm 'gyam' jñānāya namaḥ; ōm 'vaim' vairāgyāya namaḥ; ōm 'aim' aiśvaryāya namaḥ." Thus pūjā is done thinking that He has four arms, simha's face, with the first pair of hands as doing anjali, with the other two as adopting the yōga pīṭha. (These are white in colour). Then pūjā is to be done.

The pūjā is done saying:—

"Dharmāya namaḥ ... ... āgnēyam
Jñānāya namaḥ ... ... nairṛti
Aiśvaryāya namaḥ ... ... īśānam
Vairāgyāya namaḥ ... ... vāyu."

Next he says:—

"Am adharmāya namaḥ ... ... east
Am ajñānāya namaḥ ... ... south
Am avairāgyāya namaḥ ... ... west
Am anaiśvaryāya namaḥ ... ... north and
Om sadāśivāya namaḥ ... ... centre"

These are to be thought of as of the colour of dharmādis of reddish colour and to be worshipped as such. He thinks that these are in the nine-legged pīṭha supporting the plank.

Then he should say the following and do what is enjoined along with it:—

(1) Ōm bham bhautika ahankārāya namaḥ;
(2) Ōm taim tējasē ahankārāyā namaḥ;
(3) Ōm vaim vaikārika ahankārāya namaḥ.

He is to imagine these to be ropes (pāśams or kayiru) and worship them. Instead of the above some Archakas substitute the following:—

(1) Ōm bham ... ... bhautika ahankārāya namaḥ;
(2) Ōm vyūm ... ... tējasē ahankārāya namaḥ;
(3) Ōm voum ... ... vaikārika ahankārāya namaḥ.

He is to imagine these also as ropes and worship them.

Then he should repeat,

"Ōm—sam—satvaguṇāya namaḥ"
"Om—ram—rajōguṇāya namaḥ"
"Om—tam—tamō guṇāya namaḥ."

He is to imagine these as guṇas and do pūjā to them as such.

He is to imagine the five panchabhūtās as forming a mattress of cotton and repeat the following:—

(1) Om—prīm—prithivyātmanē—hum phaṭ namaḥ;
(2) Om—ām—apātmanē—hum phaṭ namaḥ;
(3) Om—ram (tam)—tējasātmanē—hum phaṭ namaḥ;
(4) Om—vām—Vāyvātmanē—hum phaṭ namaḥ;
(5) Om ām—ākāśātmanē—hum phaṭ namaḥ.

He imagines the mattress to be covered by a cloth and says "Om mam" and does āvāhanam of "Jīvātma" and uses the cloth.

Saying "Om—ram—agnimaṇḍalāya namaḥ" he thinks of agnimaṇḍala.

Saying "Om—sōm—sōmamaṇḍalāya namaḥ" he thinks that it is the maṇḍalam of moon.

Saying "Om—ham—sūrya maṇḍalāya namaḥ" he thinks of sūrya maṇḍalam.

Saying "Om—pam—padmāyai namaḥ" he thinks that in a lotus twelve white petals are present and does ārādhanam. (He imagines the flower to have kēsarams also.)

Pūja is done to these, as stated above, using sandal paste, flowers and light. (In the same manner the Tengalai Sri Vaishnavas do pūjā in karmārchādi pīṭhams also. This is especially done at Srirangam.)

Pūjā is done with sandal paste, etc., as detailed below to the various dēvatās:—

To the south of the mūla pīṭha he does pūjā to Brahmādis repeating "Om—am—Vishṇavē namaḥ" and "Om—īm—īśāya namaḥ." To the north of mūla pīṭha he does pūjā to Sanatkumārādis repeating "Om Sanatkumārāya namaḥ" "Om Sanakāya namaḥ and "Om Sanandanāya namaḥ." To the west of the mūla pīṭha pūjā is done to the durgādis repeating "Om Durgāyai namaḥ," "Om Vighnēśāya namaḥ" and "Om asmadgurubhyō namaḥ."

Then he cleans with good water the āvāhana pātram (vessel), repeats the mūla mantra and fills the vessel with arghya water. Then taking this vessel with both the hands he lifts it up to the face of God and does āvāhanam.

In the mūla bimba he imagines God to be present in its heart, but with innumerable faces on every side, legs and hands. This is considered to be "Viśvākāram." Next he thinks of God as effulgent light (*i.e.*, divya rūpa) and also as a small indissoluble being having some inseparable avayavās (*i.e.*, as sūkshma rūpa).

Afterwards he looks at the vigraha and imagines a form exactly like that of the image and thinks of a sthūla rūpa. If one gets another image (being) from the mūla bimba the mūla bimba does not lose any of its lustre. If from a light (dīpa) another light is lit, the first dīpa does not decrease in its light-emitting strength. Similarly in the bimba also this śakti does not become less.

Thinking of such a God in the mind he says four times "Om namō nārāyaṇāya āgaccha āgaccha." Then he thinks that God has entered the āvāhanapātra, pours or sprinkles the water in the vessel on the head of the karmārcha and then imagines that he has āvāhanamed God. He must think that God has entered it.

To the karmārcha āvāhana mudra and then śṛshṭi mudra are shown. Next the praṇāmā mudra is shown (*i.e.*, praying by lifting the hands). After the salutation he shows "Svāgata mudra" and "Pratimā mudra." Then he prays to God that "Sānnidhya" should be obtained by him and salutes him. He requests God to be present till the close of the Ārādhana. He then shows the prārthana mudra.

He does prārthana to God repeating "Puṇḍarīkāksha mantra." (He thinks that God is in his front and prays to Him.)

Then he repeats the mūla mantra and thinks that he is presenting the pādukais. Then he presents to God "Nyāsa mudra."

Then in God's body he does "Sthiti" nyāsa by repeating the mūla mantra; he does also "Shaḍanganyāsam." He shows the appropriate mudras of padmam, śankham, chakram, gadā and vanamālā. He repeats the Sāma "Archatapprārchata" and throws flowers repeating "Om namō bhagavatē vāsudēvāya phalam bhavatu mē pushpairnamasva."

Pūjās to other images are also done. Then pūjā for the image of Goddess is done as follows:—

He does the Ṛshyādi nyāsa to the Goddess repeating the mantra "Śriyaḥ Śrī mantrasya dhanādhyaksharshiḥ, Śrīcchandaḥ, Śrīdēvatā, Srīmbījam."

Then repeating the mantra "Om—srīm—Śriyai namaḥ" he does āvāhana of Lakshmi from the Śrīvatsa. Then he thinks of Lakshmī.

He meditates on her repeating:—

"Om—śrām—hṛdayāya namaḥ."
"Om—śrīm—śirasēsvāhā."
"Om—śrūm—śikhāyai vaushaṭ."
"Om—śraim—kavachāya hum."
"Om—śrowm—nētrābhyām vaushat."
"Om—śiraḥ—astrāya phaṭ."

and does these six anganyāsams.

He shows the padma mudra and does pushpāñjalī by repeating the Śrīmantra.

He does the same pūjā to Bhūdēvī also and does to her the following six anganyāsas:—

"Om—bham—hṛdayāya namaḥ."
"Om—bhīm—śirasēsvāhā."
"Om—bhūm—śikhāyai vaushaṭ."
"Om—bhaim—kavachāya hum."
"Om—bhowm—nētrāya vaushaṭ."
"Om—bhaḥ—astrāya phaṭ."

Then repeating " Vibhō sakalalōkēśa . . ." he does obeisance to God. Next repeating the mantra " Divyēnāryō " again he prays and does obeisance to God. Afterwards bending his head he offers an arghya. Then repeating " Divya pādyoya charane" he prays and offers his respects. Then he does obeisance with both his hands; he offers pādyam with water at the feet twice. Then he repeats " Divyapādyēna charaṇē " and prays and offers his respects. Then he cleans the feet of God with clean cloth or vastram. Then repeating " Divyēnāchamanīyēna yathāśakti," he prays to God and does obeisance. Then he imagines that materials mentioned below are given for mukhāvāsam—*viz.*, cloves, cardamoms, kasturi, betel and nuts. He offers sandal paste, flowers, incense and lamp with light in it; sprinkles water over madhuparkam; does śōshaṇa, dāhana and plāvana and then offers the madhuparkam by placing it near the dakshiṇa hand (*i.e.*, right hand) of God. He gives āchamanam and tāmbūlam, prostrates before God and repeats the following mantra :—" Dāsōham . . ." and says that he is praying.

In flowers having twelve dalams, in each dala, he imagines a śakti to have come and occupied it, by the prayer.

Then he repeats the following :—

" Om—śrīm vatsāyai namaḥ."
" Om—vam vanamālāyai namaḥ."
" Om—mam māyāyai yōgātmikāyai namaḥ."
" Om vaim—māyāyai yogātmikāyai namaḥ."

First round.—Beginning with east he goes round the eight corners repeating " Om vyāptyai namaḥ . . . Om Śāntyai namaḥ " and imagines chāmarams to be offered.

Second round.—He imagines them as having eight āyudhas and repeats " Om Śankhadharāya namaḥ . . . Vajradharāyanamaḥ."

Third round.—He goes round, and thinks of Indras repeating. " Om Indrāya namaḥ . . . Om Īśānāyanamaḥ."

Then Garuḍa is prayed to in front of God and next Vishvaksēna who is also in front of God.

Then the śaṭhāri (pādukai) is placed in snānāsana after showing it to God. He sprinkles with puṇyāham water the kumbham and snapanadravyās.

In front of God he places nine kalaśams. In the centre a ghee vessel; east, pādyam; āgnēyam, curds; south, arghyam; nairṛti, milk; west, āchamanam; vāyūvyam, honey; north, panchagavya; īśānyam, fruits. He imagines Vāsudēva, Vishṇu, Madhusūdana, Trivikrama and Vāmana in the centre and four directions respectively; imagines Śrīdhara, Hṛshīkēśa, Padmanābha and Satyavān in the four corners respectively, beginning with āgnēyam; āvāhanams of these Gods are done in respective places and upachārams as detailed below :—

Alankārāsanam—Arghyam, pādyam, āchamanam, drying the hair of the head, putting on of tilakam, sandal paste, ornaments, flowers, akshata, collyrium, mirror, incense, light and mātradānam (in a tray taking rice, betel and nuts, fruits, ghee and honey).

He offers the above mentioned things in the tray, after performing the rites mentioned above as upachārams to God, saying "Govinda prasādam." Then these things are taken away.

The things mentioned above may be offered to God repeating the mūla mantra, or they may be offered by repeating other ordinary mantras.

The cloth used as a "Tirai" (cover) is removed now and recitations of Vedas, Vedāngas, stōtras, dancing and music are done and God is considered to be pleased with these offerings.

Then repeating "Om Rām namaḥ parāya viśvātmanē namaḥ" over kumbha-hārati it is waved thrice round repeating guṇa mantras.

Then Bhōjyāsanam is occupied by God. He offers to God in this āsanam arghyam, pādyam, āchamanam, madhuparkam, āchamanam and tāmbūlam.

Then he prays to God, offers padmāsanam (also called svastikāsanam) and imagines God to have occupied this āsanam. Then with astramantra he sprinkles water over nivēdana articles (various eatables, etc., offered to God for nivēdanam).

The balamantra is then repeated and arghya water sprinkled over the materials offered Repeating the mantra "Arganambhu" water is offered to God. He does śōshaṇa, dāhana and plāvana, shows Surabhimudra and thinks that in His hand a lotus flower with dalams and karṇika is placed. Placing his left hand over his right hand in God's right hand he shows "Grāsamudra" repeating the mantra "Dēvasyatvā."

Then pānakam, karkaṇḍu (sugar-candy) pānīyam, āchamanam (all cold things) are offered to God. Pradakshina and stōtram are done.

Then, as before, he does ashṭākshara japa and hōmams and other things and closes the pūjā.

17. Brahmōtsavam or Car Festival.

The Brahmōtsavam ceremony in a temple is usually performed during a particular month, and this varies with the locality. For example the Brahmōtsavam at Conjeeveram and Lakshmipuram (near Kuppam) is celebrated on the same day. It is performed during the month of Vaikāsi every year. In this month the festival days are fixed with reference to the avabhṛtasnānam or Tīrtavāri day.

At Conjeeveram and Lakshmipuram the tīrtavāri day is the "Śrāvaṇam", *i.e.*, the day on which this star is predominant. This day is usually the ninth day of the festival. In other words the festival is begun nine days prior to the Śrāvaṇam.

Utsavams are performed to God occasionally and also periodically.

The avabhṛtasnānam day may be fixed according to the nakshatra. It may be fixed on "Śrāvaṇam," "Rōhiṇi" or "Punarvasu." It may be on the day on which praṭishṭha was done, or on the birthday of the Raja. It is also done on the Mahā sankramaṇam day.

Utsavams may last any number of days from one to thirty days. If it lasts one to five days no dhvajārōhaṇam ceremony is performed. If the utsavam lasts longer and is from five days to thirty days then dhvajārōhaṇam ceremony is performed.

Vishṇu's Brahmōtsavam should not run concurrently with that of any other deity. If the utsavam of any other deity has already commenced, the Vishṇu utsavam may be begun subsequently. The utsavam of any other deity should not be begun after the beginning of the Vishṇu utsavam and before its close.

The utsavam begins with the ankurārpaṇam ceremony. According to strict rules the ankurārpaṇam ceremony should be done at least a week before the beginning of the Brahmōtsavam. But in practice, at the present time, the ankurārpaṇam ceremony is performed on the day just previous to the beginning of the utsavam. In fact the utsavam is begun with the performance of this ceremony.

The details of the ankurārpaṇam ceremony are the same as are described under the Dīkshā and Pratishṭhā ceremonies.

On the ankurārpaṇam day kaṅkaṇams are tied on to the bērams (utsava Vigrahas) and the Āchāryas who take part in the worship of God. The wrist thread has to be prepared by twisting five or seven threads. After twisting it it is placed along with a coconut, betel leaves, nuts on a settle of rice. Usually one thread is used for a person, and the coconuts should be equal in number to the number of threads or kaṅkaṇams. Then flowers, coconuts, plantains and betel with nuts are carried in procession round the prākāram once and these things are placed in front of the deity. During the procession, chatram and chāmaram should be taken and "Śākunasūtra" is chanted. Vādyams are also sounded. Towards the close of the procession the wrist threads, coconuts and other things carried are kept down. The wrist threads are usually deposited on coconuts, one thread on each coconut and these coconuts are placed by the side of a settle of paddy or rice. The wrist threads and other articles should be placed by the side of God.

Puṇyāham is done and with this holy puṇyāham water the kaṅkaṇams are sprinkled repeating the astramantra. The lower end of the thread is held down by the thumb and its neighbour of the left hand and with the fingers of the right hand the thread is smeared with sandal paste. Then placing the thread on the cocoanut, Ananta is āvahanamed and upachārams are done to him.

The wrist threads or rakshais are purified by chanting the astramantra eight times. The first ślōka of the Jitantē stōtra is also repeated. Then the wrist thread is taken and it is tied to the wrist of the right hand of the male God (Vigraha). Then repeating the "Śrī sūktam" the wrist thread is tied to the left wrist of the Goddess. After tying the kaṅkaṇams to God and Goddess the Archaka ties it on his right hand to the wrist. Then the Archaka does nivēdanam and upachārams to God. Lastly he offers śayanam to God. This offering of śayanam is usually done as in Pratishṭhā.

The selection of the Ṛtviks or persons to help the Āchārya in the worship of God is done on the ankurārpaṇam day, during the night.

The preparation of dhvajam (flag) for hoisting up on the pole (dhvajastambham) is usually done on the ankurārpaṇam day only. The dhvajam or the flag to be hoisted should be strictly speaking, ten yards long and five yards broad. The least is the length of the mūla bēram (fixed idol in the temple) and the door way near the mūlavar. The dhvajam should never be less than the height of the door way near the mūla vigraha. The cloth is folded into four folds and the upper and the lower folds are left free and a figure of Garuḍa should be drawn in the middle (2nd and 3rd parts). A margin on each side about one-eighth part of the breadth of the cloth is left all round. The figure of Garuḍa has to be drawn in the manner described below.

The Garuḍa that is to be drawn on the flag or dhvajam should have its hands in the anjali form with flowers in his hand; his right leg should be in the front and his left leg behind. His wings are spread out on both sides. In the left foot Anantan is shown. The serpent Vāsuki is to be represented on the breast as the sacred thread; the Kārkōṭaka is to be represented on the chest; in the waist Takshaka is drawn; Padma nagām is to be shown as a kuṇḍalam in his right ear; Mahāpadmanāgam is to be represented in his left ear; on the head the Śankhanāga and in the upper arms Kuligai nāgas are to be represented. The colours in which the figure of Garuḍa is to be written is as follows:—śpaṭikam, śonitam, pītam, dhūmram, raktāmbujīyam, pingaḷam, dhuhinam and brahmaraletam are the colours. An umbrella is to be drawn over the head, two chāmaras on the two side and a lotus flower below the feet have to be drawn. Below the lotus is to be drawn the pūrṇakumbham. By the sides of the kumbham pāligais with seedlings should be drawn. Two lamps also are drawn, one on each side. The figure of Garuḍa has to be ready on the ankurārpaṇam day.

The following are the ceremonies through which the flag or dhvaja has to be taken through:—

(1) Unmānōnmāna pramāṇa śānti hōmam.
(2) Jalādhivāsam (mirror reflection)
(3) Nētrōnmīlanam (mirror reflection).
(4) Dhānyādhivāsam.
(5) Sayyādhivāsam.
(6) Tatvahōmam.
(7) Kumbhaprōkshaṇam.

All the above ceremonies have to be done on the ankurārpaṇam day only.

The flag is to be kept in the yāga śālā. Garuḍa is invoked, ārādhana is done and prayers are offerred. Nivēdanam is performed. Garuḍa stōtram is chanted in honour of Garuḍa.

The commencement of the utsavam.—God is roused from sleep by repeating the mantras "Uttishṭēti" and Sākuna Sūktam. God is then put on a palanquin or any seat repeating the mantra "Idam Vishṇur vichakramē" and is taken round the prakāram in procession. Then God is seated in the maṇḍapam. In the maṇḍapam nine kalaśams are placed and tirumanjanam or snapanam is carried out in the usual way. Sometimes a kūrcha is made to represent God and then it is bathed instead of the image of God. This is done often to save time, trouble and expense.

The Garuḍa dhvajam is taken out this day. It is placed near the dhvajastambham and then nivēdanams and upachārams are done to the flag of Garuḍa. Repeating the mantra "Suparṇōsīti" the flag is hoisted on the top of the flag staff in front of the door of the temple. After hoisting the flag the mantra "Khagēśa mala" is repeated Prayers are offered to Garuḍa that he should be present throughout the period of the utsavam. To Indra and the eight ḍēvatās of the eight cardinal points bali of pongal is offered. Every day during the festival Ārādhanam is done to the flag-staff and the digdēvatās.

The flag-staff should be between one hundred tālams and the height a little more than that of the temple. It may be seventy tālams or mānāngulas. On the day on which the utsavam begins this flag-staff is sprinkled with puṇyāham water and water from the other kalaśams established and kept at the base of the flag-staff. Usually the flag-staff has some structure round it at the base, and also some structures near it.

Towards the close of the day arrangements are done for going through the bhērītāḍanam ceremony (drum beating ceremony). When it is dark in the evening the utsava bēram is seated close to the flag-staff and to the south of it. Chakrat Āzhvār is placed just in front of the dhvajastambham. Then Ārādhanam and nivēdanam to God are performed. Afterwards close to the dhvajam and in front of the God (the utsava bēram) paddy is spread on the ground. On this spread of paddy an ashṭadaḷa padmam or chakram is drawn by the Archaka. Then on this spread of paddy the drum used by the barber musicians or meḷakkārans is deposited. This drum is covered over with a new cloth. Puṇyāham water is sprinkled over the drum now covered with the new cloth. Then Vishṇu is āvāhanamed on the southern side and on the northern or left side Śrī is made to be present by āvāhanam. The centre of the drum, which is really a mixture of satva, rajas and tamas, prakṛti is āvāhanamed. Then the bhērītāḍana stick is sprinkled with puṇyāham water. Some upachāram also is done to it afterwards. Next the "Saptatanmātra" mantram is chanted over the bhērī and it is beaten and sounded three times with the stick. While striking the drum with this stick the trimūrti mantram is chanted. The beating of the bhērī is began on the right side. The drummer is then called over and as soon as he comes puṇyāham water is sprinkled over him. He is then allowed to take on his bhērī and he is then expected to play on the bhērī to the accompaniment of nāgaswarams.

Just in front of the utsava vigraha a settle of rice is made on the floor. Over it a kumbham (pot) is placed. This pot or kumbham is filled with water and decorated in the usual way. The following dēvatās are invoked and they are requestd to be present:—

Indrādis, divyāyudhās, vaikunṭhanityas, parivārams of Vishṇu, kumudādis, marīchyādi ṛshis, Brahma, dwellers in the fourteen lōkas, vidyās and vedas. This pot is placed in the yāga śālā afterwards.

Nityōtsavam.—Brahma is requested to be present in the centre of the village, and upachārams are shown to him there. He is requested to remain till the close of the utsavam. For Indrādis bali is offered round the village as detailed below:—Brahma, Indra, Agni, Yama, Nirṛti, Varuṇa, Vāyu, Kubēran and Īśānan (Brahma in the centre of the village and the others their places round—eight corners). These dēvatās are āvāhanamed in their proper places and bali is given to each of them in order. The music (rāgam and tālam) should be the ones appropriate to each, but in practice this is ignored and only the ordinary drum is sounded. The giving of bali is done only after the hōmam and before the procession of God.

The various items gone through in the yaga śālai are as follows:—

I. The Dwāras are worshipped as in the Dīkshai ceremony.

(1) Then a kumbham is set up on the vēdikai. Vishṇu is invited and is requested to be present in the kumbham. Usually a settle of paddy is made on the vēdikai and on it the kumbham decorated with kūrcham, vastram, ratnam, leaves and flowers are deposited. The invitation to Vishṇu is made only after placing the kumbham on the settle of paddy.

(2) On the right side of the kumbham a karagam (a smaller pot) is placed and Sudarśanar is requested to be present in the karagam.

(3) On the vēdikai eight small kalaśams for the eight directions are placed as detailed below:—

East (Vāsudēva); south (Śankara); west (Pradyumna); north (Aniruddha); south-east (Āgnēya-satyar); south-west (Nirṛti); north-west (Purusha Vāyu); north-east (Īśānam—Anantar). These dēvatās are invoked and upachārams are done to them.

II. *Maṇḍalārādhanam* (Chakrābjamaṇḍalam).—Ārādhanam is performed and it is similar to that done on pratishṭhā ceremonies.

III. *Bimbārādhanam.*—Pūjā is done to chakratāzhvār or other idol used. (Yāga bēram.)

IV. Hōmam is done in the yāgakuṇḍam. The Āchārya sits to the west of the kuṇḍam facing east He does sankalpam for the hōmam Vāsudēva is āvāhanamed and he is requested to be present, all the nine days.

The following things-Ghee, flowers, incense, samit, milk, curds, sesamum, paddy and yavam (wheat) are sacrificed, eight times each, repeating the mūla mantra. Finally jaggery, rice and pāyasam are offered. During these offerings purusha sūkta is repeated. Then ghee offerings are made in the kuṇḍam for the following dēvatās:—Prajāpati, Rūdra, Sarvadēvas, Chandas, Vedas, Ṛshis, Gandharvas, Yakshakas, Apsaras, year, month, rivers, oceans, mountains, bhūtas, cows, trees, plants, herbs found in the forest, svēdajams, aṇḍajams, udbhidas, jarāyujas, bhūrādi seven worlds and the chaṇḍādi parivāra dēvatās.

Finally Pūrṇāhuti is made repeating "Idam Vishṇur vichakramē." During these nine days of the utsavam, hōmam is done every day once in the morning and once in the evening.

The utsavams are usually done as detailed below on nine days at Lakshmipuram :—

1st day—During the night—the utsavam was sūryaprabhā. During the day time dhvajārōhaṇam is usually performed.

2nd day—Ordinary utsavam without any vāhanam during the day time. (See Pl. VII-B). During the night God was seated on simha vāhanam.

3rd day—During the day time Garuḍōtsavam. This is generally done on a larger scale and attendance of people this day is very large. In fact this is considered to be an important utsavam. (See Pl. VII-A.) In the night Hanumanta vāhanam is used.

4th day—During the day time ordinary utsavam without any vāhanam. During the evening marriage ceremonies are commenced. In the night God is taken on śēsha vāhana in utsavam.

5th day—Ordinary utsavam during the day time is carried on. In the night Hamsa vāhana utsavam is carried on.

6th day—Ordinary utsavam in the day and in the evening gajēndra mōksham is celebrated. In the night elephant is used as the vāhanam during the procession.

7th day—During the day time the car festival (rathōtsavam, See Pl. VIII-B). In the night pallakku utsavam is done. (See Pl. XI-B.)

8th day—Alankāra tirumanjanam is done during the day time and ḍōḷōtsavam is performed in the evening. In the night tōpputsavam is done and the vāhanam used is the horse.

9th day—day time—tīrthavāri or tīrthōtsavam is done. In the night ordinary utsavam.

10th day—day time—mahā manjanam is performed and in the night saptābharaṇam is performed.

11th day—During the night ēkāṇtasēvai and śayanōtsavam are performed.

The vāhanams may be varied a little in other temples. For example at Budugur the vāhanams were used as follows :—

1st day— hamsam;
2nd day— simham;
3rd day—Hanumān;
4th day—chandraprabhā (śesha);
5th day—Garuḍa;
6th day—elephant:
7th day—car festival;
8th day—horse;
9th day—yāḷi or pallakku.

During the utsavam every day a flag of Garuda, if one is available, is carried. Behind God Vishvaksēna is taken in a palanquin.

Every day bali is offered. According to the Śāstras it should be offered as follows :—

1st day—cooked rice dyed with turmeric powder and mixed with sesamum seeds powdered is offered.

2nd day—cooked rice mixed with sesamum.

3rd day—cooked rice with nine dhānyams and bhakshyams.

4th day—cooked rice with tender coconut, avil and kunukku are offered.

5th day—cooked rice with padma bījam, pāyāsam and taṇdulam.

6th day—cooked rice with sojjiappam (a prepared cake with jaggery).

7th to 9th day :—Milk food mixed with sesamum, jaggery, and mudga. On eight days bali is offered both in the morning and in the evening before the utsavam and on the ninth day it is offered only during the day time.

On the ninth day tīrthavāri or avabhṛtasnānam is performed. Near the dhvajastambham a small space is cleared and afterwards on this space on a spread of rice a mortar and a pestle are placed. Then Lakshmi is invoked and she is requested to be present. Along with these in front of the dhvajastambham turmeric powder is placed. In the mortar a small quantity of turmeric is powdered and this powder is put in a small kumbham and it is placed on a settle of paddy. The mūla mantra is repeated and Śrī or Lakshmī is requested to be in the pot. This kumbham contains water coloured with turmeric powder and this water is used later to do abhishēkam to God. Then turmeric is distributed to all present in the temple at that time.

Then God is taken in procession to the lake (or tank) close to the water. An abhishēkabēram if one is available, or the chakratāzhvār when the abhishēkabēram is not available, is taken close to the water. These five or nine kalaśams are established in the usual way for tirumanjanam. The water for tirumanjanam is sprinkled over the utsavabēram and over the chakratāzhvār. Then the chakratāzhvār (or snānabēram) is bathed in water. Just when the chakratāzhvār is bathed all people bathe in water.

After the tirthavāri utsavam they come to the Yāgaśālai and purṇāhuti is to be done. At first the purṇāhuti is done and then one after the other the Āchārya does śānti-hōmam, prāyaśchittahōmam and prāṇāhutihōmam.

Towards the evening the Archakas proceed with the dhvajāvarōhaṇam. The flag is lowered and all the dēvatās are requested to go to their places, after doing upachārams to them. Then the Āchārya does samhāra nyāsam to the flag. Then it is folded and placed at the feet of God.

Mūkabali is done afterwards. For this music is played only at places where bali is actually offered. On the ninth day all the persons occupying the corners are given bali and are requested to leave the place and proceed to their own places.

Lastly the Āchārya should do japam repeating the ashṭākshara mantram.

INDEX.

PAGE

A

Abhigamanam 49
Abhigamana ārādhanam 83
Āchamanam 52
Āchāryas 17
Achyutar 126
Ādhāra śakti tarpaṇam . 70
Āgama siddhāntis 100
Agni prakaraṇa mudra 122
Āhāra niyamam 95
Ahōbila maṭṭ 7, 35
Akkiāḻvān ... 18
Alankārāsanam .. 90, 148
Alavandār 6, 8, 17, 18, 21, 22, 23
Amōda 27
Amśumāli ... 123
Ānandar 106, 129
Anantar ... 110, 121, 126, 130
Ananta Sūri 38
Ananta vaļayam 130
Āṇḍāl Gōdā) 9
Aniruddha 27, 28, 41, 100, 127
Ankurārpaṇam 103, 115, 150
Antaryāmi 110
Apachārams 76
Apāna 94, 96
Appullar 37, 38
Ārādhanam 87
Arakshetra 130
Archakas 99
Archa 110
Archa vigraha 28
Arthapanchaka 28
Ashṭākshari 68, 121
Āsuri Keśava Sōmayāji ... 19
Atreya Rāmānuja (Appullar) 38
Āpāsanam 79
Avabhṛta snānam 149
Āyudha hōmam ... 134
Āzhvārs 9
Āzhvar, Poigai (Sāra yōgin) 6, 9, 16, 29

B

Bala 113
Barnett 3, 4, 14
Bathing 53

PAGE

Bālāgni 110
Bell, in Tengalai worship 46
Bhadrāksha 17
Bhadra 130
Bhagavat Sastras .. 100
Bhandarkar, Dr. .. 2
Bhaṭṭar (Bhaṭṭaraka) 113, 114
Bhaṭṭar (Parāśara) ... 42
Bhōjyāsanam ... 90, 93, 142, 149
Bhuvana 27
Bhūsūktam 103, 116
Bhūtat Āzhvār (Bhūta Yogin). 6, 9, 16
Bhūtapuri (Śrīperumbudur) ... 19
Bimbārādhanam ... 153
Bōdhāyana 23
Brahma yajñam 74
Brahmōtsavam (car festival). 149, 150
Buthugur 99

C

Caste, Āzhvārs on 14
Chakrat Āzhvār .. 103, 116, 152, 155
Chakra Mudra 123
Chakravarthis 2
Chandan 130
Chatuślōki 6, 18

D

Dāsa 113
Defaecation 50, 51
Deva 113
Dhanush kuṇḍam 102
Dhātā 130
Dhvajārōhaṇam 150
Divāgni 131
Dīkshai, chakrābja maṇḍala... 107
Durga 123
Dwārasthānam 107

E

Embār 42, 43
Emberumānār 8
Engal Āzhvān (Vishṇu Chittan) 37
"Epic India" 14
Esanur 2
Etiquette within temple ... 78

PAGE

F

Factions among the Srī vaishṇavas ... 37
Flowers used in worship 84

G

Garuḍa 18, 103, 110
Garuḍadhvajam 152
Garuḍōtsavam 154
Gītāchārya 6
Govindāchārya... 1
Gōshṭi Pūrna ... 22, 23
Gurus, Caste of 48

H

Hanuman 103
Hayagrīva 130
"Heart of India" .. 14
Hṛshīkeśa 127

I

Idols, divine energy in ... 28
Idols, description of 28
Ijyai 49
Initiation 34–5
Initiation of women and non-Brahmans 46
Iyarpa, quoted from 29

J

Jalādhivāsam 122, 151
Jaya 130
Jayākhya samhitai 100
Jashadhvajan 123
Jīva, qualities of 31

K

Kāḍambi Acchan 43
Kangundi 122, 123, 124
Kankaṇams 150
Karṇikā kshētram 107
Kādhi varṇam 110
Kāntimati 19
Kōvilar 44
Kshatrabandhu 5
Kshetranāthan 123, 124
Kuberar... ... ... 106, 124, 129

PAGE

Kula Śekhara Āzhvār 9, 16
Kumāran 123
Kumilam village .. . 44
Kumudāksha 129
Kumuda 17, 107, 110, 129
Kūreśa 43

L

Lakshmī 6, 8, 45, 117
Lakshmīpuram .. 106, 115, 122, 123, 124, 128, 129, 154
"Life of Rāmānuja," quoted. 19, 20, 21
Līlāvibhūti 11, 27

M

Mādhyāhnika snānam 85
Madurakavi Āzhvār 6, 9, 16, 17
Madurakavi Āzhvār, his śūdra master ... 48
Mahā Pūrṇa (Periya Nambi). 8, 21, 22
Maṇakkāl Nambi ... 8, 17, 18
Maṇavāḷa Mahāmuni 7, 8, 14
Maṇḍalarādhanam ... 153
Mantra, Ashṭākshari 22
Mantradva 139
Mantra Siddhāntis 100
Māran 16
Māya 33
Mōksha, Vaishṇavā idea of 32
Morning Sandhyāvandanam ... 60
Mṛttika snānam ... 124
Mudras 136, 138, 141, 144, 147
Mūkabali 155
Mukkāniars 2
Mūla vigraha 134
Mūrti Kumbha sthāpanam or Mahākumbha sthāpanam ... 130

N

Naḍadur Ammāḷ Varadāchāriar) 37
Nālāyira Prabandham 9, 10
Nammāzhvār (Saṭhakōpan). 6, 9, 15, 16, 17
Nampillai 42, 43, 44
Nandana 129
Nandar 106
Nanjiyar 42, 43
Narasimhāchārya Swāmi ... 49

PAGE

Nāthamuni 8, 17, 23, 48
Nāvalpākkattārs 2
Nayanōnmīlanam ... 124, 151
Netrōtghāṭanam 115
Nitya vibhūti 11, 27
"Nityam" Rāmānujā's ... 49
Nityōtsavam 152
Nyāsa mudra 140, 147

O

Obeisance, Vaḍagalai and Tengalai, way of 47
Ōshadhi Sūktam 107

P

Padmāsanam (swastikāsanam). 149
Pādhur 2
Panappākam 2
Panchamahāyajñam ... 92
Pāncharātra śāstras 6
Pāncharātra system of worship. 99
Panchasamskāra ... 35, 36, 45
Para 110
Parakāla 6
Para Rūpa 27, 41
Para Vāsudeva... 19, 27, 28
Parānkuśa dāsa 17
Parānkusa 6
Parāśara Bhaṭṭar 42, 43
Parārtha Yajñam ... 99
Parichāraka 115
Paryankāsana 91
Pāsuram 10, 17
Paushkara Samhitai 100
Pavgee, N. B. 5
Perangiyur 2
Periya Acchan Pillai 42, 43
Periya Āzhvār (Vishṇu Chitta . 9, 19
Periya Āzhvār Tirumozhi 36
Pey Āzhvār (Mahat or Bhrānta Yōgin) ... 6, 9, 16
Pillai Lōkāchārya ... 28, 37, 42
Pinbalagiya Jīyār ... 43, 44
Pīṭha Samyōjana Hómam ... 122
Prabandhams 37-8, 39, 43, 44
Prabhava 129
Prachanḍan 130
Pradyumna 27, 28, 41, 100, 127
Prakṛti 33
Pramōda 27
Praṇāhutihōmam 155

PAGE

Prāṇāyāmam, way of doing .. 136
Prāṇa 94
Prapannāmṛtam, Extracts from. 22
Prapanna. Status of a Non-Brahman 46
Prapatti, Doctrine of ... 21, 23, 41
Prapatti, Tengalai view of ... 47
Prasūti mudra 111
Pratima mudra 147
Pratisarabandhana ... 111, 121
Pratishṭhā ceremony 114
Prāyaśchitta hōmam ... 155
Punḍarīkāksha ... 5, 8, 17
Punḍarīkar 106
Punḍra (caste mark) 35, 53
Pūrṇa 129
Purusha sūktam ... 106, 121, 124, 128
Purusha 126
Pushkara ... 106, 129

R

Rādhākrishnan, Prof. ... 30, 31, 32
Rahasyāmnāyam 5, 100
Rahasyatrayasāram 5
Rājasa samhita 100
Rakshābandhanam 111
Rāmānuja .. 19-27, 32, 33, 34, 36, 37, 38, 39, 40, 42, 43
Rāma Miśra 8, 17, 18
Rāsa krīḍa 14
Rathōtsavam 154
Ṛtviks 115, 150
Rudra 123

S

"Sacred Books of the East". 24, 31
Sākuna sūktam ... 103, 116, 123, 150, 151
Samāna 94
Samāśrayana ceremony ... 101
Sambandha 129
Sambhava 129
Sambhavāya 106
Samhāra mudra ... 136, 137
Sankarshaṇa 2, 27, 28, 41, 100
Sandhyāvandanam 97
Śankhasthānam 107
Sankukarṇar 106, 129
Śanti hōmam 155
Sanyāsa, Vaishṇava mode of ... 22

PAGE

Sanyāsins, Vaḍagalai and Tengalai 46
Ṣaptadasa kalaśa sthāpanam ... 125
Saraṇāgati (Prapatti) 45
Sarpanetrar 129
Sarvanétrar 106
Saṭhakōpan (Nammāzhvār) ... 6, 8, 17, 48
Śātvata samhitai 100
Sātvika tyāgam 135
Satyar 126
Savalai 2
Śayyādhivāsam (Bimbādhivāsam) ... 128, 151
Senaināthan 8, 16, 128
Setlur 49
Shaḍanganyāsam 134, 141
Śishyādhivāsam 107, 109
Snānāsanam 142
Sōma juice 5
Soul 30, 32
Sōzhiers 2
Śrāddha on Ekādaśi day 46, 47
Śribhāshya 23, 24
Śrīdhara 126
Śrīnagari 16
Srī Pāda tīrtha 47
Srī Perumbudur 8, 18
Śrī sūktam ... 103, 116, 150
Śrī Vatsānka Miśra 23
Śrōtrāchamana 50, 93
Subandhu 106
Subhadraka 106, 129, 130
Sudarśana 121, 130, 131
Suhōtrakar 106, 129
Sumukhar 106, 129
Supratishṭhitar ... 106, 129
Susenar 105, 106, 129
Susōbhanar 129
Svāgata mudra 147
Swayam āchārya purusha ... 48
Swādhyāyam 49, 97
Swarthayajñam 99

T

Tanka (Vakyakāra) 23
Tantrāntra Siddhāntis ... 100
Tantra Siddhāntis 100
Tāpa (branding) 35
Tarpaṇam, oblations to manes. 59
Tātāchars 2
Tatva hōmam 131, 151
Tatva mudra 137
Teeth, cleaning of 53
Tekkalur 2
Tengalai 7, 44, 45, 91
Tengalai āchāryas 42
Tengalai non-Brāhman as a priest 48
Thothārambhā 38
Thummagunta Drāvidas ... 2
Tirucchanda Vṛttam 11, 12
Tirukachi Nambi 21, 48
Tirukkoilur 17
Tirukkoṭṭiyur temple 23
Tirukkurukaippillan 37
Tirumazhisai Āzhvār ...6, 7, 9, 11, 16
Tirumālai 15
Tirumangai Āzhvār (Parakāla). 9, 16
Tirunarayana Bhaṭar 113
Tiruppāni Āzhvār (Yōgi Vāhana) 9
Tiruvāymozhi 13, 15, 16, 17
Tīrthahāri 56
Tīrthavāri (avabhṛtasnānam) .. 155
Tondaraḍippoḍi Āzhvār (Bhaktaṅghri reṇu) 9, 15, 16
Trivikarma 126
Tūppil 38
Turīya mūrtis 110

U

Udāna 94, 96
Upabrāhmaṇam 100
Upādānam 49, 84
Ūrdhva puṇḍram 56 8
Utsavam 151
Uttarāpōśam 95
Uyyakkondār 8, 17

V

Vaḍagalais 6, 7, 37, 43, 45, 91, 95
Vaḍakku Tiruvīdhippillai ... 42
Vaikhānasa mode of temple worship 99
Vaiśvadevam 92
Valavanūr 2
Vāmanar 106, 126
Vānamāmalai Jīyar 48
Vānamāmalai muṭṭ 48
Vanniyan (Kovilar) 44
Varaḍa Raja clearing Rāmānuja's doubts 21
Varuṇa 106, 124, 127
Vāstu hōmam 123, 124
Vāsudeva, Attributes of ... 28, 125, 127
Vēdānta Deśika ... 5, 6, 7, 8, 9, 37, 38, 39, 40, 41, 58, 100
Vedas, Vaishnava view of .. 2
Veda Veyāsa Bhaṭṭa 43
Vibhava 110
Vibhavāntara... ... 110
Vibhava vigrahas 28
Vidhātā 130
Vidyāraṇya 39
Vijaya 130
Vināyaka 123
Vīranārāyanapuram 17
Vīrasena ... 106, 129
Vishvaksēna 8, 16, 91, 103, 130
Vṛddhāgni 110
Vṛttikuṇḍam 102
Vyāna 94, 96
Vyūhas 7, 41 42, 110

W

Widowhood, Tengalai and Vaḍagalai differences about. 47

Y

Yādavābhyudayam ... 40
Yādavaprakāśa ... 1, 19, 21, 43
Yāgabheram 103
Yāgamaṇḍapam 102
Yama . 106, 124
Yāmunāchārya 17, 18, 22
Yauvanāgni 110
Yōga 49, 98
Yōga mudra 136
Yōgapīṭham 129
Yōga sampuṭa mudra 136
Yōni kuṇḍam 102

PLATES

PLATE I.

A.—A Vaḍagalai Sri Vaishnava Brahman who has passed through the ceremony of Prapatti doing japam.

B.—Tengalai Sri Vaishnava Brahmans proceeding to their guru, the Vānamāmalai Jiyar, to pay their respects.

A

B

PLATE II.

A.—A Tengalai Sri Vaishnava Brahman with Dīkshai proceeding to pay his respects to his guru, the Vānamāmalai Jiyar.

B.—The successive Jiyars of Vānamāmalai maṭham from Sri Ramanuja are represented in this picture of Ādi Śesha. It is generally believed by the Tengalai Sri Vaishnavas that Sri Ramanuja is an Avatar of Śesha who is carrying God.

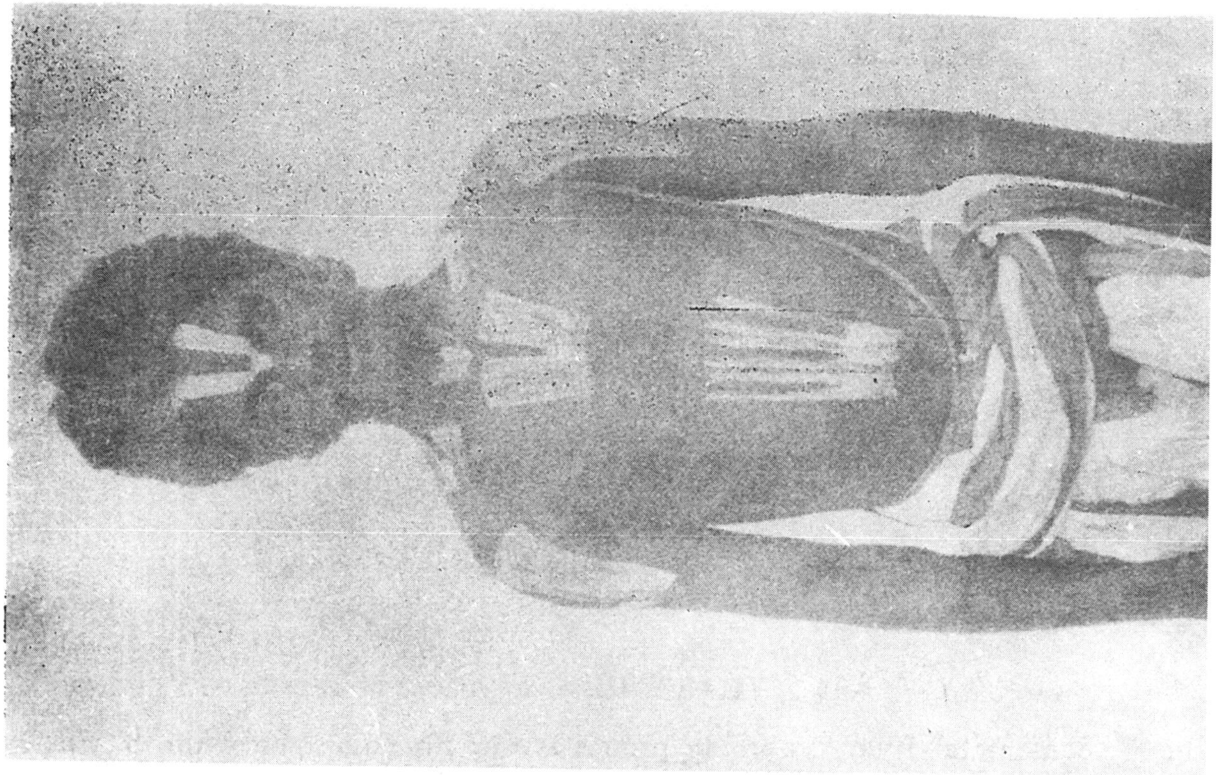

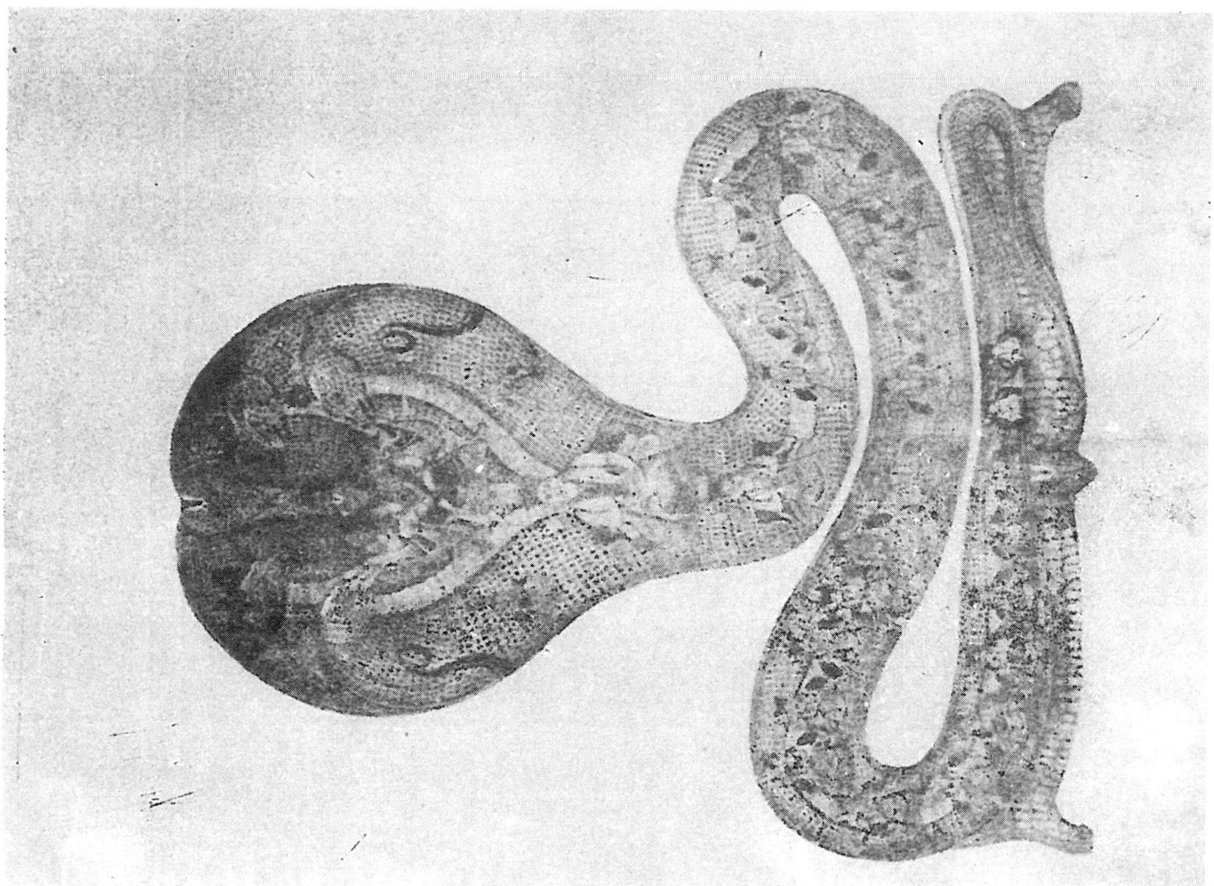

PLATE III.

A.—The Vānamāmalai Jiyar Swami in procession in his palanquin while staying in Triplicane.

B.—The Vānamāmalai Jiyar receiving his disciples.

A

PLATE IV.

A.—A Vaḍagalai Sṛi Vaishnava Brahman with the mark of chakram on his right shoulder made ḍuring the ceremony of Pancha Samskāra.

B.—A Tengalai Sri Vaishnava Brahman who is a Swayam Achāryapurusha.

A

B

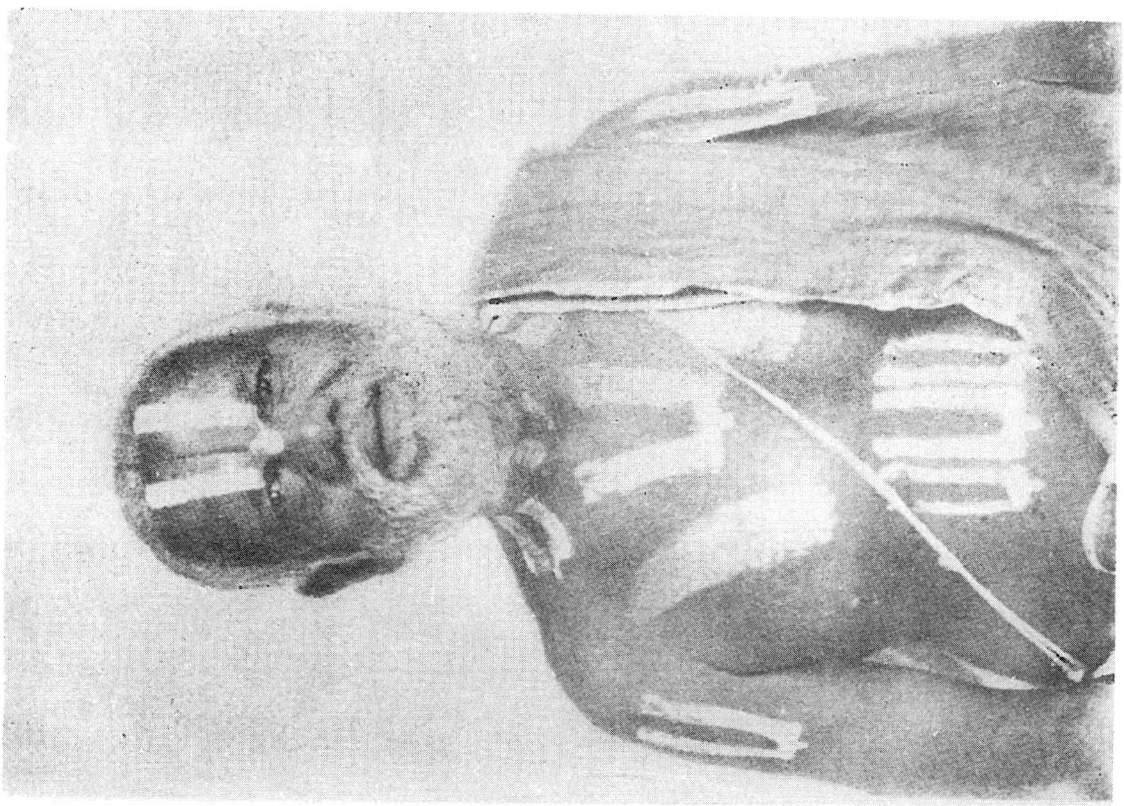

PLATE V.

A.—The Śayyādhivāsam of God Varadarājaswāmi and his consorts during the Pratishṭhā ceremony. The Archaka is sitting with sruk, etc., in front of the kuṇḍam of fire.

B.—Jalādhivāsam of God and his consorts. The vigrahas are immersed in water in large metallic vessels.

A

B

PLATE VI.

A.—The seedlings in paligais set up during the Ankurārpaṇam of the Pratishṭhā ceremony.

B.—The kalaśams established during the kalaśasthāpana ceremony in connexion with the Pratishṭhā.

A

B

PLATE VII.

A.—The Garuḍōtsavam of Varadarājaswami at Lakshmipuram on the third day of the festival.

B.—The ordinary utsavam of Varadarājaswami at Lakshmipuram on the second day of the festival.

A

B

PLATE VIII.

A.—The Archaka who conducted the ceremony of Śayyādhivāsam at Lakshmipuram during the Pratishthā ceremony.

B.—The car in which God Varadarāja is seated and drawn on the seventh festival day of the ūtsavam.

A

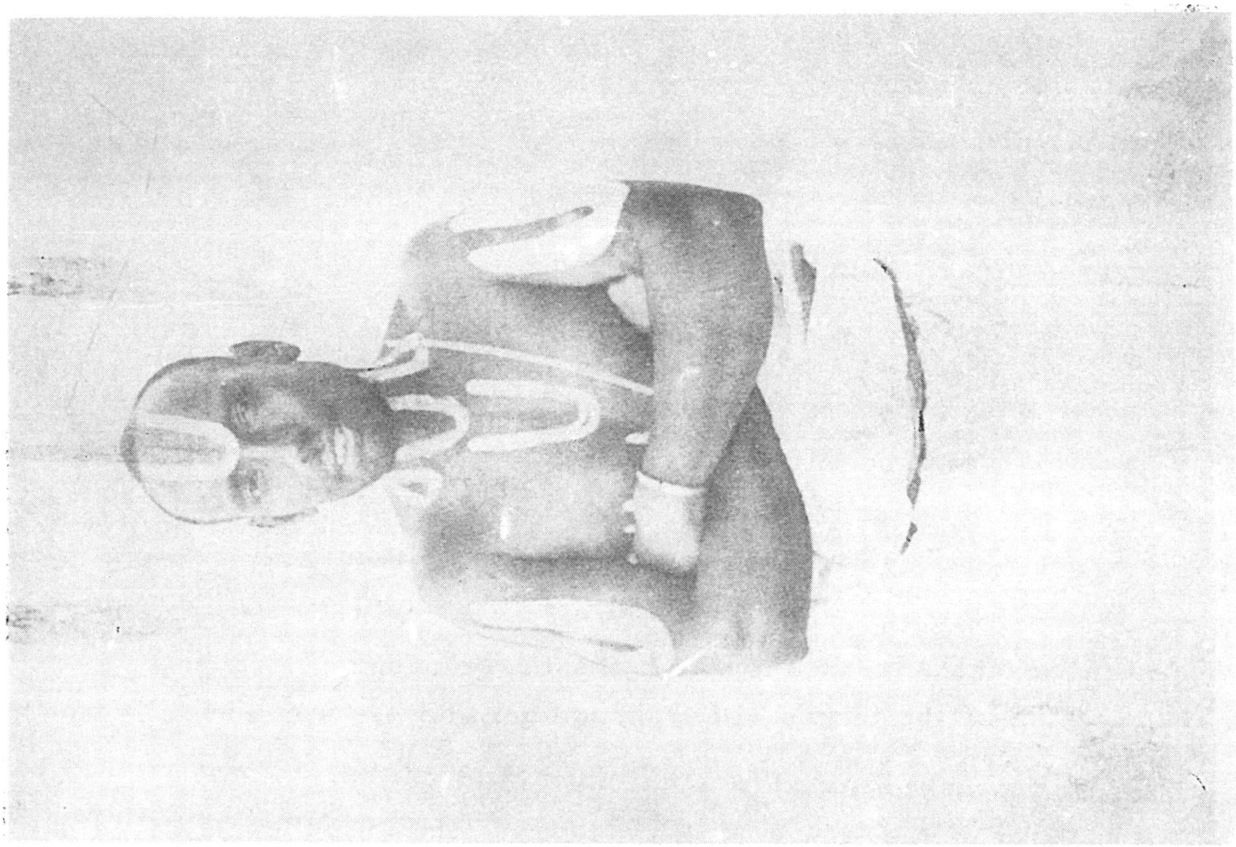

B

PLATE IX.

A.—The Chief Archaka selected for the Pratishtha ceremony.

B.—The Archaka of the temple at Lakshmipuram who performs the daily worship of God.

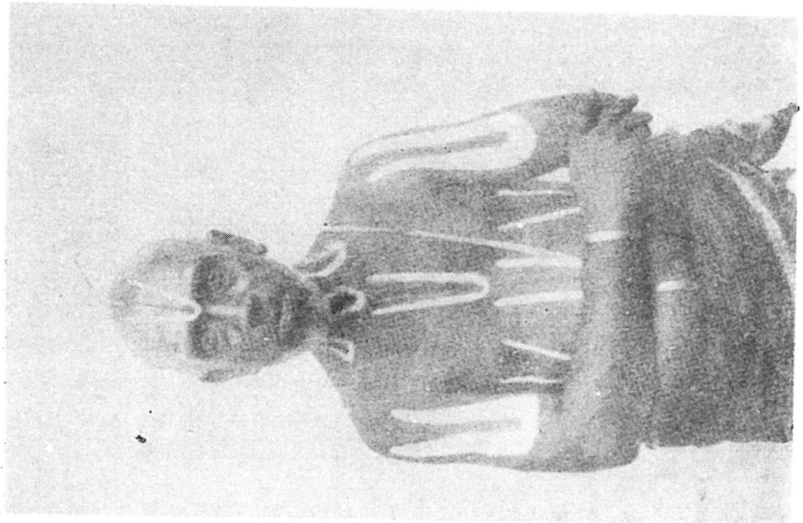

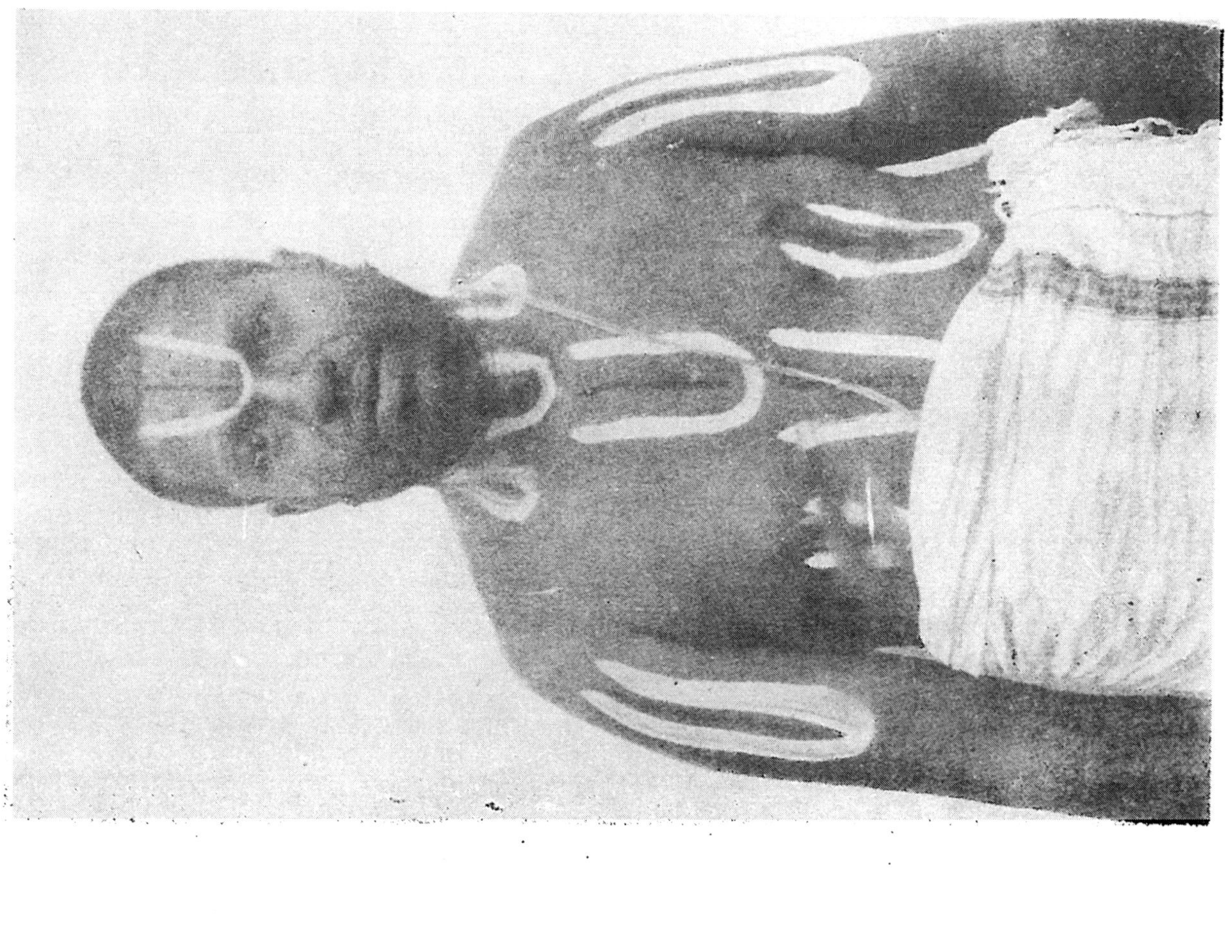

PLATE X.

A.—The Chief Archaka who was selected to perform the Pratishṭhā ceremony at Kangunḍi Village.

B.—An Archaka of Conjeeveram, who assisted the Chief Archaka during the Pratishṭhā ceremony at Kangunḍi Village.

A

B

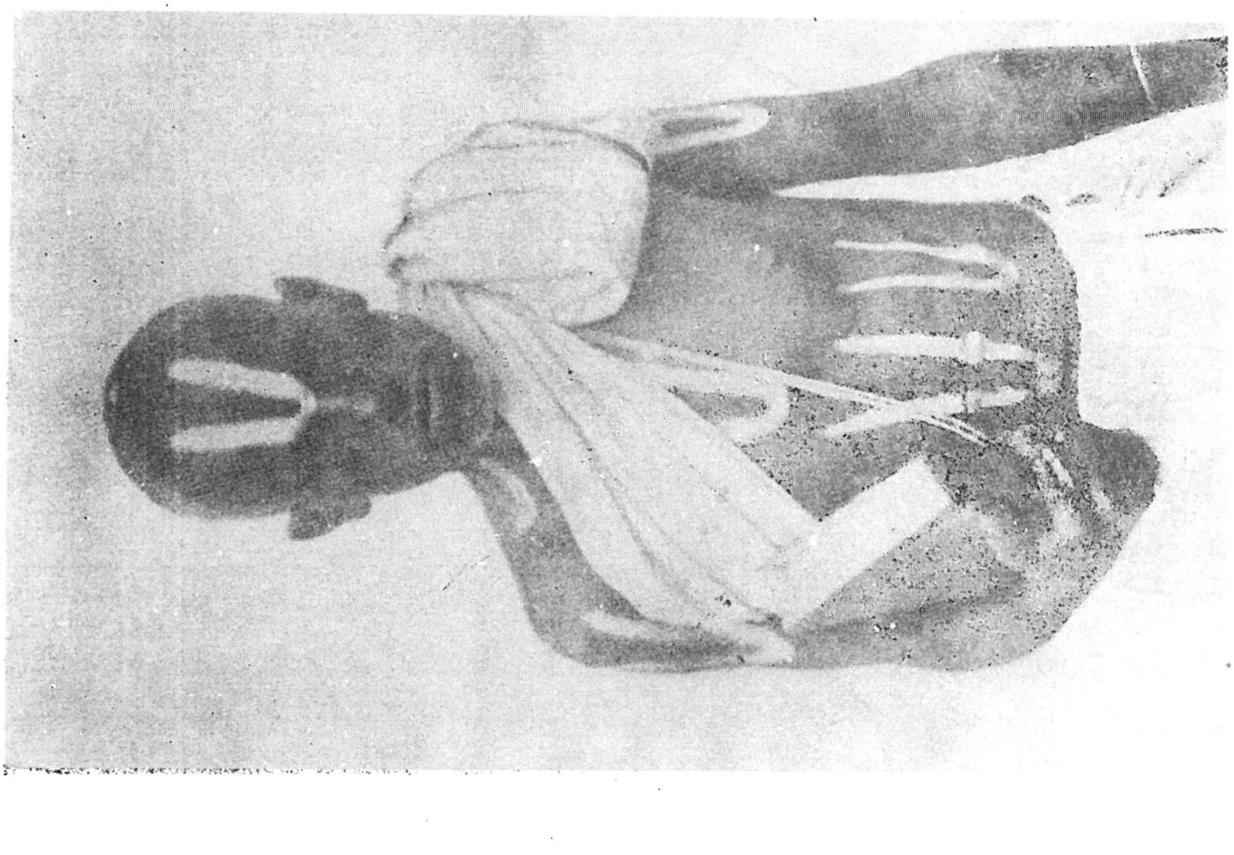

PLATE XI.

A.—The Chakrābja Manḍalam drawn on a cloth. Such a cloth is used, instead of drawing the Manḍalam.

B.—God Varadarāja carried in a palanquin on the seventh day of the festival during the night after the car festival.

B

PLATE XII.

A.—The Kovilars of the Kumilam Village who are really Vanniyans that have adopted Vaishnavism of the Tengalais and claim superiority over the ordinary Vanniyans.

B.—Three Vanniyans of the Kumilam Village engaged in temple worship and calling themselves Kovilars and claiming equality with the Tengalai Brahmans.

A

B

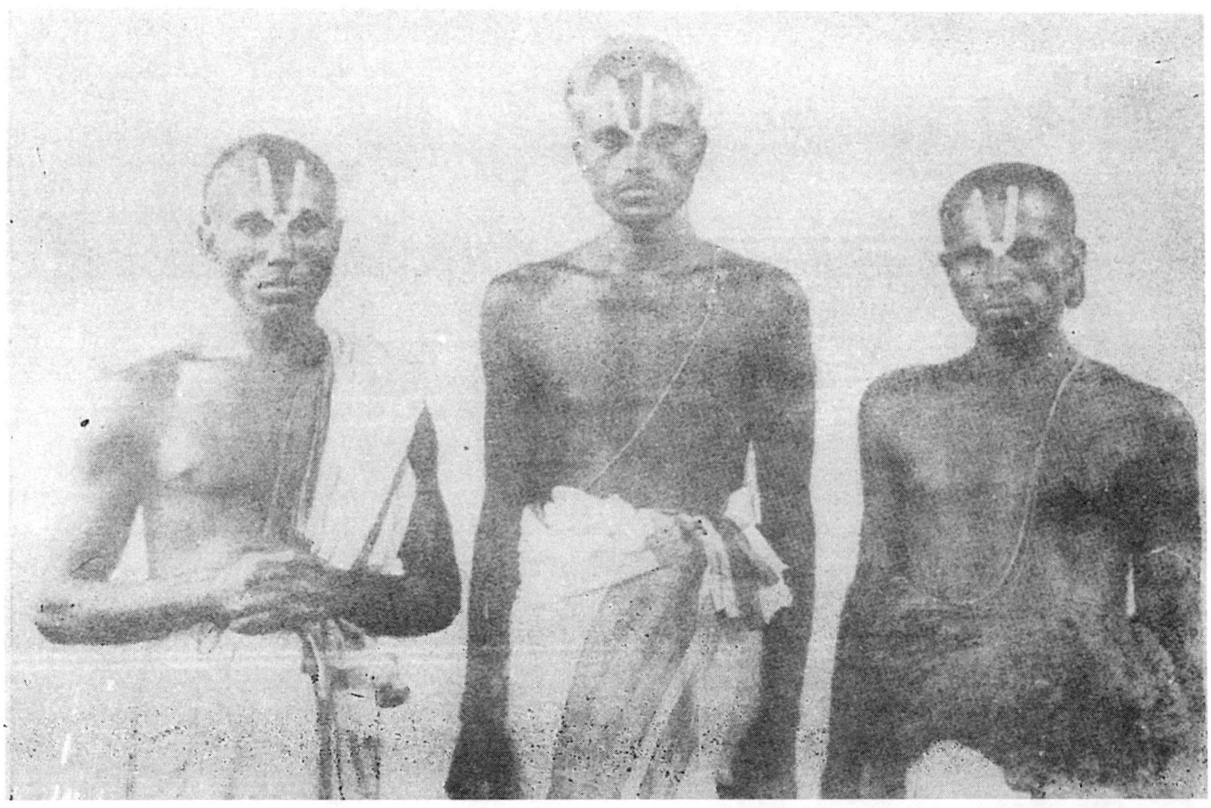